The Political Economy
of Collective Farms

Aspects of Political Economy

Series Editor: Geoffrey Harcourt

Published

A. Asimakopulos, *Investment, Employment and Income Distribution*
Pat Devine, *Democracy and Economic Planning*
Richard M. Goodwin and Lionello F. Punzo, *The Dynamics of a Capitalist Economy*
Marc Jarsulic, *Effective Demand and Income Distribution*
Peter Nolan, *The Political Economy of Collective Farms*
Bob Rowthorn and Naomi Wayne, *Northern Ireland: The Political Economy of Conflict*
Christopher Torr, *Equilibrium, Expectations and Information*
Warren Young, *Interpreting Mr Keynes*

Forthcoming

Paul Dunne (ed.), *Quantitative Marxism*
Grazia Ietto-Gillies, *Causes and Effects of International Production*
Ravi Kanbur, *Risk Taking, Income Distribution and Poverty*
Heinz Kurz, *Capital, Distribution and Effective Demand*
Jose Salazar, *Pricing Policy and Economic Development*
Ian Steedman, *From Exploitation to Altruism*

The Political Economy of Collective Farms

An Analysis of China's
Post-Mao Rural Reforms

PETER NOLAN

WESTVIEW PRESS
Boulder, Colorado

First published 1988 by Polity Press
in association with Basil Blackwell.

First published in the US in 1988 by
WESTVIEW PRESS
Frederick A. Praeger, Publisher,
5500 Central Avenue
Boulder, Colorado 80301

Library of Congress Cataloging-in-Publication Data

Nolan, Peter.
    The political economy of collective farms: analysis of China's
post-Mao rural reforms / by Peter Nolan.
        p.   cm. − (Aspects of political economy)
    Bibliography: p.
    ISBN 0−8133−0745−7
    1. Collective farms − China − History − 20th century. 2. Rural
development − China − History − 20th century.   I. Title.   II. Series.
    HD 1492.C5N65 1988
    338.7′63′0951 − dc19   88−15371
                                                                                CIP

Typeset in 10 on 12 pt Baskerville
by Setrite Typesetters Ltd., H.K.
Printed in Great Britain by T. J. Press Ltd, Padstow

Contents

*For my mother, Barbara, and in memory
of my father, Charles*

Acknowledgements

Research for this book was assisted greatly by three trips to China. In the summer of 1979 I was a participant in the Queen Elizabeth House (Oxford) China Study Group which spent three weeks in different parts of the countryside. I am grateful to Neville Maxwell and Keith Griffin for their roles in organizing this trip and the Chinese Academy of Social Sciences, Institute of Agricultural Economics, and, especially, to Wang Gengjin, Deputy Head of the Institute, for arranging our research in China. At that time 'de-collectivization' of agriculture was in its early phase of 'contracting output to the group' (*bao chan dao zu*). In the summer of 1983 I spent two months in Sichuan province looking at close quarters at the countryside in that part of China which had most rapidly completed the transition to 'contracting work to the household' (*bao gan dao hu*), the most dramatic stage of China's 'de-collectivization'. I would like to thank the British Academy for financing this trip and the Sichuan Chinese Academy of Social Sciences for arranging my stay in Sichuan. In 1986 I spent three weeks at the Economics Research Institute of the Chinese Academy of Social Sciences in Peking, collecting materials on, and discussing, China's rural reforms. I wish to thank the British Academy for financing this trip also, and the Economics Research Institute for its kind hospitality. I would like to thank, especially, Dong Fureng, Head of the Economics Research Institute, for his invitation to work there. Shang Lie, also of the Economics Research Institute, was of immense help in my research. My research has been assisted also by financial support from Jesus College, Cambridge, and the Department of Applied Economics, Cambridge.

The motive to write this book stemmed mainly from the discussions I have had at a large number of seminars on this topic over the years. The following people have all helped shape my views and I, accordingly (with the usual *caveat*), thank them: Bob Ash, John Barber, Melanie

Beresford, Krishna Bharadwaj, Francesca Bray, Lisa Croll, John Dunn, Michael Ellman, Adam Fforde, Ajit Ghose, Paul Ginsborg, Jack Gray, Keith Griffin, Chris Hann, Caroline Humphrey, Y.Y. Kueh, James Kung, Liu Minquan, Bruce MacFarfane, Neville Maxwell, Louis Putterman, Bob Rowthorn, Ashwani Saith, John Sender, Ajit Singh, Janice Stargardt, Sadie Ward, Gordon White and John Wells. I owe a special debt to the late Suzy Paine, with whom the issues in this book were argued about on innumerable occasions. I wish also to thank members of the Cambridge Research Group on the Chinese Economy, including Chris Bramall, Li Feifei, Sheng Yuming, Wing Shing Tang, Wang Hong, the late Wang Lin, Zhang Xunhai and Zhu Zhongdi. Wang Hong, Wang Lin and Zhang Xunhai provided me with a great deal of information and gave me numerous insights into the workings of the Chinese rural economy. Both Chris Bramall and Andrew Watson were kind enough to read the entire first draft of this book with immense care and I am much indebted to them for their extensive criticisms. The comments of Geoff Harcourt, the general editor of this series, were of great help. John Thompson of Polity Press was an invaluable source of enthusiasm and expert assistance from start to finish of the project. I wish also to thank both Terry Byres and Charles Curwen for their support of my work over many years. Jenny Woodhouse undertook the laborious task of typing successive drafts of the manuscript and provided a constant source of critical feedback on the contents.

Most especially, I wish to thank my wife Siobain Mulligan and our son Dermot for their consideration and support during the preparation of this book.

Introduction

This book examines the case for and against collective farms in developing countries' economic strategies in the light of China's post-Mao rural economic reforms. It concludes that collective farms are not, usually, a useful institutional form for poor countries. I did not always hold this position,[1] but the mounting evidence on China both pre- and post-1978 has forced me to rethink my views. I have been criticized by many people, including close friends, for changing my views on this, one of the most fundamental issues in development economics. The only defence I am able to offer is to repeat Joan Robinson's favourite anecdote about J.M. Keynes. When someone remonstrated with him for being inconsistent, he responded: 'When someone persuades me that I am wrong, I change my mind. What do you do?'[2]

The main arguments of this book are simple and seem to me to be common sense. I feel impelled to write it, nevertheless, because in giving talks over the past few years in a wide variety of places (to academics and non-academics), I have encountered much hostility to my views. Commitment to collective farms, in whatever guise, as a suitable institutional form for poor countries' rural areas still runs surprisingly deep among a wide assortment of groups in the West. It is powerful also in some important intellectual circles in the Third World. This is the case, for example, among a large number of left-wing Indian economists. They believe that collective farms offer a desirable alternative to the Indian structure of rural organization,[3] and, consequently, there is a deep desire to believe that the Chinese rural economy under Mao performed well.

The importance of rural co-operation in developing countries is widely recognized among development economists. There are many activities in which it is agreed that individual farm households often can benefit from

co-operation. These include irrigation, credit, purchasing industrial products, processing and marketing farm output, and welfare provision.
However, the desirability of collective ownership and operation of farmland, animals and other farm assets, and of collective income distribution,
has been much disputed. China's long experiment with collective farms
from the mid-1950s to the early 1980s produced widely divergent responses
from outside observers. An early and especially interesting example of
this was the report in the mid-1950s of the Indian Planning Commission's
delegation to study China's collective farms. The majority report concluded
that India should follow the Chinese path, calling for pooling of land,
manpower and capital resources 'so that it may be possible to fully
utilise the available resources and also to obtain economies of large scale
production' (GOI, 1957, 182). The 'minute of dissent' argued strongly
against collective farms, suggesting that the Japanese path to agricultural
development was more relevant: 'The Japanese experience shows that a
combination of family farming and service cooperatives with liberal aid
from the welfare state would be the correct policy to follow for increasing
production per acre in over populated developing countries' (GOI, 1957,
211).

In the late 1970s and early 1980s China abandoned collective farming
and returned to a structure similar to that of the early 1950s, in which
individual family farming was combined with extensive co-operation in
ancillary activities. This phenomenon is, obviously, of immense importance for both theory and policy in developing countries. Its analysis is
the main task of this volume.

While the central focus of the book is upon the issue of collective
farms, I feel that this issue is best seen against the background of debates
in the broader political economy of 'socialist' countries that go back to
the Soviet Union in the 1920s (chapter 1). Over the past two decades a
sea change has occurred both in the 'socialist' countries and in the
thinking of a large part of what might be loosely termed Western 'socialist'
economists. By 'socialist', unless otherwise indicated, I mean simply
those countries ruled by communist parties which describe themselves as
'socialist countries'. Faced with the obvious, terrible facts of mass poverty
and starvation in the Third World, to a whole generation of socialists,
including myself, the solutions seemed to lie along the path of the
Stalinist–Maoist administratively planned economy. There were serious
qualms about the system's political authoritarianism, but ultimately it
was felt that the finer points of Western democracy were worth sacrificing
in the interests of establishing a planned economy that could break loose
from Western 'neo-colonialism', and achieve rapid, independent growth
and the elimination of mass poverty. No book was more influential at
that time in propounding this view than Paul Baran's *Political Economy of*

Growth (Baran, 1957), and few articles summarized so effectively the feelings of a whole generation than John Gurley's passionate polemic on China (Gurley, 1969, 345):

> The truth is that China over the past two decades has made very remarkable economic advances (though not steadily) on almost all fronts. The basic, overriding economic fact about China is that for twenty years they have all been fed, clothed, and housed, have kept themselves healthy, and have educated most. Millions have *not* starved, sidewalks have *not* been covered with multitudes of sleeping, begging, hungry, and illiterate human beings; millions are *not* disease-ridden. To find such deplorable conditions, one does not look to China these days but rather to India, Pakistan, and almost anywhere in the underdeveloped world. These facts are so basic, so fundamentally important, that they completely dominate China's economic picture, even if one grants all of the erratic and irrational policies alleged by her numerous critics. The Chinese, all of them, now have what is in effect an insurance policy against pestilence, famine, and other disaster. In this respect China has outperformed every underdeveloped country in the world; and, even with respect to the richest ones it would not be far fetched to claim that there has been less malnutrition due to maldistribution of food in China over the past twenty years than there has been in the United States.

Few, if any, of the advocates of administrative planning in the fifties could have anticipated the explosion of the productive forces that was to be unleashed in the non-socialist Third World (or, indeed, in the advanced capitalist countries) in the subsequent period. Despite immense regional inequalities in the pace of growth, once capitalism began to gain a foothold, in the search for profit it unleashed the productive forces in the way that Marx himself anticipated, but which a wide array of later socialist economists did not. By contrast, the inadequacies of administrative planning systems became steadily more obvious. Such systems were unable to fulfil the promise of rapid long-term growth of mass living standards in poor countries, locked into a development path systematically orientated towards heavy industry. Worse still, the system was capable of making gigantic errors that could, indeed, result in mass starvation.

By the early 1980s it had become clear for anyone with eyes to see that rapid long-term growth with reasonably efficient use of resources, upon which the relief of the condition of the masses of poor people in the developing countries depended, required harnessing rather than suppressing market forces. Some variant of 'market socialism' with the state and market working in tandem was essential if growth of the desired pace and type was to be achieved. The tragedy for the socialist world is that this lesson was not learned in the Soviet Union during War Communism in 1917—21, when the costs of attempting to suppress the dynamic force of market competition were first revealed. The possibility of a 'Bukharinist' path to development which combined strong state planning through a variety of levers, with the dynamism of market competition, was ruled out by Stalin's rise to power in the 1920s. The 'NEP' path to development was not again to become an acceptable model in the socialist countries until Hungary's tentative experiments in the 1960s, and was not to flower fully until after Mao Tsetung died in 1976. The cost of these wasted years was enormous.

No mistake is more serious for a poor country than one committed in respect of agriculture. Chapter 2 examines the theoretical debates in the socialist countries concerning this issue. At the end of the 1920s, the victory of Stalinism in the USSR led to the defeat not only of the 'Bukharinist' market socialist approach towards the economy in general, but also to the triumph of the Stalinist view of the rural economy, and rural institutions in particular. Instead of taking the 'Japanese' path of combining individual enterprise with co-operation and state action in non-cultivation activities, the Soviet Union and the other socialist countries took the path of large-scale collective organization of virtually all of the rural economy confident in the existence of substantial 'economies of scale'. The Marxist—Leninist—Stalinist—Maoist tradition failed to appreciate the fundamental difference between agriculture and industry. In agriculture there are enormous problems in trying to supervise the labour of a large number of workers. Indeed, managerial diseconomies of scale quickly set in as farm size expands (in terms of number of workers). Errors of all kinds have been made in the socialist countries' rural policies, but this book argues that none has been so important as the misplaced belief in the virtues of large-scale (in terms of numbers of workers) units of production. Not only are there managerial diseconomies of scale, but a potentially powerful weapon in propelling forward a poor, capital-scarce economy is lost, namely, the dynamism of myriads of 'petty commodity producers' struggling to improve their families' situation. Under the Stalinist—Maoist system this force was consistently suppressed at great cost to the growth of the rural economy, which includes not just farming, but a myriad of non-farm activities from domestic handicrafts to petty trading.

Chapter 3 analyses the record of China's rural economy under Maoist policies. Over the long term China's collective farms did not perform disastrously. A great deal was achieved in relieving local poverty and constructing a rudimentary rural welfare system, and farm output was able to keep up with China's fast-growing population. However, the system encountered many problems, notably inefficiencies arising from the managerial diseconomies of large-scale production. Consequently, a very rapid increase in the supply of capital goods was required to sustain the growth of farm output. Moreover, to guarantee the country's basic needs in grain supply under these inefficient institutions a large proportion of collective resources had to be devoted to grain production. Over the long term China's collective farms were unable to raise rural labour productivity or to achieve any growth in output per person for the whole Chinese population. Without such growth not only did well located peasants only slowly (if at all) improve their condition, but, most importantly, the condition of the hundreds of millions of people living in more poorly located areas could not be relieved. While outside observers correctly praised the communes' ability to solve local poverty (though collectives are not the only way in which this can be achieved), they failed to appreciate how little the lot of those living in poor areas had altered over the long term, once a national system of basic grain distribution had been set up in the early 1950s. It is now clear that the dimensions of poverty at the end of the Maoist period were enormous, and concentrated in areas never visited by foreigners. Moreover, the collective farm system tied peasants to those areas, since rural migration was almost impossible under the commune system.

Most seriously of all, a collective farm system, with direct channels of control from (in China's case) production team to brigade to commune to *xian* to district (*diqu*) to province to the central authorities, contains the potentialities for colossal errors to be made. For years, outside observers attributed the disasters of 1959–61 primarily to natural causes, and Western supporters of the commune system praised its ability to prevent mass starvation at that time. As Edgar Snow's highly influential account put it:

Throughout 1959–62 many Western press editorials and headings referred to 'mass starvation' in China and continued to cite no supporting facts. As far as I know, no report by a non-communist visitor to China provided an authenticated instance of starvation during this period ... What was new was that millions of people were not starving, as they did throughout the chronic famine in the twenties, thirties and forties. What was new was that an equitable rationing system had been enforced for the first time'. [Snow, 1970, 585–6]

It is now clear that (as I argue in chapter 3) most of the responsibility for the disastrous collapse of farm output is attributable to policy errors by the central leadership, which could be put into effect through the commune system. Moreover, far from being able to prevent mass starvation, the food distribution system broke down under the severity of the crisis. The precise dimensions of starvation in 1959—62 probably will never be known. However, the abundance of new evidence available (anecdotal as well as statistical) shows that many millions of people did indeed die of starvation in China in those years. That the two worst famines of the twentieth century (the USSR in the early 1930s and China in 1959—62) occurred under colllective farming provides cause for reflection.

Beginning in 1978 and accelerating through into 1982—83 there occurred a series of massive reforms of China's rural economy, examined in chapter 4. These culminated in the contracting out of collective farm land for operation by individual households. A mass of collectively owned agricultural means of production was sold off to the peasants. Controls on income distribution were lifted. Indeed, instead of a constant barrage of propaganda to 'serve the people', China's peasants were urged to 'take the lead in getting rich'. A large number of peasants' production decisions were now in the hands of each household. The 'labour process' changed dramatically, with cadres no longer directing day-to-day work or controlling income distribution. In the rural non-farm economy, too, big changes occurred. Collective non-farm enterprises were encouraged to respond to market forces, and a myriad of new individual and co-operative non-farm enterprises sprang up. Labour migration controls weakened drastically with decollectivization, and peasants went on the move in large numbers. This was nothing less than a revolution in the Chinese countryside. Long-suppressed forces of 'petty commodity production' burst back into life. The texture of China's economy and society altered in a short space of time in a way unimaginable prior to Mao's death and the political convulsion that followed.

Not only rural institutions altered. Relative prices moved in favour of China's farmers, and the supply of industrial incentive goods rose extremely rapidly. Moreover, the Chinese leadership remained committed to following the 'Japanese path' rather than allowing everything in China's villages to be determined by the market relationships of millions of micro-economic units. The 'state' (whether in the form of the central authorities, the province or the *xian*) continued to play an extremely important role in supplementing individual households' efforts, through assistance to poor areas, irrigation, research, communications, power supply, credit, publishing, marketing, etc. It is debatable whether post-reform local 'collective' institutions (*hezuoshe* (co-op), *cun* (village) and *xiang* (administrative village)) could genuinely be termed 'co-operative'. They were still far from fully autonomous and free from control by the party which, despite a severe loss of morale during the sharp change in policy in the late 1970s, remained an immensely powerful force in China's rural life, with many avenues of control still in its hands. However, over a large part of rural China, collective actions (especially those of the *xiang*) continued to play an important and necessary role in supplementing the inadequacies of the free market, in respect, for example, of welfare provision, purchase of lumpy inputs, construction and maintenance of irrigation facilities, running a myriad of 'collective' non-farm enterprises, etc.

Chapter 5 outlines the transformation of the rural economy that accompanied and followed the reforms. In the late seventies and early eighties an extraordinarily high rate of growth of agricultural output was achieved. This showed vividly the enormous unutilised 'slack' within the collective farm economy. It provided the basis for a rapid improvement in the Chinese people's diet, which in turn cemented popular support for the post-Mao Chinese leadership. The rapid increase in farm output together with improved relative farm prices led to a sharp rise in peasant average real incomes after two decades of stagnation. In the early 1980s the rural non-farm economy began also to increase its pace of growth. By the mid-1980s this had become the fastest-growing area of the whole economy. In hindsight the performance of Maoist 'commune and brigade enterprises' appeared paltry, with expansion occurring in only a narrow range of enterprises. By the mid-eighties the rapid growth of the rural non-farm sector was quickly drawing off labour from the agricultural sector and altering the structure of rural employment. Most important of all, the direct and indirect effects of the rural reforms enabled China's poorest regions to improve their situation, so that a rapid decline occurred in the numbers in poverty.

A wide array of problems has been alleged to have appeared following the reforms, and these are examined at length in Chapter 6. These fall into different categories. Some of them are real, but cannot be attributed mainly to the institutional reforms. For example, huge regional differentials in levels of rural economic development opened up in the 1980s. There is no doubt that even after the rural reforms a great number of Chinese peasants were still living in abysmal poverty. However, it should be emphasised that absolute improvements did occur in most poor areas after 1978 — as is stressed throughout this book, 'unequal growth' and 'polarization' are two different phenomena. In the same category is the renewed upward trend in population growth in the mid-1980s. Under the commune system as much as in the mid-1980s there were strong incentives for peasants to have large families. The main underlying cause of the increase in the natural rate of growth was the 'echo effect' from the mid and late 1960s when birthrates were exceptionally high. This meant that a relatively large cohort was reaching marriageable age from the mid-1980s to the early 1990s. The party's post-reform capacity to control population growth was demonstrated in the 'one child' campaign, which reached a crescendo in 1983. Thereafter, the adverse popular reaction forced a partial retreat. In the same category as these problems is the undoubted decline in the agricultural growth rate in the mid-1980s. Given reasonable assumptions about population growth and the income elasticity of demand, it would have been most odd to have continued agricultural growth over a long period at over 8 per cent per annum. However, it is surely reasonable to ask whether a higher annual rate than that of 1984−6 (3 to 4 per cent) is desirable. By and large China seemed to have established a suitable rural institutional structure by the mid 1980s. The principal problem in sustaining agricultural growth at a reasonable rate was the price structure. The state could allow farm purchase prices to rise by increasing the role of the free market (the state still had a big influence on post-reform purchase prices) or by itself sharply increasing purchase prices. This would help raise farm profitability and sustain farm investment and output. The leadership, however, was frightened of the political implications of this in relation to urban food prices: the 'Polish' problem was never far from its mind. At the time of writing it seemed most likely that the state would steer a middle course of allowing purchase prices (and urban food prices) to rise gradually (in real terms) thereby helping to sustain a 'reasonable' but not a rapid, growth of farm output.

A second category of alleged problems is those which have been greatly exaggerated or just do not exist. For example, the idea that only collective farms can ensure a high level of rural capital accummulation is flatly contradicted by the huge expansion of the rural capital stock post-1978. The main issue is its structure (farm versus non-farm), not the capacity of farm households individually and co-operatively to save and invest voluntarily. The former issue is, more than anything, related to the price question, which has just been discussed. Also in this category of problems is the notion that without collective farms the state cannot ensure that basic grain needs are met. The most effective way to ensure high grain output is to raise prices substantially, but the Chinese state in the mid-1980s was afraid to do this. However, the Chinese leadership was united in its commitment to ensuring that grain output was maintained at least at the average per caput level of the mid-1980s. After the reforms a much smaller proportion of farm resources was required to achieve this than pre-1978. In the absence of a preparedness to rely mainly on price policy, the state still possessed a wide array of administrative powers (e.g. through direct compulsory purchase orders as well as through its control of the supply of petrol and chemical fertilizers) through which to ensure that sufficient farm resources were devoted to grain production.

Also in the second category of problems is the idea that rapid expansion of the rural non-farm economy is damaging to the farm sector. It is hard to see why this should be so. Indeed, by drawing off labour from agriculture, expansion of this sector assists the possibilities for raising farm labour productivity, and its expansion provides resources upon which local authorities can draw to support the farm economy. It was alleged also that without collective farms it would be impossible to sustain a strong system of rural welfare. The evidence does not support this. Some of the most successful programmes to provide rural welfare in other parts of the Third World (e.g. Sri Lanka, Kerala) have not required collective farms. Moreover, in much of rural China in the 1980s provision of rural welfare improved. The increased prosperity of the rural economy provided extra resources upon which collective and state authorities could draw to fund welfare programmes. It is true that in poor areas the provision of rural welfare was still extremely inadequate, but it is difficult to identify clearly whether in these areas the situation had altered much compared to pre-1978, when welfare provision in such areas also was much below that in richer regions.

A third category of alleged problems is where new difficulties have arisen and can, indeed, be linked to de-collectivization. The most obvious is the alteration in rural class relations. The re-emergence of private rural labour hiring, of usury, and of greatly increased income differentials within most villages, were linked closely to the rural reforms of the late seventies and early eighties. However, even if intra-village inequality had increased, it can be argued that this was a price worth paying for the acceleration in the pace of growth and rapid reduction in absolute poverty. Moreover, while it is true that intra-village economic inequalities had, broadly speaking, increased compared to the Maoist days, rural China in the late 1980s and 1990s was likely to be characterized by considerable fluidity in stratificational positions and was most unlikely to exhibit steadily widening class polarization. This was a highly competitive economy with ease of entry to most activities and few economies of scale, where land ownership was fairly equal, where state and collective authorities were able to raise a relatively large volume of resources to provide public goods, where the state was committed to steep progressive taxation of high individual business incomes, where the state was opposed to the development of a stratum living purely on 'non-labour income', and where the rural non-farm sector was expanding rapidly in many areas so as to provide employment for most rural strata in those areas.

Almost invariably, when China's recent rural reforms are being discussed, someone will ask: 'I admit that in many respects they have been successful, but is it socialism?' One reasonable answer to this is that the finer points of defining socialism are not very interesting in a country as poor as China still is. Most Chinese peasants under Mao, despite some improvements since pre-1949, still lived in abysmal poverty. Common sense rather than socialist principles is all that is required for one to support as the best policy that which raises mass living standards fastest. By that criterion the post-reform structures seem vastly better than Maoist communes.

However, one can take the argument beyond this. Socialism is about human freedom: freedom from the tyrannies of nature; freedom to live a fulfilled life giving expression to the individual's enormous human potentialities, a freedom which is enhanced with the increased security, welfare and cultural level associated with advances in living standards;[4] freedom from exploitation of one class, race, sex or region by another; freedom for citizens to participate equally in the political process. These notions are not simple and can be debated *ad nauseam*. However, the socialist concept of freedom is, clearly, quite different from the conservative concept which identifies 'freedom' primarily with rights to exchange commodities freely in the marketplace − a process which socialists rightly criticize as freedom for some at the expense of unfreedom for others.

As War Communism in the Soviet Union and Mao's Great Leap Forward demonstrated, it is impossible for a poor peasant economy to leap straight into the realm of socialist utopia. In practice, all socialist goals cannot be reached at once. Maoist communes did achieve certain socialist goals, which is why so many Western socialists enthused about them. They eliminated a great many local inequalities and provided security and dignity to disadvantaged people. However, they did so only through authoritarian control by the Chinese Communist Party. It is transparently not the case that Chinese peasants participated equally in the political process with the party in general or its leaders in particular. Most importantly, Chinese communes proved poor vehicles for advancing the productive forces and, consequently, raising popular living standards − surely, the most fundamental socialist goal in a poor country.

Stimulating the productive forces, and, consequently the possibilities for human self-fulfilment, in a poor peasant economy (indeed, in any economy) requires harnessing the dynamic potentialities inherent in market competition. A socialist strategy in a poor country involves recognition of this fact. This does not mean that the market should be left to work without intervention. In the interest of both equity and growth there is an enormous amount to be done to compensate for market failure. This requires a strong state, both locally and nationally, to raise resources and use them for a variety of purposes, both growth and distributional. It can be argued that this requires restrictions of the full, equal participation of citizens in the political process in the early stages of development, since with full political liberties strong varied interest groups (classes, races or regions) may be able to manipulate the political system to prevent the requisite state intervention into the market to raise resources (e.g. through taxation). This is a dangerous line of argument, and much oppression has been justified using this reasoning. Moreover, given the immense variety of politico-economic settings, such generalization is of questionable value. However, even if this argument were accepted it should be recognized that successful growth of output and mass living standards brings its own solution to political unfreedom. As a consequence of increased incomes, culture and leisure, together with the habits of independence acquired in dealing with the market, the citizens of poor countries (initially mostly peasants) are likely themselves to demand democratic rights and ensure that the party 'withers away' through popular pressure from below, whatever the views on the matter held by the party leadership.

1

Bukharinism and Stalinism: Contrasting Paths in the Political Economy of Development

> The private property of the labourer in his means of production is the foundation of petty industry, whether agricultural, manufacturing, or both; petty industry, again, is an essential condition for the development of social production and of the free individuality of the labourer himself ... But it flourishes, it lets loose its whole energy, it attains its adequate classical form, only where the labourer is the private owner of his own means of labour set in action by himself: the peasant of the land which he cultivates, the artisan of the tool which he handles as a virtuoso. This mode of production pre-supposes parcelling of soil, and scattering of the other means of production.
>
> Marx, 1967

The re-evaluation of collective farms, which is at the heart of this book, is best seen as part of a broader reassessment of political-economic strategy currently taking place in the socialist countries and, indeed, among socialists in the advanced economies of the West. Although there were major disputes within the socialist movement prior to 1917, the most important divide probably opened up in the Soviet Union during the 'Great Debate' of the 1920s. This split and the manner of its resolution had consequences not only for Soviet citizens, but also for those of all countries that were to have socialist revolutions, as well as for the socialist movement in the developed countries.

At the heart of the split was the clash between the Bukharinist 'market socialist' vision and the Stalinist 'administrative planning' vision of the long path of transition to some vaguely considered, distant millennium, the possible characteristics of which were then, and are still in the 1980s, of little practical interest for the real-world tasks of shaping current political-economic strategy in either the poor or the advanced economies.

The terms 'Bukharinist' and 'Stalinist' are used in this book to indicate broad schools of thought rather than the precise views held by these people. Indeed, one of the most 'Stalinist' documents in socialist history is Bukharin and Preobrazhensky's famous *The ABC of Communism* 1969, first published in 1920. In the light of the practical difficulties faced by the USSR during War Communism (1917–21) and in the early 1920s, Bukharin (as we shall see below) developed a quite different view of what constituted a desirable set of economic institutions and policies in a poor economy.

The precise reasons for the victory of Stalinism in the 1920s need not concern us here. What is of interest is the fact that, with certain qualifications (e.g. the defection of Yugoslavia from the Stalinist camp; the Maoist reformulation of Stalinism) the Stalinist vision was fundamentally dominant in the socialist countries, including China, from the late 1920s through to the Chinese post-Mao reforms. Moreover, important elements of the Stalinist vision, especially those concerning methods of economic organisation, remained embedded in Western mainstream socialist thinking. It was, for example, not simply because Sidney and Beatrice Webb were unobservant that they were able to write their eulogistic book about the Soviet Union (*Soviet Communism: a New Civilisation* (1937)), but because they wished to believe that under the enlightened leadership of the Soviet Communist Party a rational, planned, non-capitalist, co-operative society was being successfully constructed. The book tells us far more about the Webbs' (and a large body of Western socialists') view of socialism than it does about the Soviet Union. Despite the sea change in thinking among Western socialists in the 1980s, there still remains a large body of people who think that a socialist economy should eliminate the market, and that it is possible to combine direct state administration of the economy with economic efficiency.

Maoism, with its deep, and, in many ways, well-founded, critique of the Stalinist approach to enterprise management and division of labour, seemed to many people to offer a fundamentally different path to Stalinism. However, in many essentials the outlook was the same.[2] The main features of the Stalinist vision of socialism may be summarized as follows:

1   Confidence that a minority, vanguard party can lead the country successfully through the socialist 'transition' period. Western-style elections are denounced as 'bourgeois' devices through which anti-socialist forces might be able to influence national policy. Even Mao's Cultural Revolution attack on the party was short-lived, and aimed simply at getting the party to pursue the 'correct' line rather than questioning the leading role of the party unhindered by elections. Not even the most sympathetic

Maoists deny this. Bettelheim, for example, while hoping that the party's line is the 'correct' one (i.e. tries to move towards 'putting power in the masses' hands'), quotes approvingly the answer which Mao gave in 1967 to his own question: 'Do we still need the party?' Mao replied: 'I think that we need it because we need a hard core, a bronze matrix to strengthen us on the road we still have to travel. You can call it what you like, Communist Party or Socialist Party, but we must have a party. This must not be forgotten' (Bettelheim and Burton, 1978, 102–31). Neither Bettelheim nor Mao is able to give a convincing explanation (Bettelheim in theory, Mao in practice) of how the party can both 'centralist' and democratic simultaneously (see Schram, 1974, 11–18, for a careful discussion of Mao's views). Once one has accepted the necessity of a non-elected, tightly-disciplined, well-organized, centralized 'vanguard' party, all that remains is a question of leadership style ('persuasion and explanation ... and not wielding of an authority imposed by coercive means' (Bettelheim and Burton, 1978, 106) rather than the substance of who really makes the key decisions.

2   Deep hostility to permitting market forces (whether domestic or international) to influence resource allocation. Direct, administrative planning is regarded as the only way in which the anarchy of the capitalist economy can be overcome, i.e. planners issue direct instructions to enterprises concerning all important aspects of production (production mix, inputs to be used, price of inputs and outputs, etc.), enterprises are cut off from direct contact with markets (except, that is, for the black market, which necessarily flourishes in such a system, where it is impossible administratively to match demand and supply for different products), and 'entrepreneurship' has virtually no role:

> The basis of communist society must be the social ownership of the means of production and exchange ... All these means of production must be under the control of society as a whole, and not ... [that of] individual capitalists or combines. ... There will be neither disintegration of production nor anarchy of production. In such a social order, production will be organized. No longer will one enterprise compete with another; the factories, workshops, mines, and other productive institutions will all be subdivisions, as it were, of one vast people's workshop, which will embrace the entire national economy of production. [Bukharin and Preobrazhensky, 1969, 114]

3   Deep suspicion both of private and genuinely co-operative (as opposed to the pseudo co-operation of collective farms) ownership and operation.

Mostly, such activity is discouraged if not made illegal. These economic forms are harder to plan directly than larger-scale state and collective entities. They are regarded as encouraging the co-operatives' 'syndicalist' outlook, which considers the co-operative's interests first and society's second, or, even worse, the individualistic 'petty capitalist' outlook:

> Lenin said: 'Unfortunately, small production is still very, very widespread in the world and small production *engenders* capitalism and the bourgeoisie continuously, daily, hourly, spontaneously and on a mass scale' ... Small production refers to production done in a scattered way by individual peasants and individual handicraft labourers. It is based on personal appropriation of the means of production and individual (including family members') labour ... If small production is not entirely transformed into large-scale socialist production through the dictatorship of the proletariat, there is the possibility of capitalist restoration. This being the case, the proletariat can consolidate and develop the socialist system and finally triumph over the bourgeoisie only through a protracted struggle to completely fulfil the task of educating and remoulding the small producers. ['Marx, Engels and Lenin', 1975]

4   Strong bias in favor of large-scale enterprises. This was not just for ideological reasons but also because these are easier to plan directly than a myriad of small enterprises. Moreover, the Stalinist approach took it for granted that in most economic activity, from steel-making to restaurants, there were substantial economies of scale ('gigantism'). It seemed self-evident that rapid growth required giving high priority to 'modern' industry and that 'modern' industry was large-scale:

> To change from the muzhik horse of poverty to the horse of large-scale machine industry — such was the aim of the Party in drawing up the five-year plan, and striving for its fulfilment.... [O]nly a modern, large-scale industry, one not merely inferior to but capable of surpassing the industries of the capitalist countries, can serve as a real and reliable foundation for the Soviet regime ... [W]e have not only created these new great industries, but have created them on a scale and in dimensions that eclipse the dimensions of European industry. [Stalin, 1933]

5   Belief that the mainspring of economic growth is capital accumulation, which, in turn, is thought to be most securely sustained through administrative planning. The system, unlike capitalism, is said to be able to

achieve 'macro-economic efficiency' by sustaining a high rate of savings and investment:

> ... [T]he rate of growth is very largely (though not, of course, exclusively) dependent on the rate of investment that an economy can achieve ... To raise the growth rate to an adequate level and to maintain it there for a decade or two decades ... requires planning ... and it requires the appropriate type of political and social organisation capable of inspiring human endeavour and mobilising economic resources to the desired ends, especially in the early years of the 'push off'. [Dobb, 1967, 94; 1963, 44]

In a large, poor economy with limited foreign trade potential, sustaining a high level of investment is seen, in the Stalinist approach, to require that a high share of investment be allocated to the capital goods sector:

> '[W]hatever investment-potential one has should be concentrated upon methods and lines of production which will increase this investment potential still further. Insofar as the limiting factor consists in the output capacity of the industries which produce capital goods (machines and constructional materials), the possible growth-rate in the future will be higher the larger the proportion of current investment that is diverted towards expanding this sector of industry (Marx's Department I industries). This is for the simple reason that one will have a larger output of steel and machines in future years with which to construct and equip new factories and power-plants and steel-mills. [Dobb, 1963, 50]

Insofar as technical progress is regarded as important for growth this too, it is thought, can best be achieved in an administratively planned economy, where the state can ensure directly that a high proportion of national resources is devoted to this purpose, and where access to new technology is not limited by the privatization of knowledge characteristic of capitalism.

The Bukharinist vision was radically different. Though Bukharin did not develop a formal model,[3] he produced in the 1920s a reasonably coherent view of an alternative approach to development. Others at the time and since then have built on his insights and produced more rigorous schema.[4]

Bukharin did not question the Bolsheviks' post-revolutionary monopoly of political power (Lewin, 1975, 64). However, from his pre-revolutionary analysis of the advanced capitalist economies' 'Leviathan' state, he retained a consistently sceptical view of the modern state, possessing a 'streak of hostility to state power common to many socialists' (Lewin, 1975, 7). Bukharin was deeply aware of the dangers for democratic life in a backward country deriving from a highly centralized mechanism of economic administration. He warned in 1928: 'If [the state] takes too much upon itself, it is forced to create a colossal administrative apparatus' (quoted in Lewin, 1975, 63). Lewin summarises Bukharin's late 1920s counterprogramme to Stalinism as follows: 'less centralization, more party democracy, more rationality and scientific approach to problems, no mass coercion, less reliance on strictly administrative state measures, priority to gradualism and persuasion' (Lewin, 1975, 66). Under the Soviet NEP of the mid-1920s, the party-state was limited and relatively tolerant, and there was more social, cultural and intellectual pluralism than existed in the USSR at any point thereafter. It is no wonder that many Soviet citizens looked back upon it as a 'golden age' in Soviet politics as well as economics (Cohen, 1982, xii).

The Stalinist 'vanguard' party system combined with a system of state administration of a largely state-owned (*de facto* or *de jure*) economy contains peculiarly severe dangers of concentrations of power and lack of democracy in all walks of social life. When the legislature, the executive and ownership and disposition of the means of production all essentially are party controlled it is extremely hard for any independent centres of opposition to policies determined at the highest levels of the party to develop.[5] Bukharin's own criticisms (not extended to a full critique of the vanguard party concept) foreshadowed later, more sophisticated and penetrating analysis, frequently from socialists (see, especially, Brus, 1975; Bahro, 1978; Horvat, 1982). The central goal of a socialist society is, surely, democratic control of political, social and economic life? As Kitching has put it: 'Socialism is the greatest degree of conscious human control over the personal, social and natural environment exercised democratically. Everything that impedes advance towards such control is immoral, unjust, pernicious and unreasonable and a retrogression from socialism. Everything that advances such control and its democratic exercise is moral, just, reasonable and beneficial, and an advance towards socialism' (Kitching, 1983, 30).[6] It would be a singularly obtuse socialist who, in the light of the mass of theoretical and concrete evidence from the socialist countries from the past half-century, could argue that such a social formation offered a favourable structure within which this could develop.

The Stalinist politico-economic structure not only is undemocratic, but also prevents rapid growth of popular living standards from which long-term demands from below for political reform might emerge. This is not to deny that important advances in the popular living standard are possible under Stalinism, but, simply, to assert that real income growth generally has not been rapid and has been a lot slower in most instances than might reasonably be considered possible. International comparisons and counter-factual analysis (especially looking at the countries' potential in the light of the pre-socialist economic development) are extraordinarily hazardous. Nevertheless, I believe that serious examination of virtually all socialist countries, from the relatively advanced economies of Eastern Europe, to countries such as North Korea, Vietnam, Burma and Laos, despite considerable economic achievements in many respects, supports such a statement. Detailed justification of this statement would go far beyond the scope of this book.

In recent years a segment of the Western socialist movement has become more aware of the democratizing capacity of the market. The market place can prevent the corruption, arbitrariness and use of connections that tend to flourish when economic resources are administratively allocated (see, e.g., Paine, 1986; Gould, 1985). Even in the most politically authoritarian of non-socialist developing countries there are relatively large areas of independence for groups and individuals (and not just employers). For example, compared to the socialist countries, it is much easier for workers to change jobs, move their place of residence, or even obtain the materials needed to publish works expressing their views. Neither the state nor the market should any longer be regarded by socialists as a 'good thing' in their own right: 'the state should be treated essentially like the market — a necessary, but imperfect and occasionally dangerous way of achieving socio-economic goals. . . . Historically, the state has proved as flawed and dangerous as the market. . . . Awareness of the actual evils . . . and intrinsic theoretical limitations of [both] the state-owned and controlled economy . . . [and] the market mechanism . . . should be central to socialism' (Paine, 1986, 62 and 64).

The degree to which particular forms of political system influence economic growth is as important as it is difficult to generalise about. While fearing the concentrations of power that he observed, Bukharin (like Lenin, Mao and Stalin) felt that the process of accelerating economic growth in a poor country required strong rule by a single party. Others since him have argued in a more explicit and sophisticated fashion that the long-term interests of the masses are, indeed, best served by an undemocratic system in which tough decisions can be taken by a strong state to override sectional interests (and even the short-term interests of a majority of the population) (see, e.g., Macpherson, 1966). A key element in the accelerated growth of states as different as Meiji Japan (1868–1912) and Singapore since the mid-1960s has been the ability of the state to tax effectively (in one form or another) and ensure that a relatively high proportion of national income is at the state's disposal to use for developmental purposes. A striking characteristic too of the most successful Asian NICs (Newly Industrialising Countries) has been the suppression of an independent trade union movement, which has allowed 'Lewis-type' growth (rapid absorption of low wage labour in high accumulating industry) to proceed rapidly without strong worker pressure on wages and conditions of work[7] — the 'free market' has been ensured through a tough, undemocratic state. Of course, a strong state is not, necessarily, undemocratic. The rise of the welfare state and state intervention in the economy in the advanced economies after the Second World War showed that it is quite possible for the population to vote for a state which plays an increasingly important role in socio economic life. Nor is an undemocratic state necessarily strong, in the sense of being able to raise resources for development. Moreover, the degree of strength displayed by the state, both domestically and in international economic relationships varies from case to case. The most that one can say is that the state in a developing country needs to intervene as far as is necessary in each case to supplement market failure. The philosophy of Sun Yatsen which has guided the Taiwanese leadership is, for all its vagueness, a good guide in this respect: 'Rather than allow the free market forces of supply and demand or the dictates of central planners entirely to direct the flow of resources and determine various economic activities, there must be *planning within the context of a free economy (jihuaxing de ziyou jingji)*' (Myers, 1984, 522). South Korea and Singapore have also held broadly true to this approach. The state needs also to be relatively uncorrupt and must use well the resources it generates for its own use. A vast array of factors is needed to explain why these conditions may or may not be met in different circumstances.

It is possible that in many poor countries a necessary condition of an initial acceleration in the rate of growth is a strong, perhaps even, initially, a one-party, state. It should be stressed that the absence of democratic elections is compatible with a wide range of possibilities for inner party democracy and democratic life outside the ruling party, though the potentialities for crushing democratic rights seem, self-evidently, to be much greater where there are no genuinely contested elections between separate political parties. However, successful growth tends to bring its own solution to the undemocratic character of fast growing, authoritarian states. A rapidly rising level of industrial employment, growth of popular living standards (including, especially, formal and informal[8] education) which occurs after a certain point, together with individual independence acquired in an economy where market forces play a strong role, tend to produce demands from below for popular democracy and mass action in opposition to unpopular official decisions.[9] Examples can be found in each of the Asian NICs in the 1980s, from the resistance of Singapore's university-educated women to being treated as state 'baby factories', to Hong Kong's democracy movement and mass protests over the Daya Bay nuclear power station, from Taiwan's newly-founded (1986) opposition party and the mass protest over the siting of a large chemical plant, to the powerful opposition movement in South Korea, which in 1987 forced the government to undertake fundamental reforms, democratising the political system.

The most rapidly growing developing countries generally have not only had undemocratic systems, but have pursued intelligent policies enabling rapid growth. This is not meant to imply that everything depends on 'state policies'. Accidents of size, location, resource base, ethnic composition, legacies of entrepreneurial abilities and workers' skills, assistance from friendly powers, stationing of foreign troops, etc., all play a role in determining the range of policies available to the state and the given society's response to those policies. However, even the most cursory comparison of non-socialist countries with each other, or socialist with non-socialist countries, suggests that, whatever the cause and whatever the differences in effect, state economic policies do matter. In the most rapidly growing developing countries, not only has the large role for state-guided market forces stimulated growth,[10] but it has frequently helped provide (mostly unintentionally) a setting conducive to the development from below of a democratic movement.

The most obvious problem for democracy in systems with a large role for market forces is the unequal ownership of physical assets and the unequal chances available (because of differences in physical assets, income etc.) to develop 'human capital' (see, e.g., Plant, 1984; Forbes, 1986). As John Lloyd puts it:

> Liberty does not consist merely in the absence of restraints (usually defined as restraints of the State) but in the positive possession of 'positional' and economic goods. ... Real freedom encompasses not just the freedom money can buy but also that which bestows access to services or other resources. The fact that the unemployed factory worker in Gateshead is free to send his sons to Eton has no meaning in the real world. [Lloyd, 1986]

In poor developing countries the authoritarian, 'planning plus free market' structure, for all its problems, if practised effectively, provides a setting for the development of a mass democratic movement which might in turn take action from below to influence the distribution of assets and incomes so as to produce meaningful equality of opportunity. In an unreformed Stalinist political economy with its unity of economics and politics, relatively slow growth of mass living standards, and international isolation, it is hard for such a mass movement to emerge.

Bukharin's conflict with Stalin primarily sprang from and was strongest over relationships with the peasantry, and that is this book's central theme. However, behind the conflict lay a broader argument about economic strategy, and in periods when the spectrum of economic debate in socialist countries was allowed to widen, the 'Bukharinist' model rapidly resurfaced to challenged the Stalinist orthodoxy.

In the 1920s, the Bukharinist critique of administrative planning did not seem so convincing. Probably a majority of Soviet economists believed that a directly administered economy would be more economical in its use of resources than capitalism, and better able to sustain technical progress. Bukharin, however, grasped intuitively the dangers involved in the elimination of competition — the key to capitalism's dynamism:

> [I]f we, who in essence ... have a state super-monopoly, do not push, press and whip our cadres, spurring them to cheapen production, to produce better, then ... we have before us all the prerequisites of monopolistic decay. The role played by competition in capitalist society ... must with us be played by the constant pressure arising from the needs of the masses. [quoted in Cohen, 1974, 178]

Bukharin is unclear as to how 'socialist competition' is to be achieved, but it is only a short step from such statements to the general spirit of the 'market socialist' ideas of post-Stalin reformist economists in Eastern Europe. It has become increasingly clear that Bukharin's intuitions were correct. There is now a mass of evidence to demonstrate that it is extremely difficult in an administratively planned economy effectively to stimulate cost-cutting and the search for new, better products, to sustain technical progress, and maintain product quality.[11] Competition, both domestic and international, for all its problems, ensures a direct, powerful stimulus to these vital aspects of the economic process. It is worth noting that competitive enterprises are not necessarily privately owned.

While Stalinism believed in the virtues of large scale in all economic activities, Bukharin asserted the need to maintain a balance of economic forms. He agreed that the state ought to control directly the 'commanding heights' of the economy (major industry, banks, transportation and foreign trade), but he considered that the small-scale, private, petty-commodity producing sector (encompassing not just farming, but handicraft industries, petty trade, service activities, etc.) had a large role to play in the development process,[12] whose diverse forms he likened to 'an enormous socioeconomic salad' (quoted in Cohen, 1974, 180). In Bukharin's view, NEP's mixed economy with a central role for the market, enabled the Soviet state to benefit from the private pursuits of its 'mass of semi-friends and semi-enemies and open enemies in economic life' (Cohen, 1974, 181). He considered that NEP had established 'the correct combination of the private interests of the small producer and the general interests of socialist construction', stimulating the personal incentives of peasants, artisans, workers, 'and even the bourgeoisie', so as to 'put them objectively to the service of socialist state industry and the economy as a whole' (quoted in Cohen, 1974, 181).

Bukharin's misgivings about exclusive concentration on the large-scale sector proved well founded. There is wide variety of evidence to show that the rural, small-scale (often handicraft) industrial sector in both large and small non-socialist developing countries is extremely resilient. Unless the state intervenes to inhibit its advance (as in China after 1955) or to suppress it (as in the Soviet First Five Year Plan), it can expand alongside a growing modern large-scale industrial sector, and, indeed, perform a vital economic role. There is plenty of evidence to show that even traditional handicrafts can resist modern factory competition (Lockwood, 1968; Crisp, 1976, ch. 1; Feuerwerker, 1968, ch. 2, and 1977, ch. 5),[13] benefiting from lower transport costs and specialized local demand for inferior products, and have often been able to compete on international markets and make an important contribution to export earnings in the early stages of development (Lockwood, 1968; Feuerwerker, 1968, 1977). Of course, integration into world markets brings new types of production relations to handicrafts, and greatly increases the instability of production. There have been many examples of devastating blows dealt to particular areas' handicraft products as world market conditions have altered. Modern rural industries, using more sophisticated machine technology and more advanced business methods, have also made important contributions in a variety of contexts, sometimes building on traditional handicraft skills, and sometimes introducing completely new production methods (see, e.g., Saith, 1986; Crisp, 1976; Lockwood, 1968; Ranis, 1978). Subcontracting from large modern firms has been an important channel through which rural, non-handicraft industries have been stimulated (see, e.g., Saith, 1986; Ranis, 1978; Lockwood, 1968).

State policy can do much to influence rural industrialization, but there are many factors which, even working through market forces, without state influence, will tend to sustain rural industries. One of the most important is the fact that there may be a large pool of rural 'surplus' labour which is prepared to work for a very low income — indeed, rural labour is often prepared to work (inside or outside the family) for any net addition, however small, to family income. Given that living costs are lower for a rural than an urban worker (the rural worker lives in the original family home, has negligible transport costs, shares family food irrespective of his/her income, etc.), the income needed to attract him/her into employment is generally (peak harvest seasons apart) lower than in the cities. Moreover, such labour (often female or child) is likely to be much more docile than an urban workforce. Factory rents, too, are likely to be lower away from urban centres. Transport costs are a key element in rural industrialization. High transport costs in a poor economy may protect a wide variety of industries producing in relatively small units (not necessarily handicraft) for local needs, often making use of dispersed sources of raw materials. High transport costs will lead to certain areas (those near big cities and ports) developing small modern rural industries for urban needs or export (either direct production or through subcontracting) much more rapidly than others.[14]

In addition to the factors that would in many poor countries in the early stages of development[15] tend to promote the expansion of rural small-scale industries simply through the normal workings of the market, there are other external benefits which might lead the state to support their expansion in appropriate sectors. Most importantly, such industries often employ a large amount of labour per unit of capital — this is especially true if one takes into account not just 'industry', but the wide array of other rural non-farm enterprises, from transport to roadside food stalls. Thus, within a given time period, the structure of employment can be shifted away from agriculture more quickly than under a strategy which gives exclusive emphasis to large-scale urban industry. This factor alone has multiple, dynamic benefits for the growth process that should be considered in any social cost—benefit analysis of these activities. For example, drawing women into full time work outside the home tends to bring down the birth rate. Rapidly raising the level of non-farm employment tends to make it easier to raise farm labour productivity and, hence, rural incomes. Indeed, some authors have visualised the possibility of a dynamic virtuous circle of rural industrialization, in which increased rural non-farm employment assists the growth of farm labour productivity leading to increased rural incomes and demand for the products of rural non-farm enterprises leading to increased rural non-farm employment, etc. (Mellor, 1976). By generating greater non-farm employment per unit of capital, such a 'balanced growth' strategy may provide a greater number of people with the stimulus to improve their human capital to meet the varied needs of the non-farm sector. This stimulus may well be enhanced by the small size of rural enterprises and the much greater chances of setting up an individual private enterprise (i.e. a high 'entrepreneur—output ratio') than under alternative strategies. In addition to the employment factor, and the dynamic benefits that might stem from this, other 'externalities' to be taken into account include the reduced pressure on urban resources, and the short gestation period of rural small-scale industries.

Rural industrialization is often unpleasant. Many authors have correctly drawn attention to the high level of female and child labour, to the absence of protection from trade unions, to poor safety standards, to the long hours and harsh conditions for low incomes (see, e.g., Lockwood, 1968; Saith, 1986). However, the grinding effort of traditional agricultural work at low standards of living is not pleasant either. A balanced growth strategy (in respect to large urban and small rural plants) may often, for all the short-term harshness, be the best way to sustain rapid growth of output and living standards. This raises difficult questions, familiar to socialists in advanced economies, about the degree to which the state ought to intervene to protect workers in such sectors. The frequent response of capital to such protection is to move to regions where workers are less well protected and the 'price' of labour is reduced accordingly. In the area from which capital migrates, workers are well protected but the level of employment falls. Moreover, it should be stressed that the economic advantages of small-scale industries do not apply to all (or even most) types of industrial activities (see e.g., Little, 1987). In a wide range of industries (especially heavy industries) economies of scale and lower energy consumption per unit of output in more modern plants often tip the balance in favour of the modern large-scale sector. However, especially in the early stages of development, when transport is poorly developed and needs are relatively simple, there are a great many activities in which the small-scale sector can play a most important role.

The Bukharinist approach is suspicious too of Stalinism's stress on high rates of accumulation and heavy industry as the mainspring of economic growth in a socialist country. Under Stalin these postulates were raised to the status almost of laws of socialist development, but with little contemporary theoretical justification.[16] As the acceleration in the rate of investment and increasing emphasis on heavy industry took place in the USSR at the end of the 1920s, Bukharin launched a forceful attack on such an 'unbalanced' strategy. He asked: 'Does everything, or almost, have to be invested in heavy industry—however desirable its growth? Will the desirable economic growth be achieved in fact by maximum investments in a short span of time?' (quoted in Lewin, 1975, 55). His answer was negative. He argued that it was quite possible for an economy to over-invest: the economy might simply lack the absorptive capacity, workers' motivation and capacity to work might be affected adversely by the short-term squeezing of the consumption share (neither 'a unilateral interest in accumulation in a given lapse of time [nor] a unilateral interest in consumption' was appropriate to maximising the growth of total product (Lewin, 1975, 52)), and the combination of a high rate of investment and emphasis on large-scale, heavy industry projects would lead to a large volume of resources tied up in projects with long gestation periods (Lewin, 1975, 55).

Bukharin's strictures against excessive concentration on heavy industry were in part directed at the demand-side problems likely to emerge in a NEP-type framework: [If agriculture and industry are prevented from interacting'] you will have silent factories ... you will have a declining peasant economy; you will have general recession' (quoted in Cohen 1974, 175). These problems were 'resolved' by the comprehensively and administratively planned system in which the state itself provided the demand for its own products. However, in part Bukharin's attack on this strategy and his positive defence of 'balanced growth' of heavy industry, light industry and agriculture, stemmed from his conviction that it might be possible to become locked into a vicious circle which lost sight of the fact that the main object of growth was not industrialization *per se* but, rather, improvement in mass living standards. The 'chain' of production, he insisted, must always 'end with the production of the means of consumption ... which enter into the process of personal consumption ...' (quoted in Cohen 1974, 174). For Bukharin, the true indicator of growth was not just heavy industry, but 'the sum of the national incomes, on the basis of which everything grows, beginning with production and ending with the army and the schools' (quoted in Cohen, 1974, 175).

The twin dangers of over-investment and heavy industry bias are fundamental problems in administratively planned economies. A high degree of emphasis on a broad range of heavy industries has been shown convincingly to be justified only on non-economic grounds,[17] or in the special case where the economy is closed or where there is a 'pure or near pure' foreign exchange constraint on growth (Stewart, 1981). This is not to deny that there may often be a justification for a selective, carefully constructed programme emphasising certain types of capital goods likely to stimulate technical progress (Stewart, 1981). Rather than demonstrating the superiority of planning over the anarchy of the free market, the long-term bias towards heavy industry in the socialist countries increasingly can be seen to reflect the very problems of administratively planned systems. Their inefficiency in resource use led these economies to require relatively large amounts of capital to generate a unit of output. Moreover, the heavy industry sectors themselves in all economies use relatively large amounts of heavy industry's products per unit of output. The combination of initial intentional stress and these factors helped to produce a long-term vicious circle of heavy industry bias (and over-investment) in the socialist economies, from which only fundamental system reform can enable them to escape. It has, too, been argued that the administratively planned economies are highly conservative (for reasons to do with theories of bureaucracies rather than economics), with a powerful tendency to simply replicate existing patterns of resource al-location. Indeed, the French Sovietologist, Zaleski (1980), prefers to describe the Soviet economy as 'centrally administered' rather than 'centrally planned': [T]he existence of a central national plan, coherent and perfect, to be subdivided and implemented at all levels is only a *myth*. What actually exists, as in any *centrally administered* economy, is an endless number of plans, constantly evolving, that are co-ordinated *ex post*, after they have been put into operation' (Zaleski, 1980, 484).

The question of whether a high rate of investment is a necessary condition for rapid economic growth is still hotly debated.[18] Some eco-nomies have grown quite fast without high rates of investment, and some with high rates of investment have grown quite slowly.[19] Few economists would dispute that a high rate of investment is not sufficient for rapid growth: the effectiveness with which investment is used is critical. Unfor-tunately, in its obsession with achieving 'macro-economic efficiency' (i.e. generating, through administrative planning, a high rate of investment) the Stalinist model lost sight of the factors likely to contribute to micro-economic efficiency. Indeed, the very institutions designed to force up the rate of investment contributed fundamentally to these 'supply-side' problems. Consideration of the supply-side factors likely to sustain the efficient use of resources was striking absent from the Stalinist tradition both inside and outside the socialist countries.

'Micro-economic efficiency' is not the narrow textbook question of static allocational efficiency in an illusory world of perfect competition. I have already mentioned the Bukharinist approach's emphasis on the importance of competition for raising product quality, stimulating the search for better products and for technical progress. It also involves analysis of ways in which human beings attempt to improve their pro-ductive capacity. Human capital is generally reduced in socialist countries' plans to figures on state outlays for education, health, culture etc., much of which is categorised as 'unproductive' investment. However, much more is involved than this. It is arguable that one of the most potent forces in poor countries' development is the individual desire to acquire knowledge and use it well. When capital is relatively scarce it is especially important that the maximum output is wrung from it, and a vital part of economic analysis (generally missing in the Stalinist approach) is attempting to understand the range of factors that play upon human motivation and affect human capital in the broadest sense. Maoism is an important exception to this, but, unfortunately, however well-intentioned, the Maoist attempts to stimulate micro-economic efficiency were (as we shall see) crude and, ultimately, strikingly unsuccessful. Within the sphere of competitive, small-scale petty commodity production, so despised by the Stalinist tradition, the individual drive for improvement of human capital is especially strong. The fact that measurement of its impact may be difficult is no excuse for ignoring it.

A principal justification for the Stalinist state ownership (*de facto* or *de jure*) and control of most areas of the economy is the prevention of inequalities in asset ownership and the ability to avoid wide differences in incomes. Under the Maoist version of the Stalinist model, income differentials were in most respects kept very narrow indeed. Early in the day, Bukharin produced a penetrating critique of such an approach, arguing that the main developmental goal was to raise labour productivity and living standards, thereby laying the basis for elimination of mass poverty. If growth would be better stimulated by allowing certain aspects of inequality to increase, then to him this was an acceptable price to pay. In a phrase that was strikingly replicated in the Chinese, post-Mao critique of Maoist communes' distribution policy, he argued that the goal of a poor socialist country should not be 'equality in poverty': 'Our aim is not reducing the more prosperous upper stratum but ... pulling the lower strata up to this high level: poor peasant socialism is wretched socialism ... only idiots can say there must always be the poor' (quoted in Cohen, 1974, 176). Such views surfaced repeatedly in the socialist countries when controls on debate were relaxed. They find their modern counterparts in the slogan of China's brief 'NEP' period in the early 1950s – 'expand the household and become rich' (*fa jia zhi fu*), and in the Chinese slogan of the 1980s – 'take the lead in getting rich' (*xian fuqilai*). The view is paralleled too in the writings of those development economists who argue that controlling inequality should be of secondary importance compared to the goal of relieving poverty (see, especially, Fields, 1980).

The Stalinist view of development is now everywhere on the retreat in the socialist countries: the Hungarian reforms of the late 1960s were the first cautious steps in dismantling the administrative planning system. The Chinese post-1978 reforms opened the floodgates, and fundamental system reform is on the agenda throughout the socialist world, from

Cuba to Vietnam, from Algeria to Rumania. In late 1986/early 1987 the Soviet Union itself took the first steps along the path. In turning towards some form or other of market socialism, these countries were, in effect, returning to the Bukharinist path of the Soviet NEP, which was eliminated from the agenda in the socialist countries by Stalin's victory in the political struggle and by the influence of Stalin's ideas on his Soviet successors and on the leaders of the other socialist countries.

This book is concerned with rural reform. Reforming agriculture and small-scale non-farm enterprises by giving greater economic rights to individuals, groups and enterprises, and increasing the role of market forces, is less difficult to accomplish than reform of large-scale enterprises. In China's case, for example, the most far-reaching reforms began in agriculture and by the mid-1980s had affected also most small-scale non-farm enterprises, including leasing-out of the majority of small state enterprises. However, in the large-scale non-farm sector, progress was much slower: for example although for most products of large-scale industry a portion of output could be sold at free market prices (Chinese Academy of Social Sciences, 1987), the state fixed the limits within which products sold at 'floating' prices could move, and a large proportion of the products of large-scale industry still was sold at state-fixed prices.[20] The much greater importance of agriculture and small-scale non-farm enterprises in the Chinese economy than in the developed socialist European economies meant that it was easier in China to attain a relatively fast overall pace of reform.

Agricultural de-collectivization in China involved individual households being given direct control over land and rights to the usufruct from it, as well as rights to own other means of production, while in the small-scale non-farm sector either individual households or small groups were generally the beneficiaries of such changes. Under individual agriculture in China in the 1980s, incomes may rise and fall, but the possibility of bankruptcy and unemployment is small, especially as each farm household is given the right to use land rent free and the agricultural tax absorbs only a tiny portion of farm income. Also, because of the special inefficiencies related to collective farm agriculture, enormous gains to productive efficiency are achieved in agriculture simply through de-collectivizing the work organization and payment systems. Moreover, in agriculture and the small-scale non-farm sector reduced state control of markets tends to be spontaneously replaced by a high degree of competition (with beneficial economic and social results), since it is difficult to establish oligopolies or monopolies in most of these activities, especially in a poor, labour-abundant economy.

In agriculture and the small-scale non-farm sector peasants and employees almost universally respond positively to economic reform. Indeed, there is plenty of evidence in China's reforms of the late 1970s/ early 1980s that there was enormous pressure from peasants (though there often was opposition from lower-level cadres) at each stage to push the reform process further (Watson, 1983). Conversely, there is much greater opposition to economic reform of large-scale enterprises. This comes not simply from bureaucratic and Stalinist party leaders, but also from employees at all levels. In a large enterprise any gains to the unit of production from increased enterprise rights are likely to be diffused widely among a large workforce, especially when it is difficult to change traditional egalitarian payment systems (as in China in the 1980s). Moreover, there are likely to be much smaller gains than in agriculture from internal changes in work organization and payment systems: collective agriculture exhibits large managerial diseconomies of scale, whereas the inefficiencies in socialist countries' industry attributable purely to methods of internal enterprise management and payment systems are often relatively small. In socialist industry, increased inter-enterprise competition may bring gains to society as a whole, but for many individual enterprise reform brings no benefits at all; indeed it creates a serious possibility of bankruptcy and unemployment − it is much more difficult to separate an owner-operator household from its productive assets than it is to separate an industrial worker. Unsurprisingly, bankruptcy is an immensely contentious issue in socialist countries' industrial reforms. In China for example, a first draft (in 1986) of the Enterprise Bankruptcy Act was withdrawn, and the second draft (approved in December 1986) contained so many qualifying clauses designed to keep the potentially 'bankrupt' enterprise in business that it appeared to have been designed more to prevent, than to facilitate, bankruptcy ('Enterprise Bankruptcy Act', 1987).

In large-scale industry, granting enterprises economic rights (notably the right to retain a proportion of profits, or to retain all profits after tax) and increasing the operation of market forces does not necessarily increase competition. Indeed, there is the distinct possibility that large state enterprises might behave in an oligopolistic or even monopolistic fashion, especially in a huge economy such as China's, with a poorly developed transport system (even for a poor country), which is, effectively, divided into several regional markets. Moreover, without simultaneous reform of the price system, increased enterprise rights in industry can produce perverse, undesirable results, whereas in agriculture there can be considerable gains without reform of the price system. For example, there may be high profits and incomes for industrial enterprises that are fortunate enough to produce goods in particularly short supply and/or for which historically the price was set far above costs of production. These sorts of problems provide fuel to anti-reformers and contribute to a slowing of the reform process. Unfortunately, trying to reform the industrial price system step by step also produces big problems. For example, if price reforms proceed more rapidly in one sector than in another, then shortages may quickly develop in the unreformed sector, resulting, for example, in pressures to increase imports (especially in the case of necessary capital goods) leading to balance of payments problems (Chinese Academy of Social Sciences, 1987).

This book argues that reforming collective agriculture is a difficult, complex process: simply de-collectivizing collective farms is not a sufficient basis for sustained, efficient growth of the rural economy. However, in large-scale industry the process is much more complex, and even countries like China and Hungary, which had taken giant strides by the mid-1980s, still were in the middle of a long, turbulent process evoking huge social and political tensions. While the shortcomings of the Stalinist system are fairly clear, the manner in which to resolve them is not.

2

Theoretical Arguments concerning Collective Farms

Although Marxist agricultural theory has been criticised since the time of Bernstein and David in the late nineteenth century ... Marxist-Leninists have remained unmoved. Each new state socialist country has been surprised to discover that large-scale socialist agriculture suffers from serious problems.

Ellman, 1981

... [T]he advantage offered by a vigorous co-operative movement can hardly be exaggerated. ... It is needless to dwell on the vital importance of improving farming technique, which has very properly claimed a large share of the attention devoted to agricultural questions in China ... The foundation on which other indispensable improvements are most easily and securely built is machinery through which credit can be secured on reasonable terms, and orderly marketing substituted for the alternating periods of glut and scarcity which make farming a gamble, and a gamble with the dice heavily loaded against the farmer ... Once co-operation is firmly established, it can be extended from agriculture to the crafts carried on in connection with it ... The course of wisdom ... is to retain, where possible, ... the small production units which are the traditional form of industrial organization in China, but to secure for them the advantages of large-scale methods in finance and commerce, by taking steps to promote the formation of co-operative societies for credit, marketing and the purchase of raw materials.

Tawney, 1932

The collective farm has been the dominant form of rural organization in the socialist countries. Although there have been variations in

their nature both within and between socialist countries, there have
been many common characteristics. Among the most important are
the following:

- most rural means of production are owned by the collective;
- a large proportion of personal income is distributed by the collective;
- most collective labour occurs under the direction of collective farm
  officials, who generally are appointed (*de facto* or *de jure*) by party or
  state officials from outside the collective farm;
- the most important decisions about income distribution (the
  balance between consumption and accumulation, the payments system) are strongly affected by central party policy, in
  the formation of which collective peasants play little role;
- a large part of collective farm marketing occurs in order to meet (*de
  facto* or *de jure*) mandatory targets set by state or quasi-state purchasing authorities;
- collective farm members have no right to change their place of
  residence.

These are the characteristics which Soviet, Chinese, and other socialist
countries' collective farms have exhibited for most of their history. These
characteristics fundamentally differentiate these institutions from
co-operatives, in which, ideally, membership is voluntary, officials are
elected by the membership, and key policies (e.g. income distribution)
are democratically determined.[1] Indeed, the word collective is a misnomer.
Although the ownership of their assets, their work organization and
income distribution are formally collective, in practice they are generally,
in effect, state farms, except that members are not paid wages (as in
'state farms' proper) but have fluctuating incomes depending on the
harvest. As various observers have pointed out, the form of rural social
organization with which they have most in common is the idealized form
of the medieval European manor.

The governments of most socialist countries have attempted to go
beyond voluntary co-operation towards full-scale collectivization. There
are a number of reasons why in principle they have considered this to be
desirable.

*The political and ideological threat posed by an economically independent peasan-
try*   A powerful stream running through pro-collective writings since the
Soviet debates of the 1920s has been the conception that peasant consciousness is inferior to that of the urban industrial proletariat. Shaped
by the environment of individualist 'petty commodity production', the

peasantry is considered incapable of talking broad social interests into account. Consequently peasants may oppose policies which they consider harmful to their short-term interests, but which the state considers to be in the long-term interest of the whole nation. Collectivization resolves this problem in an effective fashion:

> There can be no doubt that such a revolutionary break [as collectivization] with the centuries-old backwardness of the antediluvian Russian village could not have been achieved with the consent of the irrational, illiterate, and ignorant peasant ... [I]n fact, compulsion and terror were decisive in achieving this 'profound revolutionary overturn' ... As in all situations in which the objective requirements of social developments collide with the individuals appraisal of those requirements, the latter may obstruct and delay the historical process; they cannot stop it altogether. [Baran, 1957, 278−9]

In a poor country with fast population growth it is likely to take a long time before the majority of the population is employed in the modern sector. The time required for this is lengthened if the country follows a capital-intensive heavy industry strategy such as China did from the early 1950s to the 1980s. Under such a strategy the structure of employment shifts only slowly, so that collectivization of agriculture can be viewed as an alternative method of 'proletarianizing' the peasantry necessitated by the slow growth of non-farm employment.

Agricultural collectives are viewed as vehicles through which the peasants' consciousness may be transformed (i.e. 'proletarianized') without waiting to be absorbed into modern sector employment. A central role is visualised for the communist party in 'leading' the peasantry into agricultural collectives and instilling proletarian values in peasants once they are inside the collectives. Although socialist countries' leaderships speak of agricultural collectives as though they were independent self-governing bodies, such statements sit uneasily beside the notion espoused by most socialist governments of leading peasants towards 'higher' forms of organization and consciousness: 'A great deal of work has to be done to remould the collective-farm peasant, to correct his individualistic mentality and to transform him into a real working member of a socialist society' (Stalin, 1929b, 469).

Such a position, in which a country's minority rulers feel they are justified in taking control of the day-to-day lives of the mass of the population in order to transform their consciousness and prevent them acting against what the minority rulers conceive of as the long-term common interest is deeply problematic from the standpoint of fundamental democratic principles. An important example of ethically based opposition to increased state control over the peasantry is found in the evolution of Bukharin's opposition in the 1920s to Stalin's anti-peasant approach (Cohen, 1974, 165−73). As Cohen observes; 'From the moment in December 1924 when he first denounced Preobrazhenskii's law as a "monstrous analogy" and "a frightful dream", to his charge in 1929 that Stalin's program amounted to "military-feudal exploitation of the peasantry", "ethical rhetoric" was part of his opposition to anti-peasant policies' (Cohen, 1974, 168). The only possible defence of such policies is the attainment of rapid growth of output and, eventually, living standards: as I will argue later, collective farms have proved a fundamental problem on both counts.

It is, of course, in principle possible to have truly independent self-governing fully collective farms. These have rarely (if ever) existed in socialist countries and have been far less numerous outside those countries than various forms of voluntary co-operation, which fall short of full collective farms. This book argues that there are few advantages and a great many disadvantages to full collective organization of the rural economy, so that it is most unlikely that peasants would voluntarily adopt such an institution.

Collectives can raise the rate of rural saving and investment Most administratively planned economies have placed high accumulation rates at the centre of their economic programme, and it is thought that collective agriculture can raise the rural accumulation rate compared to its performance under private farming. In part, there is a belief that this might occur voluntarily. Purchase of large, lumpy inputs which were impossible for individuals to undertake become possible for the collective farm. Large investment projects, such as irrigation works which benefit the whole local farming community, may be hard to organise due to differential benefits accruing to individual farm households. These may be more easily undertaken (voluntarily) where the means of production are owned in common and the benefits accrue more evenly within the community.

However, with income collectively distributed and most labour time centrally organized, if party control is sufficiently strong collectives can be used as vehicles for pushing up the accumulation rate (both through the purchase of inputs and through labour accumulation) against the wishes of peasants, but in order to achieve goals that the national leadership believes are in the whole country's long-term interest.

There are many problems in principle with such an accumulation-oriented approach to rural collectives. Firstly, there may be institutional possibilities other than collective farms which can enable private farmers to benefit from the purchase of lumpy inputs or from large-scale labour construction projects. For example, already by the early nineteenth century China had built up a sophisticated irrigation system alongside private agriculture (Perkins, 1969, 60-70). Densely settled, rice growing areas, such as Hubei, Hunan, Zhejiang, and Guangdong provinces, all had more than three-fifths of their cultivated land irrigated by the late nineteenth century (Perkins, 1969, 67). Shiba (1977) provides a detailed, and fascinating account of the medieval development of the sophisticated irrigation system of the Ningbo Plain (Zhejiang province). Alongside individual family farming, local officials, sometimes in collaboration with powerful local lineages, from the seventh through to the thirteen century constructed with peasant labour a sophisticated system of dikes and canals which liberated the area's agricultural production potentiality (Shiba, 1977, 390−6). Secondly, when peasants are free to make independent decisions, provided an adequate supply of industrial products (both capital and consumer goods) is available at the right price and markets are well developed, then, as the experience of China post-1978 confirms, peasants do not generally lack the motivation to save and invest. Moreover, there is a serious possibility that national leaders may use the control provided by collectives to push for such a high level of labour accumulation and/or marginal reinvestment rate that current returns to collective labour are reduced and labour motivation in the collective sector is damaged.

Collectives can serve as vehicles through which the state can achieve a high rate of marketing of farm production and siphon off rural savings to finance non-farm investment In a free market setting, with individual household-based farms, it may prove difficult to extract rural savings to finance non-farm investment. It may be practically difficult to tax a dispersed peasantry, and inadequate supplies of industrial commodities at prices that peasants consider unacceptable may reduce peasant incentives to produce output for the market. Therefore, it may be argued that the only way to sustain a Preobrazhensky-type policy of squeezing rural savings to finance industrial investment may be through forcibly sustaining a high rate of farm marketings by means of the control the state is able to exercise through collective farms − the 'Stalinist' solution. As Baran (approvingly) put it:

> [I]f there were no other powerful reasons for the desirability of collectivization of agriculture, the vital need for the mobilization of the economic surplus generated in agriculture would in itself render collectivization indispensable. By transferring the disposal of agricultural output from individual peasants to government-supervised

collective farm managements, collectivization destroys the basis for peasants' resistance to the 'siphoning off' of the economic surplus. [Baran, 1957, 268]

It may, however, be difficult even with collective farms to sustain a net savings outflow (see, e.g., Ellman, 1975; Ishikawa, 1967a). Moreover, whatever the institutional setting, a rapid rate of rural population growth, together with inadequate supplies of industrial capital goods and industrial incentive goods, may limit the growth of farm output *per capita* and, hence farm marketings (Ishikawa, 1967a). A special additional problem with collective farms is that in the process of their formation there frequently occurs much destruction of rural capital stock (especially animal motive power) necessitating an even larger 'import' of capital goods from abroad or from the industrial sector. An extreme example of this is the USSR. A 'stupendous' expansion of the use of agricultural machinery occurred between the late 1920s and late 1930s (mechanical power increased from 2 per cent of total farm power in 1929 to 57 per cent in 1938 [Jasny, 1949, 451 and 458]). However, due to a disastrous decline in rural livestock during collectivization (the number of horses fell from 29 million in 1929 to 14 million in 1938), the total rural horsepower (animals plus machines) in 1938 stood at the same level (30 million) as in 1929 (Jasny, 1949, 498). This sort of problem will be exacerbated if there are institutionally induced inefficiencies in the way in which the capital stock is used in collective farms. Indeed, it may be that collectivization produces a high rate, accompanied by a relatively low volume, of farm marketings, and in so far as it is practically possible to measure it, a net inflow rather than a net outflow of savings.

Collectives can serve as vehicles for the rapid diffusion of new techniques   Instead of relying on the market to diffuse new techniques, improved farm technology can be directly and rapidly introduced through collective farms in which party cadres are in leading positions.

The problem with this is that collectives can act as a medium through which both good and bad techniques can be disseminated. In a free market setting, inappropriate new technologies will simply not be purchased or be used experimentally only by a small segment of the peasantry. Enormous nationwide errors become a real possibility with collective farms, especially when operating together with an administratively planned industry which has few incentives to produce products that peasants really want. Examples range from the influence of Lysenkoism on Soviet genetics to the Chinese experience with the two-bladed, two-wheel plough [Ellman, 1981]. In their attempt to raise agricultural productivity without full mechanization China's planners in the mid-1950s mass-produced a new 'improved' plough, with two wheels and two blades. Huge numbers of these ploughs were produced: four million were planned for 1956 alone, enough to make the new plough the major tilling instrument over about three-quarters of China's farmland (Stavis, 1978, 70). Unfortunately, the plough was unsuited to agricultural conditions over a large part of China: 'As soon as the plough was distributed in Southern China, serious technical difficulties were noted. It sank into the mud of paddy fields and was too heavy and cumbersome to be used on the small plots of paddy or terraced fields. Generally, two beasts were required to pull it, and the Chinese work buffalo refused to work in teams. It was too wide for the paths between fields' (Stavis, 1978, 70). Large numbers of these expensive ploughs which collectives had been 'urged' to buy were simply discarded, at 'incalculable cost' (Walker, 1968, 420). Despite this, large numbers stockpiled as the industrial system kept churning out a useless product until the whole episode was brought to a halt in 1958 (Chao, 1970, 103).

Collectives enable villages to avoid class polarization The differentiation issue played a central role in both China's and the Soviet Union's collectivization. Mao and Stalin each argued that following their country's land redistribution, class inequalities began to develop. Mao, for example, in his key pre-collectivization speech in 1955 maintained:

> What exists in the countryside today is capitalist ownership by individual peasants. As is clear to everyone the spontaneous forces of capitalism have been steadily growing in the countryside in recent years, with new rich peasants springing up everywhere and many well-to-do middle peasants striving to become rich peasants. On the other hand, many poor peasants are still living in poverty for shortage of the means of production, with some getting into debt and others selling or renting out their land. If this tendency goes unchecked, it is inevitable that polarization in the countryside will get worse day by day ... [The] solution to this problem ... [is] to carry out co-operation and eliminate the rich peasant economy in the countryside so that all the rural people will become increasingly well off together. [Mao, 1955, 201−2]

However, the reality of rural class polarization under farm modernization in developing countries has turned out to be much more complex than Mao or Stalin anticipated. At the spatial level it is unquestionable that certain regions have benefited much more than others, on account of advantages enjoyed at the start of the modernization. Consider, for example, the following data on India:

Table 2.1 *Selected economic indicators for Punjab, compared to All India*

	Fertilizer consumption per hectare of cropped area 1982/3 (kg)	Electricity consumption per caput 1982/3 (kwh)	Motor veh. per 10 000 population (1980/1)	Per caput bank deposits Dec. 1982 (Rs)
Punjab	128	337	193	1657
All India	37	146	76	763

Source: Tata Services, 1984, 8–9[2]

However, the situation is much more problematic in respect to changes in village class structure. Owing to the difficulties associated with supervising agricultural labour (see below), it is unlikely that there will be a widespread emergence of large 'capitalist' farms each using large numbers of hired workers. Moreover, there is plenty of evidence to suggest that Green Revolution technology can percolate quickly down through different farm sizes,[3] especially where irrigation conditions are good. However, if state policies are inappropriate (e.g. if the rate of interest and the price of capital goods are kept too low; if the state fails to establish institutions to ensure the supply of 'lumpy' inputs) there is a possibility of large 'capitalist' farms emerging in which modern mechanized inputs substitute for labour. This process may be encouraged, too, by policies which make labour hiring illegal or which 'protect' wage labourers through minimum wage and other legislation. However, what is most striking about rural class relations under modern technology in countries where most of the labour force is still located in the rural areas is the diversity of outcomes, influenced not only by state policy but also by the enormous variations in the initial social and economic setting within which the new technology takes effect.[4]

Collectives can enable 'basic needs' of poor villagers to be met   It is often argued that collective agriculture can ensure that 'basic needs' can be better met than under private agriculture. All rural workers can be provided with employment. Farm families without, or with very little labour power can be provided for out of collective funds. These funds can be used to establish collective health and educational facilities from which all peasants can benefit.

There are, however, some shortcomings in this argument. First, the greatest problems of rural poverty tend to be regionally concentrated in whole areas with adverse conditions. Static redistributive measures can only to a limited degree resolve these areas' problems. Their more complete resolution is generally dependent on growth of output per person over the whole economy. Moreover, local redistributive policies excessively oriented towards basic needs can, paradoxically, impede that objective through their effects on production incentives and growth of farm output. Secondly, it is not clear that establishing local collective health and education facilities, or providing a basic minimum supply of food is necessarily dependent on collective ownership and operation of farm assets and collective income distribution. Some poor economies have been successful at rapidly improving rural 'basic needs' provision without establishing collective farms. The most striking examples are the Indian state of Kerala under communist rule and Sri Lanka. Despite being a 'low-income' country, Sri Lanka's profile in the 1980s in terms of overall death rates, life expectancy, child death rates, infant mortality and enrolment rates in primary and secondary education is the same as that of countries in the 'upper middle income' category, with average per caput income several times Sri Lanka's level (World Bank, 1986b, World Development Indicators). Successive governments in Sri Lanka were able to mobilize a relatively large amount of resources to meet 'basic needs' without setting up collective farms, or, indeed, even pursuing far-reaching land reform:

> Since the granting of universal suffrage in 1931 and more particularly after gaining independence in 1948, the policies of major parties have been influenced by a concept of a welfare state and redistributive justice. Through programmes of welfare and social service, a redistributive mechanism was introduced in Sri Lanka without affecting the economic structure and its productive relations. [ARTI, 1978, 20, quoted in Gunasinghe, 1982, 47]

Thirdly, while collective farms do guarantee employment, open unemployment in the countryside of poor countries is rarely the alternative. Rather, peasants are likely to suffer varying degrees of underemployment depending on their access to productive assets. It is an open question whether it is better to be collectively or privately underemployed.

Collectives enable the realization of economies of scale and overcome problems of 'lumpy' investments Belief in the superior efficiency of large-scale collective agriculture was deep-rooted among post-revolutionary socialist leaderships:[5]

Such despoliation of human energies and labour as takes place in the small, individual peasant economy cannot last any longer. If a transition were to take place from this splinter economy to a socialised economy, productivity of labour could double and treble, human labour could be saved twofold and threefold both for agriculture and for the human economy at large. [Lenin, quoted in Baran, 1957, 275]

The main disputes were about the pace of advance (e.g. whether collective farms should precede or follow mechanization). It was thought that collective farms would enable farmers to co-operate in the purchase of large modern inputs, construct irrigation facilities, and improve farm efficiency in a variety of ways—by allowing all farmland to benefit from agricultural experts' decisions about crop choice and methods of cultivation; permitting crop rotations impossible on individual farms; avoiding waste of farmland through boundaries between plots of land; avoiding waste of labour caused by walking between a farm's different plots; enabling the use of large mechanized inputs on consolidated holdings thereby producing better technical results (e.g. deeper ploughing) or releasing labour for other productive activities (this especially applies to mechanization of tasks at the peak seasons in the farm calendar); permitting full utilization of the capacity of lumpy inputs; enabling increased specialization and division of labour; and permitting 'socialization' of domestic labour, thereby releasing females for other productive activities.[6]

In fact, the issue of lumpiness and economies of scale in agriculture was much more complex than was anticipated by socialist countries' leaders.[7] The degree to which large farm size is economically advantageous varies greatly with different aspects of the farm process.

For most elements of working capital (including seeds, chemical fertilizer, pesticides, etc.), for livestock and for land, there is a high degree of divisibility of factors of production. Although free access to credit and better knowledge usually enable larger farmers to be the first to adopt modern inputs of working capital,[8] in modernizing areas it is often the case that new technology quickly percolates down through different farm sizes.[9]

There is an enormous variety of farm machinery for field work, so that, unlike in many industrial activities, a wide spectrum of capital—labour ratios is feasible. Nor should it be forgotten that capacity utilization can be kept high by renting machines out. The principal influences on capital—labour ratios in farming seem to be (1) managerial diseconomies of scale in respect to labour supervision (discussed below) and (2) the relative price of capital and labour. The existence of powerful managerial diseconomies of scale in farming means that it is rare to find direct farming using large numbers of hired labourers. When labour is relatively abundant and cheap, rather than the hiring of large numbers of permanent wage labourers, managerial scale diseconomies (producing falling output per worker with expanding farm size) tend, after a certain size [10] to lead to land being rented out rather than directly cultivated by the landowner. As the economy matures and farm labour becomes relatively more expensive it becomes rational to substitute capital for labour (as opposed to the purchase of capital goods to augment labour), so that farms may expand in area, but still employ relatively few hired workers. In the USA by the mid-sixties, for example, the average farm size was over 350 acres but there was an average of just 1.9 workers per farm (Bradley and Clark, 1972, 466).

There is usually a wide array of support operations which bear greatly upon farm performance. Many such activities (e.g. irrigation, processing, credit, research, marketing) are often beyond the scope of individual households, or would be carried out much more efficiently by an agency above the household level. The development of the rural productive forces will be inhibited in economies that lack such agencies.

The vision that many socialist countries' planners had was of enormous productivity gains to be obtained in agriculture, as in industry, from the division of labour and specialization made possible in a large unit production. An extreme example of this was the rationale given in the Chinese journal *Red Flag* during the Great Leap Forward (1958) for large-scale farm organization: 'The rapid development of agriculture simply demands that [the peasants] greatly emphasise their own organizational character, demands that in their work they act faster, in a more disciplined and efficient way, that they can be better shifted around within a broad framework like the workers in a factory or the soldiers in a military unit' (quoted in Schurmann, 1968, 479). In fact, the farm economy is characterised by peculiar difficulties in supervising farm work, generally leading to powerful managerial diseconomies of scale as the numbers of workers in a production unit expands. These difficulties are especially severe in rice-growing economies (see e.g. Bray, 1983, and Wittfogel, 1971).

There are a number of reasons for this. Firstly, special problems arise from the sequential nature of work over the course of the agricultural cycle. The bulk of farm tasks change with the season, so that most farm workers shift from task to task in the course of the year, making permanent job specialization impossible. Also, the final product of labour appears long after the bulk of the labour has been expended. If many workers have contributed to a piece of land during the course of the farm cycle, then it may be extremely difficult to identify and reward the contribution made by each worker. This difficulty is reduced, though not eliminated, by contracting pieces of land to sub-groups, as in the Chinese countryside in the late 1970s/early 1980s with the 'contract production to the group' (*bao chan dao zu*) reform, and the Russian 'link' (*zveno*) reforms of the 1970s. However, the ultimate way to solve this problem is to contract the land to the individual household, as occurred in China's reforms of the early 1980s (*bao gan dao hu* – 'contract work to the household'). A particularly interesting early example of this problem was in the 'classic' manor in Western Europe in the ninth and tenth centuries. Most field work on the lord's demesne was typically undertaken on plots contracted to the service households: 'more usually [the service household] was given the responsibility for an entire season's cultivation of a given plot of land ... taken from the *demesne* arable; activities which began with preliminary ploughing, continued right until storing of the grain in the lord's barn' (Duby, 1968, 40). Moreover, the sequential nature of operations and their dispersed nature means that, in contrast to many industrial processes, it is impossible to control the pace of work by regulating the speed at which material flows from one part of the production process to another. Only a few tasks, notably harvesting, in the course of the farm cycle have an easily measurable product. For most other tasks it is extremely difficult to determine how well a particular job has been done until the results become apparent in the form of the final product. In the absence of a system of contracts for different pieces of land, farm managers can only assess the quality of most supervised workers' labour by direct inspection. Hence, the saying among tractor drivers on Soviet collective farms: 'Plough deeper: I see the director coming' (quoted in Nove, 1977, 139). The same source asks: 'Who does not watch the work of the ploughman – the accountants, the supervisor, the brigadiers, the representative of the peoples' control, the rural Soviet, the agronomist, the agitator-political-organizer and even a volunteer-quality-controller. Yet what sort of peasant is it, if it is necessary to follow him about to ensure that he ploughs and harrows properly?' (quoted in Nove, 1977, 139).

Further problems result from the spatial dispersion of work on a large farm with many workers.[11] Given the importance of direct inspection, the large area covered in supervising farm work creates particular difficulties. Moreover, the nature of farm work will vary greatly in different parts of the farm owing to local natural conditions, and it is unlikely that the farm manager's knowledge of what is required on different parts of a large farm will compare with that of individual farm households. This problem is accentuated by the unpredictability of the weather, which frequently requires a quick, flexible response that may be hard to achieve in a large centralized unit of production. The problems discussed in this paragraph were recognised clearly by Joan Robinson: 'For the deployment of labour [in the agricultural sector of an under-developed country], a rather small scale is required. Workers are spread out over space so that discipline is hard to enforce; an incentive wage system is not easy to arrange or to administer; there has to be a great diffusion of managerial responsibility; every field is different, every day is different and quick decisions have to be taken' (Robinson, 1964).

It seems, then, that the peculiar nature of agricultural production leads to special difficulties in obtaining diligent labour from a large work-force. Direct supervision is hard to put into effect, and for most farm tasks it is not possible to devise payment systems that elicit high work motivation. Beyond a certain farm size (in terms of number of workers) managerial diseconomies of scale quickly set in. These considerations suggest strongly that for the key farm tasks, especially those associated with crop production, careful, diligent and knowledgeable labour is more likely to be provided by independent relatively small-scale farms than by units each employing a large number of workers: 'For getting work out of the workers, a peasant family is hard to beat. Discipline and responsibility are imposed by the pressing incentive to secure the family livelihood' (Robinson, 1964).

The labour supervision problem in farms with large numbers of workers is resolved if workers are strongly self-motivated out of a commitment to the collective project. It is not coincidental that under Mao so much effort was devoted to trying to get Chinese peasants to change their consciousness in the hope that they would develop self-motivation for hard, diligent work, negating the need for supervision. Examples of long-term success in this endeavour are rare, the most notable being Israeli kibbutzim. However, close examination of the kibbutzim reveals that a wide array of special conditions is responsible for their ability to sustain diligent, self-motivated, unsupervised farm labour e.g. membership is voluntary; the early kibbutzniks had a high degree of commitment to socialist goals, were highly educated, and brought a strong work ethic to the kibbutzim; there is a high degre of democracy within the kibbutz; the kibbutzniks have a high level of awareness of the importance of the social experiment they are undertaking; the kibbutzim have operated in a rapidly growing economy and have been able to raise their living stan-dards greatly since they were founded (Morawetz, 1983, 230—3).

The case for collective farms in developing countries on the grounds that they enable the realization of economies of scale and overcome prob-lems of lumpiness is not at all clear-cut. There certainly does appear to be a necessity for supra-household institutions to enable farmers to benefit from a wide range of important ancillary activities that frequently are inadequately provided by individual households and, perhaps, to permit the purchase of some large, lumpy inputs. However, it is possible to imagine a wide variety of institutions apart from the collective farm which might facilitate this. In the day-to-day tasks of crop cultivation the economic efficiency arguments for collective cultivation of the soil are weak. Moreover, there are strong reasons to think that, except under special conditions, there will be powerful managerial diseconomies of scale as employment per farm rises.

CONCLUSION

Rural markets in poor countries rarely work perfectly. There are usually many ways in which such markets 'fail'. In order to achieve a satisfactory growth rate of rural output it is usually necessary for much economic activity to take place above the level of the individual farm household. Voluntary co-operation among farmers is one important method of achieving this, and can benefit peasants in a wide variety of ways, including irrigation, research, processing farm products, transport, marketing, crop-spraying, health and education. In addition, unimpeded rural markets have important distributional consequences both locally and regionally. Local co-operation *per se* will have little impact on regional disparities, but may have an important impact on differentials within villages, through democratically agreed measures such as taxation and the provisions of public goods.

These types of voluntary co-operative activities, often government initiated, and in concert with direct state action (national and local),[12] can play a central role in successful rural development strategies. A model for such government-led rural co-operation is the work of the Joint Commission of Rural Reconstruction (JCCR) in post-1949 Taiwan:

> The JCCR was actively engaged in a fully integrated program of rural development long before this concept became popular. Its activities included livestock and crop improvement, water resource development, soil conservation, agricultural organisation and extension, agricultural financing, rural health improvement and agricultural research. The JCCR was particularly successful in helping to organise and direct the activities of the farmers' associations. [Thorbecke, 1979, 182]

Under this system, Taiwanese agriculture grew rapidly and relatively efficiently in the 1950s and 1960s. However, such supra-household state and co-operative action does not require collective cultivation of the soil, collective ownership of means of production and collective income distribution, though extensive farmer involvement in such schemes is greatly assisted if land redistribution (as in Taiwan) has reduced inequalities in rural asset ownership.

This chapter has argued that there are few advantages to collective cultivation, ownership of rural assets and collective income distribution. In a small number of exceptional cases (e.g. Israeli kibbutzim) where people choose to establish such institutions because they believe in them ideologically, mutual trust among voluntary co-operators running their own organizations can be established and the institutions run successfully. However, this is an exceptionally difficult thing to achieve.

In practice, peasants in socialist countries frequently have been forced unwillingly into collective farms so that lack of independence and absence of trust between peasants and those who ran the farms existed from the start. In those cases where peasants were 'mobilized' to join collective farms voluntarily, there are likely to have been few examples where peasant members trusted each other sufficiently to avoid serious difficulties with the payments system, arising from the peculiar problems in agriculture of accurately linking income to work done. In such cases, once these problems become obvious, it is likely that tight control over peasants would be required in order to keep them in the institutions which they had joined voluntarily. Moreover, of course, in all the socialist countries, whatever the methods by which collective farms were formed (the degree of compulsion varied greatly), the central leadership was unable to resist the temptation of trying (not always successfully) to control the fundamental aspects of peasants' economic and, indeed, social, life. Constant, deep, detailed intervention in matters ranging from the principles of distribution of collective incomes to sowing patterns, eating arrangements, freedom of movement, family size, burial arrangements and marriage practices, led quickly, if it had not begun that way, to a low trust relationship between rural cadres and peasants.

The net outcome of this is that for reasons of principle as well as errors in the practice of socialist governments, the labour process in collective farms in one respect has been analogous to that in capitalist industrial enterprises: collective work is a struggle between peasants and the managers of collective farms, with peasants possessing the capacity to work ('labour power') but the leadership having to try to coax work out of them in the collective sector via, mainly, the payment system. Of course, unlike the capitalist worker, the peasant in a collective farm cannot move his/her labour to another employer. More fundamentally, for the present argument, this chapter argues that if rural labour in large units is not self-motivated and based on mutual trust but is, rather, low-trust (of each other and of cadres) and supervised, an especially severe set of problems peculiar to agriculture arises, associated with the difficulties of labour supervision. In a poor economy, dominated by agriculture, this has profound consequences.

3

The Chinese Rural Economy under Mao

It is wrong to say that the present development of the co-operatives has 'gone beyond the real possibilities' or 'gone beyond the level of political consciousness of the masses'. ... China has an enormous population with insufficient cultivated land, ... natural calamities are frequent, ... and farming methods are backward. Consequently, although the life of the peasant masses has improved since the agrarian reform ... many are still in difficulty or not well off and those who are well off are relatively few, and hence most of the peasants are enthusiastic about the socialist road. ... For them socialism is the only way out ... [T]he only way for the majority of the peasants to shake off poverty, improve their livelihood and fight natural calamities is to unite and go forward along the high road of socialism.

Mao, 1955

Petrashevsky tried to put his Fourierism to practical use, explaining it in person to the peasants on his poverty-stricken estate in the region of St Petersburg. He built a large communal house for them with collective services, to replace the wretched huts in his village. One night he found it in ashes. It had probably been burnt down by the peasants themselves.

V.R. Leykina, quoted in Venturi, 1960

Ganbu shi na dajiade, jiti shi dajia nade — The cadres are those who grab things from everyone; The collective is that which everyone grabs things from

Popular saying in the Cultural Revolution

This chapter examines the record of China's collective farms under Mao, from the mid-1950s to the mid-1970s. It argues that in this period the

Chinese rural economy performed only moderately in terms of its pace of growth of output, of factor productivity and farm income. After the late 1970s its performance improved dramatically (see chapter 5). Trying to disentangle the reasons for the relatively poor performance pre-1978 is not easy: as is usual in the social sciences we do not have neat 'laboratory' conditions in which to isolate and test the different elements that might be responsible. Two main sets of problems in principle may have produced this result. Firstly, there may have been difficulties arising from the institutions *per se*, and secondly, there may have been difficulties caused by the external setting in which collective farms operated. Moreover, there is the probability of interaction between these phenomena. However, many observers have argued that criteria other than growth of output are relevant to judging the degree of success of a rural development strategy. Accordingly, this chapter examines also the results of this system for rural inequality and poverty relief.

RURAL INSTITUTIONS AND THEIR POLICIES UNDER MAO

A brief history

The collectivization of agriculture in China in 1955/56 was not spontaneous. The movement was strongly led by local party cadres encouraged by the central leaders, Mao especially (Selden, 1982). Nor was it without problems: such widespread occurrences as undervaluation of assets, excessive zeal in collectivizing items that cooperative regulations specified should have remained in private hands (e.g. trees and fish ponds), as well as uncertainties about the outcome in collective farms, led to a serious fall in pig stocks (Walker, 1965) and a fall in the output of a wide range of 'minor' agricultural and sideline products (Nolan, 1981, 61 and 209−10).

Instead of consolidating the collectives established in 1955−6, Mao, in the teeth of much high level opposition, led the movement to establish large 'rural people's communes' in 1958−9 ('the Great Leap Forward'). Mao believed the new institutions could accelerate the growth of farm output through more rational use of labour and through the stimulus given to peasants' work enthusiasm by the move towards 'communist' social relationships: 'The basis for the development of the people's communes is mainly the all-round, continuous leap forward in China's agricultural production and the ever-rising political consciousness of the 500 million peasants. ... It seems that the attainment of communism in China is no longer remote event. We should actively use the form of the people's communes to explore the practical road of transition to communism' (Central Committee, 1958). The agricultural collectives of 1955—6 had contained only about 160 households each; the people's communes each contained about 5000 households (Nolan, 1983c). Within the communes in 1958—9 dramatic changes to family life occurred with the 'socialization' of domestic labour. Incomes of constituent villages were equalized; 'private plots' were abolished; a large part of collectively allocated personal income was distributed in accordance with family size ('according to need') rather then 'according to work'; vast, ill-considered schemes were undertaken to use allegedly 'surplus' labour for water conservancy schemes and to expand rural industry (Nolan, 1983c). The results were disastrous. In 1962 grain output per caput stood at only 79 per cent of its 1957 level, while for aquatic products the 1962 figure was just 69 per cent of the 1957 figure, and for cotton, edible oil and meat the 1962 figure was a mere 45—46 per cent of that of 1957 (ZGTJNJ, 1985, 273). The collapse of agricultural production was accompanied by a demographic disaster, the enormity of which only became apparent to the outside world in the early 1980s. China's official data show a fall of 10 million in the total population in 1959—60 (SYC, 1983, 103) with a rise in the death rate from 12 per 1000 in 1958 to 25 per 1000 in 1960 (SYC, 1983, 105). One estimate concludes that the extra mortality during the four years of food crisis amounted to almost 17 million (Coale, 1981, 89). Another concludes that the net loss of life in 1960—1 was no less than 23 million (Aird, 1982a, 277—8).[1] It is surely cause for reflection that the worst famines of the twentieth century (in the Soviet Union in the early 1930s and in China in 1959—62) have occurred in countries with collective agriculture.[2]

It is often suggested that the principal reasons for the post-Great Leap disasters in agriculture were the withdrawal of Soviet experts following the Sino—Soviet split in 1960 and the severe flooding of 1960 and 1961. Soviet experts were mainly working in the non-farm sector, so this withdrawal could have had no direct effect on agriculture. Moreover, there is not much of a case to suggest an indirect effect, since the industrial crisis post-dated the agricultural crisis (table 3.1).

Table 3.1 *Indices of gross value of agricultural and industrial output in China (at 'comparable' prices)*

	1957	1958	1959	1960	1961	1962	1963
Agriculture	98	100	86	75	74	78	87
Industry	65	100	136	151	94	78	85

Source: ZGTJNJ, 1984, 24

There is no doubt that there were severe 'natural' disasters in 1960 and 1961, with abnormally large areas of farmland flooded (ZGTJNJ, 1984, 190). However, as Chao (1970, 125–38) has painstakingly shown, 'it is questionable to call the calamities in that period natural' (Chao, 1970, 129). A massive, ill-conceived expansion of the irrigated area occurred during the Great Leap, followed by an equally rapid contraction thereafter. Official Chinese sources reported the index of the irrigated area to have changed as follows: 1959=100, 1959=206, 1963=96 (Chao, 1970, 121). The figure for the Great Leap is almost certainly a considerable overestimate. However, a massive expansion undoubtedly occurred, and these facilities were so poorly designed and executed, as to play a major role themselves in causing subsequent flooding. Chao concludes: 'To a large extent (the floods) were man-made, or at least, man-induced, calamities, because there would not have been so many nationwide disasters, and lasting for three years, if the government had not carried out wholesale water conservation construction. In other words human action created a new pattern of calamities unseen in Chinese history. What the Chinese Communists did in 1958 had not only destroyed most of the flood-control facilities but also had made the areas previously flood-free now vulnerable to heavy rainfall' (Chao, 1970, 130). There could be no better example of the capacity of collective farms under central direction to introduce wildly inappropriate schemes.

Following the disaster of the 'Great Leap Forward' collective institutions were modified dramatically in principle; in many areas collective agriculture broke down and virtual private farming resumed (see, e.g., Chen and Ridley, 1969). Only through a massive campaign in the early 1960s, the 'Socialist Education Movement' (Baum, 1975), were rural collectives firmly re-established. Although this campaign was successful in re-collectivizing China's villages, the considerable popular support for them which characterized the collectivization and communization campaigns of the 1950s (albeit that they were firmly led by the party) was severely eroded by the catastrophe of 1959–61. Popular trust in the party's judgement on rural matters had declined greatly. The institutional structure remained basically unchanged from then through to the late 1970s. Important functions were organized at the commune and the intermediate 'brigade' level, including hospitals, schools, road construction, water conservancy, small industries and running large agricultural means of production. However, the 'production team', rather than the commune, each containing around 25 households in the early 1960s, became the basic unit of ownership, of agricultural work organization and of income distribution (Nolan, 1983c).

Regional differences in institutions

One might expect there to have been big differences in the form of collective organization in China, to take account of the enormous regional differences in agricultural conditions. While the size of collectives varied somewhat,[3] and there were many local variations in institutional practices, a striking feature of the pre-1978 system was the narrow range of such variations. The whole of rural China operated under fundamentally the same system. This was illustrated vividly by the series of production team accountants' manuals published in each province in the early 1970s.[4] These substantial documents (80–150 pages each) provide detailed insight into the Maoist commune system, and show only small variations in the way different provinces wished rural intitutions to be run. It seems likely there would be considerable efficiency losses resulting simply from this insensitivity to regional differences.

Non-economic aspects of village life

Under Mao, the Chinese Communist Party's (CCP) membership amounted to only 2.5 to 3 per cent of the total population (though its influence extended through ancillary organizations, such as the Communist Youth League). This 'vanguard' body controlled the key positions of village political power.[5] Such control was legitimated by the Party Constitution as follows: 'State organs, the People's Liberation Army and the militia, labour unions, poor and lower-middle peasant associations, the Communist Youth League, the Red Guards, the Little Red Guards and other revolutionary mass organizations *must all accept the centralized leadership of the Party.*' (*Constitution of the Communist Party of China*, 1973, Article 7) (My emphasis — P.N.) All important village decisions ultimately had to be sanctioned by the party, and the party was the key vehicle for putting into effect state regulations on rural matters.

Pre-1978 the party not only tightly controlled the village economy, but also deeply influenced social affairs. For example, traditional village theatre and music were pushed in the direction the party wished to follow, with only a narrow range of 'revolutionary' products sanctioned. Tea houses, the traditional village male meeting places, were condemned and mostly closed down. Traditional marriage and burial practices were attacked and the party attempted (not always successfully) to change these, too, in a 'revolutionary' direction (see, especially, Parish and Whyte, 1978). The party's intervention in these areas, especially in the extreme form it took during the late sixties and early seventies, produced widespread discontent among the peasantry, and made it difficult for local party cadres to develop a relationship of trust with the peasants.

Size and supervision

Chapter 2 argued that there were fundamental labour supervision problems in agricultural units with more than a few workers. Only special conditions could overcome the necessity for such supervision. In China in the sixties and seventies, even the smallest unit of collective ownership and work organisation — the production team — contained, on average, 40−60 workers (ZGJJNJ, 1981, VI, 7 and 9). It proved impossible to devise payment systems that would produce the same kind of diligent, self-motivated labour for the collective as characterized peasants working for their own family. In part, the problem was the party's relatively egalitarian policies concerning collective labour remuneration. However, as a mass of Chinese literature in the 1980s suggests, to a substantial degree it reflected the fundamental difficulties in principle in devising payment systems for workers in labour-intensive agriculture (see, e.g., Lin, 1982).

Assigning workpoints to different tasks caused immense problems in calculation and measurement of performance. As one exasperated team cadre graphically put it:

> I have tried the system of assigning workpoints to quotas. I spent a lot of energy making different rules for how many workpoints there should be if one does this kind or that kind of work and if one performs a certain amount of work. In the case of ploughing, for instance, the rules for workpoints differed depending on whether one used a strong or weak buffalo, or one of average strength. Even for the same kind of buffalo, there were also different kinds of land; and for the same type of land, the case was also different if it had rained or if the soil was dry . . . . With so many rules, it was almost endless. If they were printed into a book, it would be quite a thick edition. They were so elaborate the peasants were not interested at all. [quoted in Lin, 1983, 65]

The complexity of the system is illustrated by the fact that in the 1970s, one brigade's list of workpoint norms included over 200 different tasks (Xin Yu Brigade, 1978). For each task there was an attempt to set a 'quantity requirement'. For example, for winnowing, weighing and putting into store the grain from one *mu* of land, two workpoints were awarded; the 'quality requirement' was that the grain was ' correctly weighed' and that there was 'no waste' in winnowing (Xin Yu Brigade, 1978). Checking such 'quality requirements' in detail for a myriad of tasks for a large number of workers operating under varied conditions was beyond the capacity of team leaders and village accountants, so that in practice there must have been only a rough relationship of work accomplished to remuneration. Moreover, there was a high probability of personal ties and corruption intervening in the workpoint recording process.

The complexity of the piece-rate system (in its various forms) was a major reason, apart from party ideology,[6] that collective remuneration in the Cultural Revolution was frequently based on the simpler time rate system. Under this the worker's collective annual workpoint total depended on time spent on collective labour plus a periodically reassessed workpoint grade allocated to the worker. Although simple, this system had the major drawback of a relatively tenuous link between labour output and remuneration.

Labour mobility

It was extremely difficult pre-1978 to move residence from one part of the countryside to another. To do so required the permission of both the local public security organ (with whom peasants were registered) and the collective to which it was intended to move. Pre-1978 collectives provided peasants with both employment and the bulk of their income. Hence, the control system was hard to evade. In general, it was said to be easy to get official permission to migrate from the city to the countryside, from the plains to the hills, or from the hills to the mountains, but difficult to obtain permission to move in the opposite direction.[7] The lack of labour mobility almost certainly had static efficiency costs, and probably inhibited the spread of ideas. It also enabled well-placed collectives to maintain their income, derived from superior location, undiminished through in-migration. It prevented peasants in poor areas improving their situation through migration and, perhaps, in turn improving the position of those left behind through remittances. Substantial ill-feeling must have been generated in backward areas as a result of this policy. This is in striking contrast with migration patterns in the 1980s after the rural reforms.

Collectives' sowing pattern

Under Mao, China's population was growing relatively rapidly; also, China adopted a sceptical approach towards international trade and was determined not to depend heavily on grain imports. Consequently, if the leadership wished to ensure that basic food needs were met, it was essential to ensure that grain production kept up with population. The poor productivity of agricultural resources (discussed below) meant that a large proportion of resources was required to achieve this fundamental goal. Even in the mid-1970s, over 80 per cent of China's sown area was planted with grain (ZGTJNJ, 1985, 252). To achieve such a high figure through the state grain price alone was impossible in the given circumstances. The state was committed to price stability in the non-farm sector, which limited the degree to which it could raise the price it paid peasants for grain without forcing the budget into substantial deficit or encroaching upon other budgetary outlays. A large share of the non-defence portion of the state budget was committed to capital construction in heavy industry (ZGTJNJ, 1984, 308 and 421). This was in part a matter of choice, but in part attributable to the low efficiency with which the capital stock was used, mainly on account of micro-economic problems derived from the administrative planning system. Moreover, the state was locked into a vicious circle of high outlays on this sector owing to the high requirements of the heavy industry sector for its own products (e.g. in 1973 the average consumption of energy (kilograms of coal equivalent) per *yuan* of output value was: agriculture = 0.58, light industry = 0.48, heavy industry = 4.33, transport = 2.26, construction = 1.01 (Chen, 1981, 7751). Substantially raising the grain price (had it been politically feasible to do so) without corresponding reforms to increase the supply of industrial wage goods at a sufficient pace, might, indeed, have produced a perverse result of even less incentive to produce and market grain. Consequently, the state intervened directly in the collectives' resource allocation process, forcing them (via planting instructions and compulsory purchase quotas) to grow more grain than they would have voluntarily chosen to grow at the given price. The preemption of a large proportion of collective resources for relatively low-return grain production contributed to lowering the relatively low level of income obtainable from the collective (particularly in relation to the private sector).

Marketing

The state began to procure grain compulsorily in October 1953, and the system of 'unified' (*tong gou*) and 'assigned' (*pai gou*) state purchase quickly expanded in the mid-1950s to include all the major farm products (Duan, 1983). Eventually, the system included over 200 farm products (Duan, 1983). The proportion of agricultural output procured by the state rose quickly in the 1950s, reaching a peak of over two-fifths of total farm output in the mid-1960s.[8] State purchases and agricultural taxation accounted for an officially estimated 92−5 per cent of farm sector sales to the non-farm sector in 1952—83 (Sheng, 1986, 12). Virtually all state procurement occurred through compulsory 'unified' or 'assigned' purchases. Even in the early 1980s (i.e. after a considerable reduction in the number of products in these categories) about 80—5 per cent of state procurements were in these categories (Duan, 1983). This left collectives with little freedom in marketing their produce.

From the mid-1960s to the mid-1970s rural free markets dealt in a relatively small volume of produce. This was not surprising given the extensive restrictions. For example, in Jiading *xian* (in the Shanghai suburbs) the following restrictions applied (Nolan, 1979). First, prices in the 'free' market were not allowed to be more than 20 per cent higher than the state price. Second, only peasants from within a certain catchment area were permitted to come and sell their produce. Third, there were certain products that were prohibited from sale on the free markets (e.g. coarse grain from private plots). Fourth, different communes made their own regulations on sales at free markets (e.g. some communes stipulated that peasants should not go to the market in the busy season, or that they were only allowed to come in the morning). Fifth, collectives were prohibited from selling at the free markets.

Collectives' saving and investment decisions

Through the local party apparatus, the central leadership under Mao pushed rural collectives towards its favoured strategy. The various model units (notably the famous Dazhai (Tachai) production brigade) which China's production teams were urged to emulate, stressed the importance of accumulation for agricultural growth, and were characterized by a high marginal investment rate. According to official policies, the optimal path for collectives to follow was to 'gradually' increase commune members' personal incomes and to 'rapidly' increase collective accumulation (Nolan, 1983c, 40). Indeed, in the case of relatively rich collectives, all increments to collective net income had to be channelled into investment, since a ceiling on personal incomes from the collective was commonly fixed in a particular area (Nolan, 1983a, 41). This dampened collective work incentives, especially in well-off areas. Such a strongly accumulation-oriented policy towards rural growth in part was made necessary by the low efficiency of collective resource use: in order to grow the system needed a lot of capital. Moreover, such a policy helped to exacerbate this very problem, since the high marginal investment rate depressed work incentives and itself reduced the effectiveness with which capital was used. In the process was formed one of the many 'vicious circles' that characterized the Maoist rural economy.

Labour accumulation

A major argument in favour of rural collectives has been their alleged capacity to mobilize Nurksian 'surplus labour' for low-cost capital construction.[9] In principle, the fact that the whole village benefits might enable this to be achieved voluntarily by the collective whereas a village with private, unequal ownership might fail to mobilize such labour.

China's collective farms were extremely 'successful' at mobilizing 'surplus' labour both in the 1950s (Schran, 1969, ch. 3) and in the 1960s and 1970s (Nickum, 1978). The most striking product of this effort was the enormous expansion of China's irrigated area from 20 million hectares in 1952 (19 per cent of the arable area) to 27 million hectares in 1957 (24 per cent of the arable area), reaching 43 million hectares in 1975 (43 per cent of the arable area (ZGJJNJ, 1981, VI, 13). However, there were problems with this policy.[10] First, labour often was not 'mobilized' voluntarily. Second, labour was often 'mobilized' for projects organized at levels above the production team, and it was difficult to devise systems that ensured that returns to localities were proportionate to their contribution. Third, it is unlikely that the opportunity costs of labour for construction work normally were assessed carefully. Returns to such work were relatively low and falling. Although annual output per agricultural worker rose a little over the long term,[11] the large increase in 'surplus' labour per worker mobilized for low productivity construction helped contribute to the long-term decline in the value of the 'workpoint' (i.e. the return per unit of collective labour). There is plenty of evidence to suggest dissatisfaction with the degree of labour mobilization achieved by the Maoist collectives. Peasants reportedly did not fear hard labour, but only feared useless labour (Ishikawa, 1982, 122).

Distribution of personal income by the collective

During the Great Leap Forward a large number of communes distributed a high proportion of personal income according to 'communist' principles, i.e. 'according to need'. This had a strong detrimental effect on work incentives, since the individual worker's effort now had little effect on his/her income. Hard work now depended crucially on either mutual trust or on a commitment to a higher goal (e.g. building a strong national economy, or 'serving the people'). Accordingly, commune regulations in the 1960s stressed the importance of keeping a quite high proportion of collectively distributed personal income allocated 'according to work'. Although collective welfare allocations were an important aspect of the Chinese collective system, they do not seem to have generally taken a large share of collective income.[12] Moreover, commune members had to pay for access to welfare facilities.[13]

However, in its determination to ensure that minimum 'basic needs' were met, the party stipulated that a sizeable segment of grain should be allocated 'according to need' (i.e. family size, often weighted by age structure). For example, in Guangdong province in the 1970s it was officially advocated that this 'basic grain ration' should not fall below 70 per cent of total collective grain distribution (Zhong, 1974, ch. 4). The grain was not provided free. Its value had to be offset against earnings from the collective and a loan made if the household 'overdrew' (i.e. the value of its grain exceeded that value of its collective workpoint earnings). In high income collectives this caused no problem, but in poor areas where most collective income was absorbed by grain consumption, adherence to party guidelines led to the bulk of personal income being allocated 'according to need' with all the incentive problems that this involved.

In respect to allocation of collective income 'according to work' big problems developed. The first is simply that (as noted in chapter 2) for most farm tasks it is extremely difficult to measure work contribution. It is not surprising that most collectives probably used a hybrid system, with piece rates often adopted for simple, easily measurable tasks (e.g. harvesting), and time rates adopted for the rest of the farm calendar, weighted by the worker's 'workpoint' rating.[14] In principle, collective workers' 'workpoint' ratings could have been extremely wide. In practice, in the atmosphere of the Cultural Revolution they were not, and it was normal for adult male workers' rating for a day's collective labour to fall between 8 and 10 points, i.e. a very narrow differential (see, especially, the discussion in Parish and Whyte, 1978, 60–5).

Official policy in the late 1960s and in the early/mid-1970s was strongly opposed to wide differences in workpoints within production teams. For example, in Guangdong province in the early seventies, on the one hand official policy affirmed the importance for work incentives of 'distribution according to work', opposed 'absolute egalitarianism', and considered it necessary to 'recognize the differences' in labour contribution when allocating collective income for personal consumption. On the other hand, it spoke as follows:

... The Lin Biao and Lin Shaoqi bunch of swindlers advocate the revisionist trash of 'workpoints in command' and 'material incentives' which expands the differences in individual incomes of commune members. While we must recognize that 'work points in command' and material incentives can sometimes stimulate some people's production enthusiasm this type of incentive definitely isn't socialist enthusiasm; it is enthusiasm of the capitalist-road type. If we do things in this way, then capitalist thinking will spread unchecked. Not only will we be unable to promote socialist development, but it might bring about a capitalist restoration. . . . 'Recognizing the differences' certainly does not mean the bigger the differences the better. If labour remuneration differentials are too great, and the differences in commune members' living standards are too wide, this will not be in conformity with the socialist system of common ownership of the means of production and the mutual relations between members; that is to say, it is detrimental to commune members' unity and even more detrimental to mobilizing all positive elements to speed up the socialist revolution and the construction of socialism. [Zhong, 1974, 12–14]

Although 'absolute egalitarianism' was probably rarely practised, the deep suspicion of 'workpoints in command' ensured that the range of workpoint differentials was so small as to constitute a serious barrier to effective work incentives in the collective sector over most of rural China in the sixties and seventies.[15]

The private sector

Following the disastrous attempt during the Great Leap Forward (1958–9) in many areas to eliminate the private sector completely (Walker, 1965), peasants thereafter were formally allowed to undertake private economic activity on their 'private plot' (generally set at about 5 per cent of arable land) and to raise a limited number of 'private' animals. Presumably, this was, in part, simply a recognition of the peasants' attachment to private property, though part of this attachment may have been as a form of insurance in case the collectives collapsed again or performed less well than was hoped. However, it probably reflected too the fact that supervision problems were more severe in some types of activity (e.g. vegetables) than in others and that total output would, accordingly, suffer severely if all production was in the collective sector . However, the private sector was viewed with great suspicion by central power-holders, as a 'soil for nurturing capitalism', which might 'contend with the collective economy for land, labour, power, time and fertilizer, encroaching upon and weakening the collective economy.' (*Socialist Collective Ownership System*, 1976, ch. 3). The appropriate policy was said to be to 'manage it well, lead it strongly under conditions in which the collective economy has absolute superiority', so as to 'increasingly restrict' its scope (Shanghai County Party Committee, 1975).

Except in extremely advanced, highly mechanized areas (such as parts of North-East China) the net income from a unit of labour time in private sector work generally was considerably higher than in the collective sector. The private sector provided some important products (notably vegetables) which the collective often could not; it gave peasants an opportunity to produce relatively high value products for sale to the state or at the village fairs; also, it provided a much greater opportunity than in the collective sector for the concealment of production to escape the state's procurement net. Many of the processes discussed above (e.g. labour supervision difficulties, ceilings on collective distributed income, state sowing plans and procurement quotas pushing collectives to produce relatively low value produce, very high marginal reinvestment rates, labour mobilization for mass construction projects with low returns) tended generally to lower collective relative to private remuneration. Under such circumstances, the private sector provided a constant lure to commune members, draining the collective sector of resources, and tending still further to reduce the collective sector's rate of pay.

Local cadres waged a constant struggle with peasants to persuade them to allocate a large share of their productive energies to the collective sector (Unger, 1978) and the struggle was a major source of conflict between them. At least about one-quarter of peasants' personal income in the late 1960s and 1970s came from the private sector (Nolan, 1983c, note 42) and to keep the figure even at this level was a massive struggle for the rural party apparatus.

THE EXTERNAL ECONOMIC SETTING

Supply of industrial inputs

Pre-1949 Chinese agriculture had already achieved a high level of development within the confines of 'traditional' technology (Ishikawa, 1967b, 57-84). By the late 1950s there were only limited possibilities for increasing output using traditional technology alone (Perkins, 1969), as was demonstrated by the disastrous failure of the attempt to expand the irrigated area in the Great Leap Forward (Chao, 1970, ch. 5). The production of industrial inputs for agriculture was given a low priority in the 1950s (*First Five Year Plan*, 1956, ch. 3), as industry concentrated on expanding its future capacity to produce capital goods. Following the Great Leap Forward the production of industrial inputs was given much higher priority and Chinese agriculture modernized rapidly in the 1960s and 1970s:

Table 3.2 *Modernization of Chinese agriculture, 1957—1975*

	1957	1975
Tractor-ploughed area as % of total ploughed area	2.4	33.3
Irrigated area as % of cultivated area	24.4	43.4
Power-irrigated area as % of total irrigated area	4.4	52.9
Chemical fertilizer applied per hectare of cultivated land (kg, nutrient weight)	3.3	53.8
Electricity used per hectare of cultivated land (kwh)	1.3	183.6

Source: ZGJJNJ, 1981, VI, 13

Indeed, in the 1960s and 1970s the countryside began to take a greatly expanded share of some important key industrial products. The share of total steel products used in agriculture and for agricultural machinery rose from 8 per cent in 1957 to 17 per cent in 1977; the share of electricity used by the villages rose from less than 1 per cent in 1957 to 11 per cent in 1977; the share of timber products used by communes and brigades rose from 5 per cent in 1957 to 13 per cent in 1977, while that of cement rose from 9 per cent to 25 per cent over the same period (Ministry of Agriculture, 1980).

A large proportion of farm industrial inputs was produced in state factories and supplied through state marketing networks at state-fixed prices. The system of tight control through administrative planning meant that there was little incentive for factories producing farm inputs to improve the quality and variety of their products.

Supply of industrial 'incentive' goods

Through their impact on peasant incentives to work, save and invest in human and physical capital, industrial 'incentive goods' can play an important part in agricultural growth. Indeed, at low levels of income the commonsense distinction between investment goods (things which improve labour productivity) and consumption goods often becomes blurred. The rate of growth of output of industrial incentive goods in China pre-1978 was impeded by, among other things: (1) a misguided belief in the virtues of heavy industry and underestimation of the importance of incentive goods in the growth process; (2) inefficiencies in the use of capital (due in turn to the problems of administrative planning and of enterprise work organization and payments systems) reinforcing the pre-emption of resources by the capital goods sector; (3) a vicious circle of heavy industry expansion attributable to the fact that heavy industry uses a relatively large amount of heavy industrial products per unit of output. Per caput availability of industrial incentive goods was further limited by the rapid growth of population that was sustained until the 1970s. Supplies to the peasantry were further limited by the peasants' low average purchasing power compared to urban workers. Starting from a very low base, rapid growth rates were recorded for certain industrial consumer durables,[16] but still, at the end of the Maoist epoch, consumption levels in the countryside were very low as may be seen in Table 3.3.

Table 3.3 *Average consumption of consumer durables per 10 000 people*

	Bicycles		Sewing machines		Radios		Watches	
	Urban	Rural	Urban	Rural	Urban	Rural	Urban	Rural
1957	90	4	19	1	22	1	108	0
1975	246	28	133	15	287	40	514	12

Purchases in the current year, i.e. not stocks.
Source: ZGNYJJGY, 1982, 211

Moreover, the range of products was very narrow indeed and the quality was generally poor.

Terms of trade between industrial and agricultural products

From the 1950s through to the 1970s a considerable improvement (for the peasants) took place in the relative price of agricultural sales to the state (which purchased most farm sector marketings). The index of procurement prices of agricultural and sideline commodities rose from 100 in 1957 to 143 in 1975, while the index of the retail price of industrial commodities sold in the villages fell from 100 to 98 over the same period (ZGJJNJ, 1985, 532). However, Chinese economists argue that this conceals some important problems. As Preobrazhensky argued in the 1920s (Preobrazhensky, 1965, 111), and many development economists have pointed out since,[17] more important than the direction of movement of the index of relative prices (the 'commodity terms of trade') is the relationship of prices to costs. Chinese economists argue that rapid increases in farmers' material costs of production substantially eroded the improvement in purchase prices. From 1965 to 1976, material expenses (at current prices)) per physical unit of product reportedly rose by 17 per cent for grain, 25 per cent for oilseeds, 89 per cent for tobacco and 92 per cent for cotton (Investigation and analysis of issues in the agricultural economy, 1982, 109). Moreover, China's farmers pre-1978 had to pay relatively high prices for industrial inputs compared to those prevailing on world markets (Liang, 1982, 72).

Inter-sectoral resource flows

There are many problems involved in analysing inter-sectoral resource flows, ranging from such conceptual issues as defining a 'resource' and a 'sector' to the difficulties involved in acquiring the necessary data. The simplest approach is to treat inter-sectoral flows in conventional balance of payments terms using either current or constant prices. Two substantial studies have been undertaken along these lines, one for the 1950s (Ishikawa, 1967a) and one for the whole 1952−1983 period (Sheng, 1986). Each examines the balance of trade between the farm and the non-farm sectors, and does not directly examine the balancing inter-sectoral 'savings' transfers (factor service payments and current transfers, and capital transfers and lending). Measured in current prices, Ishikawa (1967a) finds an export surplus for the farm sector from 1952 to 1954, turning into an import surplus from 1955 to 1957. Sheng (1986) finds the import surplus to exist throughout the period from 1952 to 1983. Choice of a base year for measuring 'real' values is difficult. However, a good case can be made for choosing 1957, since by then the relative prices of industrial and agricultural products had more or less returned to the position of 1930−36, the most normal years for the Republican economy. In the early 1950s the relative price of industrial products was high, i.e. the 'price scissors' had widened considerably compared to 1930−36 (ZGNYJJGY, 1982, 191). Over the long term, the relative price of agricultural sector 'exports' increased considerably, so that measured at 1957 prices, the size of the farm sector import surplus in 1952−57 is reduced somewhat (though not eliminated), and for the post-1957 period it expands considerably (Sheng, 1986). This seems to suggest that the farm sector in China was not (except, according to Ishikawa in the early 1950s, i.e. before collectivization) used as a source of savings to fund non-farm investment.

However, examining inter-sectoral 'resource' flows in terms of market prices (whether current or constant) may conceal important features of inter-sectoral exchange. It has been argued in respect to both China (Macrae, 1979) and the USSR in the First Five Year Plan (Barsov, discussed in Ellman, 1975) that a more appropriate approach is to examine the products exchanged in terms of embodied labour. It is hard to quantify this notion. A simpler approach is to examine the exchanged commodities in terms of the relationship to prices and costs in each sector. There is a strong feeling among Chinese economists that 'unequal exchange' in this sense increased from the 1950s through to the 1970s, and that while agriculture's exports were becoming progressively less profitable (or even making losses), the industrial sector was making large profits on its sales to agriculture often using materials purchased from that sector, (see, e.g., Dong, 1982, 47).

THE RESULTS

Output

Viewed in the simplest terms, Chinese agriculture under collectives performed well. The gross value of agricultural output reportedly rose from 64 billion *yuan* in 1952, to 79.3 billion in 1957, 129 billion in 1975 and 146 billion in 1978 (all at 1970 prices) (ZGNYJJGY, 1982, 28), giving a compound annual growth rate of 2.7 per cent from 1957 to 1975 and 3.0 per cent from 1957 to 1978. Looking at the main individual agricultural products, over the same period, only oilseeds failed to register a big increase. From 1955−7 to 1975−7 grain output reportedly grew at 2.0 per cent per annum, cotton at 1.7 per cent, jute and hemp at 5.2 per cent, sugar cane at 3.2 per cent, tobacco at 6.1 per cent, fruit at 3.1 per cent, and meat at 3.5 per cent (see table 5.1).

Obviously, to leave the story here would be unsatisfactory. China's population also expanded enormously growing from 646 million in 1957 to 924 million in 1975 (ZGTJNJ, 1985, 185). Thus, the growth rate of agricultural output was not far ahead of that of population − 2.0 per cent per annum. Indeed, the most striking thing about output per person of the main farm producuts in China from the mid-1950s to the mid-1970s is how little change there was. Grain output per caput was unchanged, cotton and oilseeds fell slightly, while meat output rose slightly (see table 5.2). The unchanging food otuput per caput is reflected in the long-term stability of nutrient intake per person in China: average daily calorie intake in both the 1950s and the late 1970s was reported to be around 2300 (ZGTJNJ, 1984, 100).

Productivity

China's government in 1949 inherited an economy in which output per hectare was already relatively high by 'traditional' standards (Ishikawa, 1967b, 57-83). Over the long term it proved extremely difficult to expand the cultivated area. Indeed, there was a reported net loss of land due to urban encroachments and other causes. The reported arable area fell from 112 million hectares in 1957 to 100 million hectares in 1975, while the number of agricultural workers increased massively from 193 million in 1957 to 295 million in 1975, resulting in a sharp decline in arable area per worker from 0.58 hectares in 1957 to just 0.34 hectares in 1975 (ZGNYJJGY, 1982, 8 and 85). After some expansion of the sown area in the 1950s (from 141 m hectares in 1952 to 157 m hectares in 1957), the reported figures for the 1960s and 1970s show a slight decline (e.g. in 1975, the sown area was reported to be 150 m hectares) (ZGNYJJGY, 1982, 9, ZGTJNJ, 1985, 292). Consequently, despite the increased number of workers per unit of farmland, the 'multiple cropping index' (sown area as a percentage of arable area) altered little after 1957 (1952=131, 1957=141, 1965=138, and 1975=150). The main path towards increasing farm output was raising yields per unit of sown area. In respect of grain the Chinese record is impressive, with an expansion of more than 60 per cent in yields from 1957 to 1975. Among the major 'economic' crops over the same period, the results were mixed: impressive improvements in yields were achieved for cotton (71 per cent), rapeseed (76 per cent), and tobacco (111 per cent), though, in the latter two cases, this followed a serious decline in the mid-1950s; for peanuts (20 per cent) and hemp (12 per cent) there was little change, while for sugar cane (−18 per cent) and sugar-beet (−13 per cent) yields actually fell (see table 5.3).

As has been shown, a rapid expansion of modern inputs took place in Chinese agriculture in the sixties and seventies following the disaster of 1959−61. The value of China's agricultural fixed assets (excluding land) expanded much more rapidly than the value of agricultural output. Consequently the capital−output ratio in agriculture (at current prices) rose form 0.29 in 1957 to 0.67 in 1978 (ZGNYJJGY, 1982, 119). At constant prices, the rise would have been much greater.

Given the long-term rapid growth of rural population, and the slow rate of absorption of rural labour into non-farm employment, the agricultural labour force expanded rapidly from the mid-1950s to the late 1970s, at around 2.4 per cent per annum compound average growth rate (ZGNYJJGY, 1982, 85). Output per worker over the long term from the mid-1950s to the mid-1970s hardly altered. The gross value of agricultural output (at 1970 prices) per agricultural worker was reported to be 367 *yuan* in 1952, 411 in 1957, 373 in 1965, 380 in 1970 and 437 *yuan* in 1952 (ZGNYJJGY, 1982, 28 and 85).

Peasant income and consumption

By 1952, Chinese official sources claimed that average peasant real incomes had recovered to their pre-1949 peak (Nolan, 1981, ch. 2), though this assertion was not supported by strong evidence.[18] There is, however, plenty of evidence that peasant average real incomes grew quite fast from 1952 to 1954/5 and that little advance occurred during and immediately after collectivization (Nolan, 1981, ch. 2.)

From the mid-1950s to the mid-1970s, growth of rural income and living standards was tightly constrained by the slow growth of farm labour productivity. In current prices, quite substantial growth of peasant income and expenditure appears to have occurred (see table 3.4).

Table 3.4 *Chinese peasant income and expenditure in 1950s and 1970s*

| | Average expenditure per caput in villages (yuan)[a] | Average per caput distributed income (yuan) per co-op/commune member[b] of which: | | Average per caput peasant consumption[c] | |
		total	ready cash	(yuan, current)	(index, at 'comparable' prices)
1952	28.6	—	—	62	85
1957	39.1	40.5	14.2	79	100
1970	49.1	59.5	—	114	121
1975	58.6	63.2	12.4	124	129

Sources: [a] ZGMYWJTJZL, 1984, 21
[b] ZGNYJJGY, 1982, 202
[c] ZGTJNJ, 1985, 552

However, a part of this simply reflects the rise in the value of peasants' self-consumed products (reflecting the rise in state purchasing prices). The real growth of average per caput peasant consumption was, reportedly, in the order of 20–30% from 1957 to the mid-1970s – not negligible, but hardly suggesting a major change in peasant living standards. Moreover, the reliability of this estimate is called into question by the much more detailed data on average per caput peasant material consumption (see table 3.5).

Table 3.5 *Consumption levels of China's peasants per caput in 1950s and 1970s*

Av. per caput consumption in villages of:[a]	Unit	1952	1957	1970	1975
Grain	kg	192.0	205.0	185.0	187.0
Edible vegetable oil	kg	1.7	1.9	1.1	1.2
Fat pork	kg	5.5	4.4	5.1	6.7
Fresh eggs	kg	0.9	1.1	1.3	1.7
Sugar	kg	0.6	1.1	1.6	1.6
Salt	kg	5.3	6.3	7.9	8.2
Cigarettes	boxes	7.2	12.1	16.1	17.6
Alcoholic drink	kg	0.7	0.9	1.0	1.2
Cloth	m	4.6	6.0	6.6	6.2
Shoes	pairs	0.1	0.1	0.4	0.5
Matches	boxes	13.0	17.0	16.0	16.0
Soap	cakes	0.5	1.1	1.5	1.9
Thermos flasks	no./100 people	0.4	2.2	3.1	2.2
Enamel mugs	no./100 people	1.1	1.9	4.7	4.8
Enamel bowls	no./100 people	0.5	1.5	4.3	5.4
Sewing machines	no./100 people	0.0	neg.	0.1	0.2
Wristwatches	no./100 people	0.0	neg.	neg.	0.1
Bicycles	no./100 people	0.0	neg.	0.2	0.3
Radios	no./100 people	0.0	0.0	0.1	0.4
Coal	kg	22.0	49.0	56.0	54.0
Av. per caput consumption for the whole population of:[a]					
Beef/mutton	kg	0.9	1.1	1.3	1.5
Poultry	kg	0.4	0.5	0.3	0.4
Tea	kg	0.08	0.12	0.09	0.12
Aquatic products	kg	2.7	4.4	3.0	3.3
Av. area of housing space per peasant[b]	sq.m	—	11.3	—	10.2 (1978)

Sources: [a] ZGMYWJTJZL, 1984, 22−50
  [b] ZGTJNJ, 1985, 570

Village average per caput consumption levels of the most fundamental items, as well as some less fundamental ones − grain, housing, edible oil, cloth, pork, coal, alcoholic drink, tea, poultry and aquatic products − either rose a negligible amount or even declined. The main advance was in the consumption of a narrow range of generally poor quality consumer durables. The base from which the advance began was virtually non-existent, and, as was shown in table 3.5 consumption per rural household of even these still was small at the end of the Maoist period.

The most striking area of progress in rural living standards in this period was in health and education (see table 3.6).

Table 3.6 *Selected indicators for health and education in China compared to other low-income countries*

	Unit	China 1960	1979	Other low-income countries (excluding India)[b] 1960[b]	1979[b]
Death rate	no/1000	9.6[1a]	6.3[2a]	24	16
Birth rate	no/1000	38.1[1a]	18.3[2a]	47	42
Life expectancy at birth	years[b]	–	64	–	51
No. enrolled in primary schools	% pop. (of primary school age)[b]	–	93	–	74
No. people per physician	no.[b]	3,010	1,160	32,290	16,380

[1] 1965.
[2] 1978.
Sources: [a] Statistical Yearbook of China 1982, 1989
     [b] World Bank, 1981a, 168–78

China's death rate is reported to have fallen much more dramatically than that in other poor countries.[19] Although it took a long time for China to turn her attention in a sustained fashion to reducing population growth, once she did so (from the late 1960s onwards) birth rates reportedly fell very rapidly – indeed the relatively low birth rate in China by the end of the Maoist period was a valuable 'legacy' to the post-Mao regime. It is hard to disentangle the degree to which different elements contributed to the decline in the birth rate in the 1970s. Some of the contributory factors are: (1) changes in sex and age composition, especially those stemming from the demographic disaster years of 1960–1; (2) expansion of contraceptive production and facilities for abortion; (3) psychological pressure to marry late, stemming from different sources; (4) the ability of team leaders to penalize (e.g. via collective food distribution) peasants who failed to conform to population policy. The expansion of medical personnel much exceeded population growth, and by the end of the Maoist period China had a very low ratio of people to doctors compared with other poor economies, and there is good reason to think that a much larger proportion of these than in other poor countries worked in rural areas (Byres and Nolan, 1976). In addition, a rapid expansion of rural paramedical services took place under Mao — by 1978, there were reported to be 1.6 million 'barefoot doctors' (World Bank, 1981b, Annex A, table 12.1), or one for every 500 rural dwellers. By the end of the Maoist epoch it is likely that average life expectancy in the Chinese countryside was significantly above that in most other low income countries.

From the mid-1960s to the mid-1970s a considerable expansion of rural education took place. Enrolments per 10 000 people reportedly rose for 994 in 1977 to over 1500 in 1978 (SYC, 1982, 494). By the mid-1970s it is likely that enrolment rates among school-age children in China's villages were high by the standards of other low income countries.

China's collectives were able to mobilize a large amount of rural resources for rural health and education. It should, however, be noted that considerable progress was made in China in these directions prior to collectivization. Moreover, a large proportion of funding for rural welfare services under Mao came from the state, rather than the collective. For example, in Sichuan province in the late 1970s/early 1980s, about one-half of the village primary schools were state-run. Of the total (i.e. all province) primary school financial outlay in 1982, 73 per cent came from the state, 11 per cent from collectives' funds, 11 per cent from students' fees and 5 per cent from enterprises' funds. These figures had altered little compared to pre-1978 (Nolan, 1983b). Moreover, substantial progress occurred in the 1960s and 1970s in some other parts of the low income Third World without collective farms, such as Sri Lanka and in the Indian state of Kerala (see the discussion in chapter 2).

Local inequality

The dimensions of, and processes affecting, intra-village inequality in pre-1949 China are much disputed. Some authors (e.g. Elvin, 1973 Myers, 1970), basing themselves more or less explicitly on the 'Chayanovian' view of the peasant economy, consider that inequality was not permanently structured. Rather, they argue, it was extremely fluid, with families shifting their position in the hierarchy as changes occurred in their family composition (principally in the worker—dependant ratio): 'Chinese rural society in the nineteenth century and the early twentieth century was ... one of the most fluid in the world ... Everywhere there was a constant competition ... in which the fortunes of individual peasant families continually rose and fell'. (Elvin, 1973, 258—9). However, other authors (e.g. Yang, 1965, vol. II; Chen, 1973; Institute of Pacific Relations, 1939) have argued instead that pre-1949 intra-village socio economic hierarchies were of a more enduring nature. The high degree of mobility which the 'Chayanovian' approach argues for, assumes a competitive market for land and financial capital, and equality of opportunity in access to human capital. In fact, the land and credit markets in poor countries' rural areas often are relatively monopolistic (see, especially, Bhaduri, 1983). Indeed, there is often considerable inter linkage between these markets (see, e.g., Bardhan and Rudra, 1978). Moreover, inequalities in 'human capital' (health, education, skills etc.) tend to be strongly related to income level and to influence future productive capabilities. Accordingly, it is often difficult for families simply to expand the scale of production as worker—dependant ratios change. At the very least, it may be concluded that in pre-1949 China, as in most pre-modern village societies, the operation of 'Chayanovian' forces was modified greatly by more permanent inequalities. Of course, as I will emphasize frequently throughout this book, regional variations were enormous, as the information in table 3.7 indicates.

Table 3.7 *Inequality in ownership of farmland in different parts of China: selected data*

		'Landlords'		'Poor and hired' and 'other peasants'	
Area	Year	% of population	% of farm land owned	% of population	% of farm land owned
Shenxi province, Wuqiang city, No. 1 administrative village (*xiang*)	1951	20.3	31.3	20.6	10.7
Hunan province, 13 villages (*cun*)	1950	3.0	55.0	62.0	7.0

These are the two most extreme pieces of information in a long table drawing information from many parts of China.
Source: Yan et al., 1955, 278—9

In pre-1949 China, enormous variations in intra-village class relations could be found within a relatively small area (see, e.g., Ash's findings on tenancy in Jiangsu province in the 1930s (1976, 11—22)).

During China's land reform (1946—52) around two-fifths of farmland was redistributed, causing a considerable reduction in intra-village inequality. Most importantly it virtually eliminated (in an economic sense) the landlord class, i.e. those who could live on rental income and who did not have to labour in the fields in order to earn a living. Given the arduous nature of work in the Chinese countryside, the distinction between those who did and those who did not have to work seems to me to be a more fundamental form of inequality than differences in material consumption, and its elimination deeply affected the texture of village life.

There is much debate about intra-village inequality in China between land reform and collectivization (just as there is about inequality in the Soviet countryside in the 1920s). As we saw in chapter 2, Mao believed that class polarisation was proceeding rapidly, and many Chinese authors tried to show that, indeed, this was the case (e.g. Su, 1965). In fact, this seems not to have been so. Most peasants now had access to farmland for which they did not have to pay rent. Institutional credit began to become available. Health and education for the mass of the population improved markedly, and mutual aid teams (to which almost three-fifths of peasants belonged by 1954) helped increase poor peasants' access to scarce means of production. In addition, a progressive agricultural tax, limits on rent payments (where these existed) and interest rates, combined with increasing state control over purchasing farm produce and marketing industrial products in the village probably helped to reduce the benefit richer peasants obtained from economic independence pre-collectivization (Nolan, 1976; Nolan, 1981; Shue, 1980).

Indeed, some of the most careful Chinese surveys in the mid-1950s draw quite different conclusions from Mao about the extent of, and trends in, intra-village inequality prior to collectivization. A major national survey of the condition of peasant households in 1954 (two years after the completion of land reform) concluded:

> It can be seen ... that from the end of land reform to the end of 1954, approximately half of the poor and hired peasants rose to become middle peasants, approximately half of the rich peasants descended to become middle peasants, and the middle peasants already (i.e. by 1954) composed over 60 per cent of the village population, becoming the most important part of the village structure: this proves that our party's policy of helping the poor and hired peasants and restricting the expansion of the rich peasants obtained a great victory. [Concise and important materials ... 1957]

A perceptive article by Zhang Youran argued that in pre-revolutionary China the rich peasant (i.e. 'kulak') economy was weaker than he understood it to have been in pre-1917 Russia, and that the conditions after land reform in China were not conducive to class polarization. He pointed out that before collectivization rich peasants had 'only about twice as much land and other means of production as the average peasant', and that generally they either did not hire labour or hired only a small amount. According to Zhang, in China 'the elimination of the rich peasants did not require a special movement like land reform, or collectivization in Russia' (Zhang, 1965).

Between collectivization (1955–6), when a system of 'collective' ownership of most means of production was set up, and the early 1960s, large fluctuations occurred in payment systems and work organization. It was not until after the debacle of the Great Leap Forward (1958–9) that a reasonably stable set-up emerged. Then, as was seen earlier in this chapter, the income distribution system had the following characteristics. First, and important component of collective income was allocated 'according to need'. A sizeable part of grain rations was distributed according to family size. A small collective fund was set up in most villages to provide some assistance to the very poorest members of the village (the 'five guarantee' households) and collective welfare funds were established also in most villages to provide access at subsidized prices to health and educational facilities [see, especially, Davis-Friedman, 1978]. Second, differentials in daily workpoint earnings between collective workers were small (as we saw above). However, this was compatible with quite wide differences in average per caput family income, arising from differences in worker–dependant ratios, as the data in table 3.8 suggest.

Table 3.8 *Distribution of collective income available for consumption in no. 7 production team of Xintang production brigade, Tangtang people's commune, Fogang xian, Guangdong province, 1978*

Range of collective income per caput (yuan)[a]	Number of:			Mean household size (persons)	Mean number of labour powers	Mean ratio of labour powers to household size
	households[b]	people	labour powers			
31–50 (lowest = 36)	3	16	4	5.3	1.3	1:4.1
51–70	14	79	29	5.6	2.1	1:2.7
71–90	6	24	13	4.0	2.2	1:1.8
91–110	2	7	5	3.5	2.5	1:1.4
> 110 (highest = 162)	3	5	5	1.7	1.7	1:1.0

[a] Excluding funds from outside the village.
[b] Excluding two households (of one person each) with negligible earned incomes but receiving collective support.
Source: Nolan, 1979

Third, despite the constant struggle by local cadres to keep the private sector under control, even at the end of the Maoist period, at least one quarter of peasants' net income came from this source.[20] On the basis of the limited data available it is difficult to be sure how this affected intra-village inequalities.

This system was one in which some sort of local floor was established to peasant consumption (albeit that in many places the floor was very low), though, as has been noted, it is debatable whether it would have been possible to establish such a welfare system without collective income distribution. Through the policy on workpoint allocation, earnings differentials were kept within a narrow range, but quite wide differences in average incomes could still exist between families. Using the available data it is hard to make comparisons, but it is at least possible that the pre-collectivization inequalities in intra-village incomes were no wider than those in the Maoist communes. Post-land reform, pre-collectivization intra-village income differentials do not seem to have been wide, as the data in table 3.9 tentatively suggest.[21]

It is likely that the mobility of income positions in the commune system was high since peasants within each village had more or less equal access to a large part of the village's land and physical capital. Also, there was fairly equal access locally to the means by which human

Table 3.9 *Average gross income of different peasant strata in China, 1954* (yuan)

	Average gross income per:		
	household	*worker*	*caput*
Co-operative members	705	271	138
Poor and hired peasants	489	244	117
Middle peasants	774	310	155
Rich peasants	1279	432	209
Former landlords	497	226	118

From a survey of over 16 000 peasant households in 25 provinces. It seems likely that peasants were grouped according to their 'class' position, so that the data provide some insight into intra-village inequalities, though the problem of confusion with spatial inequalities is far from completely avoided.
Source: Concise and important materials . . ., 1957

capital was reproduced and improved upon. The main determinant of average income, anyway, was the worker − dependant ratio.[22] It seems reasonable to suppose that the degree of mobility between income positions was much greater than in most pre-1949 Chinese villages and somewhat greater than in the villages after land reform.

Spatial inequality

As one might expect in a country of China's size there were wide spatial differences pre-1949 in rural labour productivity and income. Information was poor. The cost of migration was high. There often was local resistance to in-migration and state help for poor areas was negligible. Consequently, income inequalities were persistent. Spatial income differences among ordinary farmers were probably less than differences in labour productivity, since areas with higher labour productivity often had higher rent payments per farmer (usually a higher proportion of farmland was rented in such areas). One important effect of the land reform was that it may well have allowed (unintentionally) spatial income differences in farmers' incomes to widen by allowing better-placed areas with higher rental payments to retain for personal consumption part of the payments formerly made to landlords.[23]

Collectivization had no direct impact on these differentials and a variety of post-collectivization surveys showed wide spatial differences in peasant income, even within a single province (see table 3.10).

Table 3.10 *Average per caput net income of the agricultural population in Shenxi province, 1956* (yuan *per caput*)

Area	yuan	Proportion of agricultural population (%)
Whole province within which:	64.3	100.0
1 Industrial crop-growing areas within which: highest *xian* = 172.3 highest APC[a] = 212	125.7	15.3
2 Main grain growing area	75.2	41.4
3 Hilly area	42.8	34.6
4 Extremely poor mountainous area within which: the two poorest *xian* = 15.6	19.3	8.7

[a] APC = agricultural producer co-operative.
Source: Tan, 1957

Tan Zhenlin's survey (Tan, 1957) of peasant income concluded: 'Owing to differences in natural conditions, varieties of crops, managerial and operational experience,and to the quality of leadership, peasant incomes differ from place to place. The peasants in better districts and well-run co-operatives may receive 100—200 *yuan* per annum; the peasants in poor districts and badly-run co-operatives may receive only 20 *yuan* per year.' Indeed, there is no reason to think that collectivization would directly affect spatial income differentials. Depending on the policies adopted this institution is quite compatible with various outcomes in terms of regional differentials.

Evidence on changes in spatial inequality from the mid-1950s to the late 1970s is fragmentary.[24] It is most unlikely that spatial differences in rural labour productivity narrowed. The application of modern farm inputs rapidly increased in the 1960s and 1970s, but a disproportionately large share of these were intentionally channelled into better located 'high and stable-yield' areas such as Southern Jiangsu province and the Pearl River Delta in Guangdong province. Such areas probably had lower marginal capital-to-output ratios (principally because their irrigation systems were already highly developed); they almost certainly had a greater propensity to market increments to output; transport costs to and from large urban centres were lower, and they possessed large investible surpluses with which to buy the new inputs (in backward areas the state would have to have provided loans to enable large quantities of inputs to be bought). It is difficult to prove unambiguously that spatial differences in rural labour productivity widened, but it is certain that there were still wide local and regional differences at the end of the Maoist period (see chapter 6). For example, in 1980, the gross value of total rural social product per rural worker ranged from 1927 *yuan* in Heilongjiang province to 473 *yuan* in Guizhou province (ZGNCTJNJ, 1985, 173 and 202). In Anhui province in 1978 the gross value of agricultural and industrial output per caput ranged from 477 *yuan* in Dangtu *xian* to 126 *yuan* in Fuyang *xian* (AHJJNJ, 1985).

Spatial differences in income were restrained (as has been seen) by the strict imposition of income ceilings and by a policy of enforcing high marginal investment rates. Nevertheless there were still large differences in average incomes between provinces. In 1980, average net income per peasant ranged from 397 *yuan* in the Shanghai suburbs to 142 *yuan* in Shenxi province (ZGNCTJNJ, 1985, 173 and 202). Within Anhui province in 1978, average net income per peasant ranged from 183 *yuan* in Dangtu *xian* to 34 *yuan* in Yingshang *xian* (AHJJNJ, 1985).

Poverty

Western awareness of the dimensions of poverty in Maoist China was dim. Western visitors to China almost all visited only prosperous areas. Post-1957 the Chinese issued negligible information on the subject. Moreover, western analysis of Chinese poverty focused mostly on local mechanisms to help the poorest sections of any given village.

After 1978, a great deal of information began to be published in the Chinese press which made it possible to construct a more realistic picture of the dimensions of rural poverty in pre-1976 China. For example, a detailed study in 1978 showed that over 16 per cent of China's counties and 30 per cent of production teams could be considered 'poor', defined as an average per caput income distributed by the collective (in cash and kind) of below 50 *yuan* (Shi, 1980). At the price at which collectively distributed grain was valued in the 1970s, 50 *yuan* amounted to just 250 kilograms of rice (Nolan, 1983a, 56), and at least two-thirds of peasants' total net income came from the collective.[25] In other words, an average collective distributed income of less than 50 *yuan* was, indeed, extremely poor. Moreover, the poor *xian* were regionally concentrated. Of the 377 'poor' *xian* (with less than 50 *yuan* average per caput distributed income), 310 were located in or around ten large grain-deficit areas (Shi, 1980). The author of one detailed study on the subject commented:

> It is indeed a serious question that in China 20 years or so after communisation the poor units still occupy such a large share and, moreover, that there is such a great disparity between rich and poor, with the high-income teams standing at more than three times the level of the poorest. ... *The distribution of rich and poor xian makes one feel very uneasy.* The rich *xian* are concentrated in the suburban areas of large and medium cities and municipalities and in the border areas, while the poor *xian* are concentrated in areas whose natural resources and ecological environment have suffered severe damage. [Shi, 1980, my emphasis − P.N.]

Not only were 30 per cent of production teams at below 50 *yuan* average per caput distributed income, but many were a long way below. For example, in Guangdong province in 1975, 17 per cent of production teams had less than 40 *yuan* (see table 3.11).

Table 3.11 *Average per caput distributed income in production teams in Guangdong province, 1975*

Income level, yuan	Proportion of teams (%)
40 and less	17.2
41−50	16.9
51−100	54.0
101−50	9.5
151 and above	2.4

Source: Nolan, 1983a, 44

For teams below 40 *yuan*, even with state assistance, life was extremely harsh. Hinton (1983), for example, gives a graphic account of Fengyang *xian* (Anhui province) pre-1978. The *xian* was so poor, that even with state assistance an average of 50 000 people left home each winter to beg. In bad years, the figure rose to 150 000.

Consider the case of Qingjiang rural people's commune in the 1970s. It was situated in the poorest part of Gansu, itself China's poorest province (in 1981, the average per caput distributed income in Gansu province was just 57 *yuan* (SYC, 1982, 202)). Qingjiang commune was in the drought-stricken, central part of Gansu which suffered from severe natural disasters and soil erosion. This area contained over five million peasants (30 per cent of the province's peasant population) with grain yields per *mu* of just 156 *jin*, compared to an average of 242 *jin* per *mu* for the whole province. The central part of Gansu was so poor that over one thousand production teams were without any draft oxen at all. In 1978 (which was a moderately good year for the region), fully 43 per cent of the area's production teams had an average per caput distributed income of less than 40 *yuan*, and seven *xian* produced a personal grain ration of below 150 kilograms. In 1979, the average ready cash distribution by the collectives was just 12.6 *yuan*, and in eight *xian* it was just one *yuan* or so. In order that the area was able to survive at even a very basic level, the state sold it 103 million kilograms of grain (an average of 20 kilograms per person), or 40 per cent of the province's total grain resales to the villages. The most basic of needs — foodgrain — was met (at a low level) through the system of state supply, which is a considerable achievement of the Maoist system, but peasants in many parts of this area still were in 'great difficulties': 'not only do they not have fuel, are they short of grain and have little to wear, but, as soon as they encounter drought, both people and livestock find it hard to even get food and drink'.

Within this very poor area, Qingjiang (in Huining *xian*) was one of the poorest communes. In most years, its collective distributed income (in cash and kind) averaged less than 40 *yuan* (see table 3.12) and its grain consumption was only kept at a bare minimum level ('not enough to fill the stomach') because of state resales. The peasants mostly had no money to buy fuel and a great many peasants were normally unable even to buy salt. When they were ill they had no money to get treatment or buy medicines. Some households were even unable to buy oil for their lamps. The average household was indebted to the extent of 147 *yuan* to the collective, the bank and the credit cooperative.[26]

Apart from grain resales (usually financed by loans rather than gifts) and assistance for areas hit by extremely severe disasters, the state under

Table 3.12 *The livelihood situation in Huining xian's Qingjiang commune (Gansu province)*

	Average per caput grain output for personal consumption (kg)	Average per caput grain re-sales to peasants (kg)	Total personal grain consumption per caput (kg)	Average collective distributed income per caput (yuan)
1973	49	80	129	27.6
1974	102	47	149	26.0
1975	169	2	171	44.5
1976	87	60	147	17.9
1977	97	60	157	23.0
1978	124	18	142	27.0

Source: Yu, 1980, 27

Mao was severely constrained in what it was able to do to improve conditions in poor areas. Indeed, the key slogan for backward areas was 'self-reliance'.

CONCLUSION

This chapter argues that China's agriculture performed only modestly pre-1978. It had a quite good, though mixed, record in respect to land productivity, a quite poor performance in respect to labour productivity, and a bad record in respect to capital productivity. Over the long term there is no evidence of any improvement in China's per caput output of farm produce or in the Chinese people's diet. Peasants' average material consumption grew very slowly, though in welfare provision important advances were recorded. As chapter 5 will show, the performance post-1978 dramatically improved in most respects. To what degree is the modest performance pre-1978 attributable to collective agriculture?

At the micro-level, via the party structure the state intervened deeply in the way China's collectives were run. For some higher level cadres it was alleged, 'the production team had actually become a purely administrative unit appended to the responsible administrative organ and they consider it to be a bead on an abacus that can only move when manipulated from above' (quoted in Nolan and White, 1982, 193). Peasants in one district said: 'We have only one production team in the whole county and only one person who knows farming i.e. the first secretary of the county party committee' (quoted in Nolan and White, 1982, 193). The party established a monolithic structure with little sensitivity to regional differences in agricultural conditions; it forced production teams to allocate a large proportion of grain 'according to need'; it forced them to adopt a remuneration policy that permitted only narrow differentials in workers' collective incomes; it tightly controlled the collectives' pattern of resource allocation; it pushed teams to adopt a high marginal re-investment rate and to greatly increase per caput labour mobilization for public and collective works; and it prevented peasants shifting their place of residence. However perfectly things were run in other respects, this set of policies was likely to produce considerable peasant dissatisfaction, and to tend, *ceteris paribus*, to reduce the rate of remuneration for collective labour. Correspondingly, the relative attraction of private work increased, and a struggle between cadres and peasants over the allocation of resources (especially labour) between the collectives and the private sector followed, tending to erode further the cadre—peasant relationship. Undoubtedly, collectives could have been run better than they were, and, probably, the economic results would have been better. A brief glimpse of the possibilities was provided in 1957, when, insofar as was possible, the teething troubles of collectivization had been largely ironed out (especially in respect to policies towards the private sector).

The state's use of its political power in this way made it impossible to establish independent collectives in which there was mutual trust among co-operators, which is an extremely ambitious goal even in the most favourable circumstances. Collective labour was not, mostly, self-motivated and did require supervision. I have argued that where labour supervision is necessary in agriculture it is hard to achieve effectively and that failure in this respect has high costs. The evidence in chapter 3 tends to confirm this.

I argued earlier in this book that micro-level performance cannot be considered in isolation from the macro-setting (there is, obviously, a continuous iteration between the levels). In certain respects the macro setting for Maoist collectives was benign. Measured at market prices there was no long-term extraction of peasant savings, and there was a rapid rate of increase in the supply of industrial farm inputs. However, there were other serious problems stemming from the macro-economy. It is possible that when a more comprehensive analysis is undertaken it will be demonstrated that, indeed, there was a sustained net resource transfer out of the agricultural sector; the variety and quality of industrial farm inputs left a great deal to be desired; the non-farm sector performed hopelessly in absorbing agricultural surplus labour (though it should be noted that under the given institutional arrangements, a lot more labour was required to produce a unit of output than post-1978: the extent of 'surplus' labour cannot be assessed independently of the institutional setting); and the provision of industrial 'incentive' goods was deficient in quantity, variety and quality. These factors undoubtedly play a role in explaining the modest (though not disastrous) performance of Maoist agricultural collectives.

This analysis suggests that one cannot conclude precisely the degree of responsibility of collective institutions *per se* for China's relatively poor agricultural performance pre-1978. Excessive, heavy-handed state interventions exacerbated the problems (though, it should be stressed that it is only possible to imagine in exceptional circumstances the formation and maintenance of fully collective farms without external compulsion: 'heavy handed state interventions' generally are a necessary condition of the existence of collective farms). Moreover, shortcomings in the macro-setting also contributed to the problems identified. A necessary condition of improved farm performance in China post-1978 was changes in both these respects. However, it seems unquestionable that a major part of the problems encountered by the rural economy pre-1978 is attributable to the institution of the collective farm *per se*. The problems in principle identified in chapter 2 were, indeed, all found to have been encountered in Maoist communes.

Nothing in this account contradicts the proposition advanced in chapter 2 that there is a wide array of supra-household farm activites in poor economies in which co-operation (and/or state action) is frequently neccessary both for successful output growth (e.g. irrigation and drainage, research, transportation, processing, marketing) and welfare provision (e.g. education, health care, old age insurance). However, the analysis does tend to confirm that for many important farm activities, especially those directly related to cultivation, large size (in terms of employment per unit) in agriculture confers few benefits, and generally involves substantial costs, arising from the inability of farm managers to be familiar with the varied conditions under their control, and, especially, from the enormous difficulties (if not impossibility) involved in devising payment systems that motivate workers as effectively as they are motivated on individual family farms.

China's pre-1978 experience suggests that while co-operation in agriculture can be extremely useful, collectives generally have little to offer if one is seeking to achieve a satisfactory growth rate of the rural economy.

However, perhaps it can be argued that, despite the problems posed by collective farms for rural growth, China's collective farms enabled other objectives to be met, such as preventing excessive inequality and alleviating poverty?

This chapter showed that China's collective farms established an effective system of local poverty relief, and kept earnings differentials within narrow limits. However, this was not inconsistent with quite wide inter-family differentials in average incomes on account of differences in worker—dependant ratios. This system probably enabled a relatively high degree of inter-temporal mobility in families' income positions, in which 'Chayanovian' elements played an important role. Compared to pre-1949 China (and with what an unreformed countryside would probably have looked like) the contrast is strong. However, the contrast with the post-land reform, pre-collectivization situation in the early 1950s is much less striking.

Collectives have little to offer in resolving the question of spatial inequality. It is, in principle, quite possible under a system of collective farms to have spatial inequalities of almost any dimension, depending on the policies pursued. At the heart of the spatial question lies the issue of differential land rent. Article 17 of the USSR's law of 1918 'On the socialization of the land' decreed: 'The additional income derived from the best pieces of land as a result of their more advantageous location with respect to markets, will be devoted to social needs in accordance with the instructions of the organs of state power' (quoted in Ellman, 1973, 110). In fact, neither post-1949 China nor the Soviet Union pursued a clear, consistent policy such as is suggested by the above quotation.[27] In China, following the disastrous results consequent upon the equalisation of local spatial income differentials within the people's communes during the Great Leap Forward, China's government reacted by committing themselves emphatically to not transferring differential income away from production teams:

> In handling the distribution of differential rent, the differential rent attributable to land with favourable natural conditions should, in general, be kept by the production teams concerned; otherwise egalitarianism will follow and those production teams that produce more cannot earn more. If so, their production enthusiasm will be dampened and the development of agricultural production will be adversely affected. [Zhong, 1961]

As has been seen, China's rapidly-growing supply of modern inputs in the sixties and seventies was concentrated disproportionately in certain areas. Moreover, labour mobility was very limited. Consequently, it is possible that the spatial inequalities in differential rent incomes widened. Rather than tax away the extra income, the Maoist policy was to control (though not eliminate) rural regional income differences by forcing communes to reinvest a high proportion of their income, by directly controlling their production structure and by setting absolute limits to the average incomes distributed by collectives.[28]

The net effect of these policies, as has been seen, was to contribute to the micro-economic problems experienced under Mao in all rural areas, but whose consequences for the economy were especially serious in the well-located areas with large growth potential.

Although collective farms helped to solve local problems of poverty, it has been shown that the worst aspects of poverty in China were, as in most developing countries, regional in nature. At the end of the Maoist period, there still were large regional concentrations of poverty. Indeed, it is quite likely that the proportion of peasants in absolute poverty had not fallen since the mid-fifties and, of course, that absolute numbers had risen greatly. As I shall show in subsequent chapters, the key to eliminating spatial concentrations of poverty was a set of policies to stimulate growth in those areas, which in turn depended partly on more general acceleration of rural growth to provide resources with which better-off areas could assist growth in poor areas.

4

The Post-1978 Reforms

When I asked an elderly peasant guarding a heap of watermelons he had brought in from the countryside to sell at a market in Peking what was meant by the responsibility system, he furrowed his brow at first, and then a pleased smile creased his face. 'It means we can do what we want', he replied.

Quoted in Schell, 1984

INSTITUTIONS AND POLICIES WITHIN THE VILLAGES

Following the death of Mao Tsetung in 1976 a sea change took place in Chinese political economy. The most important event in signalling these changes was the third plenum of the Eleventh Central Committee of the CCP, held at the end of 1978. This meeting set in motion a massive programme of rural reform which was to transform the Chinese countryside step by step in the late 1970s and early 1980s. This, in its turn, laid the base for wide-ranging reforms in other areas of the economy. Within a short period, the whole edifice of Maoist political economy was demolished. A major new chapter had begun in the political economy not just of China but of all the socialist countries.

Changes

Beginning in the late 1970s, and accelerating into the early 1980s, there occurred a dramatic transformation of China's rural institutions and policies.[1] Its centrepiece was the splitting up of production teams, and the establishment of different forms of 'contract' system: either 'contracting output to the group' (*bao chan dao zu*), 'contracting output to the household' (*bao chan dao hu*), or 'contracting work to the household' (*bao gan dao hu*).

These systems spread rapidly. By the end of 1980 almost half the basic accounting units were employing some kind of 'contract' system (table 4.1).

Table 4.1 *Proportion of China's basic accounting units in people's communes employing different types of contract system prior to 1983*

| | 1980 | | 1981 | | 1982 |
	Jan.	Dec.	June	Oct.	Dec.
Bao chan dao zu	24.9	23.6	13.8	10.8	13.3
Bao chan dao hu	4.1	18.5	31.3	26.6	8.7
Bao gan dao hu	0.02	5.0	11.3	38.0	70.0
Total	29.1	47.1	56.4	75.4	92.0

Source: Kueh, 1984a, 357

Under the '*bao chan*' systems the group (*zu*) or household (*hu*) contracted with the production team to fulfil a specified amount of farm output (to be handed over to the team) for a fixed land area, with current inputs fixed and provided by the team. In return for fulfilling the contracted task the group or household was given an agreed workpoint entitlement (with proportionate reductions in workpoints for underfulfilment of the contract). Any output in excess of the contract could be retained by the group or the household (Nolan, 1983b).

In 1982–3 there occurred a full-scale return to family farming. 'Contracting work to the household' (*bao gan dao hu*) became the almost universal practice, and by the end of 1983, over 94 per cent of peasant households in China operated under this system (ZGTJNJ, 1984, 131). In its speed and importance, the de-collectivization of Chinese agriculture in 1982–3, directly parallels collectivization in 1955–6. The post-1978 reforms brought a profound transformation to daily life for China's 800 million peasants. For analysts concerned with rural policy in socialist countries and in developing, non-socialist countries, it has given cause for deep reflection. As one Chinese writer puts it: 'No matter how people look upon the fact, the tide of household management, with unprecedented breadth and speed, depth and thoroughness, has bid farewell to the unsuitable theories, concepts and feelings, *and makes everyone concerned with China's realities think*.' (Zhou, 1986, 93). (My emphasis, – P.N.). The most important changes in the villages in this period are outlined in the following pages.

The role of the party   Chapter 3 argued that before 1978 the CCP intervened deeply in all aspects of rural political, economic and social life. An important part of the post-Mao rural reforms was an attempt to increase rural economic efficiency by formally separating party from both government and economic administration in the villages. The party was now supposed to confine itself to ideological work, namely 'guaranteeing the two civilizations' (cultural and spiritual) (Nolan, 1983b). The former 'people's commune' was now to be called the *xiang* (township). Alongside the change in name went formal incorporation into the governmental structure, so that the *xiang* now had its own organs of 'people's government'. The post-reform *xiang* government was supposed to concern itself with 'protecting and educating the people', addressing itself to such issues as public security, health, education, justice, environmental protection and organizing peasants' obligatory labour on collective projects (Nolan, 1983b). Under the new set-up elections for the top positions (*xiang* head and vice-heads) were indirect, by a small minority of peasants;[2] the government officials were appointed by the *xiang* head, subject to approval by the *xian* (county) authorities. The economic activities at the *xiang* level characteristically were now supposed to be run by separate organizations (e.g. agricultural technical services, industrial and commercial) with independent accounting and independent business operation (Nolan, 1983b).

It is difficult to assess the degree to which party control over village life had changed in practice (White, 1985). Undoubtedly, the number of village cadres (both party and non-party) fell sharply in the 1980s, perhaps by as much as a half,[3] paralleling the decline in their control over daily peasant life (Nolan, 1983b). Also, the prestige of party members who formerly administered Maoist policies suffered severely with the about-turn in party policy after 1978. For years, rural party cadres had been urging peasants to 'serve the people' and shun 'material incentive'. Suddenly, they were told to encourage 'take the lead in getting rich'. The psychological disorientation was profound. Many members of this potentially discontented group received compensation in the shape of becoming privileged 'specialized households'. They were strongly encouraged to do so, and, indeed, often possessed superior skills (especially education) and, of course, connections (*guanxi*). As one Chinese writer put it: 'Party members usually have more connections and are comparatively more competent than ordinary farmers. Therefore they have more chance than the others to make money'. (Lu, 1986, 14). According to a survey of 21 000 specialized households in Ying *xian* in Shanxi province, 43 per cent of the specialized households were former production brigade or team leaders, and peasants who had once been cadres (Wan, 1984, 18). They quickly came to form a large segment of this new rural economic elite. The party's influence had waned as new, more complex village power relations emerged. One commentator argued: 'In contrast to the former "fusion" of political and economic power within the collectives, there has been a process of separation into two power systems, one based on formal institutionalized authority and one on control over economic resources (including scarce skills)' (White, 1985).

In fact, the decline in party authority and its separation from administration of rural economic affairs in the 1980s was far from complete. The Chinese leadership's determination to maintain the CCP in a position of absolute dominance in all spheres of social activity became crystal clear, if anyone had ever doubted it, in early 1987 following the demonstrations by students (sometimes joined by workers) in Shanghai, Peking and elsewhere.[4] Chen Junsheng, secretary-general of the State Council reminded the Chinese population:

Without the leadership of the Party the country would be fraught with upheavals and rent by disunity. Old China was called 'a sheet of loose sand'. . . . Only after the Communist Party came to power did the divisions in China end. . . . Today if people are allowed again to kick out the Party committees to make revolution, it will definitely ruin our four modernisations. [Chen, 1987]

The separation of the rural party from economics was far from complete by the mid-1980s. Later in this chapter, and in subsequent chapters, I will argue that despite the upheavals of the late 1970s/early 1980s there still were a number of key economic channels through which the CCP exercised power in the villages, such as the allocation of grain purchase quotas, of petrol and chemical fertilizer, power supply, administration of the 'birth plan', mediation in economic disputes, allocation of licences to set up new businesses, access to health and educational facilities, and so on.

Contracts Before 1978 most decisions on rural production and distribution were administered directly by the state or indirectly by the state's representatives in collectives. The 1980s witnessed an explosion of independent economic decision-making by individuals and groups. Integral to this process was a massive expansion of economic contracts, so that by the mid-1980s a single *xian* could have up to half a million legally binding contracts ('Handling economic disputes', 1985). The state expended a considerable effort to explain the way to go about drawing them up so that they could be legally enforceable, (see e.g., Sang, 1983). A legal framework previously lacking had to be constructed to correspond to the requirements of the new situation. The foundation of this was the general 'Economic Contract Law' of December 1981 (Law Research Institute, 1984). This 15-page document laid down general principles covering all economic law in China. Subsequent laws went in detail into different aspects of relevance to the evolving rural situation.

There were, still, plenty of problems. Events went ahead so rapidly that it was inevitable the law should lag behind. Moreover, despite considerable efforts to develop public understanding of economic law, it was admitted that due to lack of peasants' and cadres' knowledge, or failure to take the matter seriously, economic contracts were sometimes concluded which had incomplete clauses, whose contents were insufficiently concrete, in which the economic responsibilities were not made clear, which were not properly ratified by an authorized third party, and which were not, consequently, legally binding (Sang, 1983, 1–2). In addition, there was a serious lack of trained lawyers (in 1984 there were less than 15 000 in the whole of China) and legal advisers to relevant departments which might act as arbitrators in the event of disputes over contracts.

However, despite these problems the rule of law was far from absent in the Chinese rural economy in the mid-1980s. Apart from formal 'laws' (see above), a huge number of state policy documents (including 'instructions' (*biao shi*), 'notices' (*tongzhi*), 'regulations' (*guiding*), 'documents' (*wenjian*) and 'opinions' (*yijian*)) was published covering every conceivable aspect of village economic behaviour,[5] to be put into effect through the government and legal system and, especially, through the rural party apparatus. For rural business to be conducted successfully, participants in a contract must have 'legitimate expectations under contracts'. The easy availability of printed 'standard contracts' (see, e.g., Sang, 1983) in the mid-1980s was helping to solve the problem of wrongly drawn up contracts. Moreover, while there was a severe shortage of trained lawyers, the number of rural notaries, who required a much shorter period of training, was rapidly expanding – the legal equivalent of 'barefoot doctors'. Moreover, despite problems of personal connections and corruption, the huge rural party apparatus played a vital role in mediation over disputed contracts.

Land division By 1983, virtually all collectively-owned farmland (apart from 'private plots')[6] had been divided up for operation by individual farm households. Four different methods of land contracting were adopted. The proportion of land contracted directly according to household size was 70 per cent; 21 per cent was contracted partly according to household size and partly the number of workers in the household; 8 per cent was contracted according to the number of workers in the household, and 0.4

per cent according to workers' technical and managerial skill (Rural Survey Group, 1986, 9).

Initially, the period of the land contract was unspecified, but it quickly became obvious that the uncertainty thereby produced led to shortening of peasants' time horizons and problems in respect to investment in the land for long-term returns. Accordingly, in 1984 (Central Committee, 1984, Article 3(i)), the contracted period for most types of land was fixed at 15 years. Early in 1987, it seemed likely that the important decision had been taken by the State Council[7] to extend the land contract period to 50 years and to permit land contracts to be inherited by children (Han, 1987b). Land division was the heart of the 'contract system', with decisions over the multiple aspects of farm work being taken out of the hands of collective cadres and returned to individual farm households. The rural 'labour process' was fundamentally transformed by this.

'Parcelization' of holdings was integral to the process of land division. Not only did each household received a small plot, but these plots generally were subdivided into still smaller units to enable each household to receive its share of good and bad land (Nolan, 1983a). On average each household was contracted just 0.56 hectares divided into no less than 9.7 parcels (Rural Survey Group, 1986, 9). The reasons for parcelization in the 1980s are the same as in pre-1949 China: 'Land varies in quality from acre to acre; one man must not have all the best land, and another all the worst; a farmer needs both dry and wet land, hilly land for fuel and manure as well as level land for his crops; the dispersion of plots enables him to pool his risks of flood and drought' (Tawney, 1932, 39).

Land contracts were transferable from one household to another, where the transferring-out household was short of labour or wished to change occupation. Indeed the process quickly became actively encouraged by the state in the interests of 'concentrating land in the hands of farming experts' (Central Committee, 1984, Article 3(i)). The household which ceased to cultivate the land was legally permitted to require the new cultivator to supply it with a certain amount of grain at the parity (state) price (Central Committee, 1984, Article 3(i)), and, in many areas, the local authorities permitted rent payments for the use of the contracted land.

Agricultural means of production other than land   Small 'traditional' means of production (e.g. farm tools), draft animals, and most small modern means of production (including walking tractors, small sprayers, threshers, etc.) were sold off to peasants in 1982−3 (Nolan, 1983b). One of the most vivid sights encountered in the summer of 1983 during the final stage of 'de-collectivization' in parts of rural Sichuan province, was lines of collectively owned means of production, each with its price ticket, arranged on the communal threshing ground ready for sale to households.

By 1983 peasants were legally entitled to own individually, and to bequeath to children, both large and small means of agricultural production (Nolan, 1983b). Many larger collective means of production (e.g. tractors, large sprayers, trucks) also were sold off to individuals or groups of households in 1982−3. However, a large number (probably the majority) of them remained in the ownership of the *cun* ('village'),[8] or the *hezuoshe* ('co-operative'), since they were almost always beyond the financial reach of individual peasants (Nolan, 1983b; Oi, 1986a). Under the contract system individual households had to pay fees for the use of collective means of production. Collectively owned large means of farm production generally were operated under a contract between their drivers and the collective; often the price paid for the right to use collective assets was established through a collectively run auction among prospective operators. The operators of these assets were typically rewarded or penalised in relation to the degree of over- or under-fulfilment of contracts that they struck with the peasants (Nolan, 1983b), in sharp contrast to the pre-1978 system.

Technical services Both the nature and the extent of technical service work altered in the 1980s. Alongside the rapid rise in rural incomes in the 1980s (see below) went a considerable expansion of rural technical services provision, though there were big regional differences depending on the level of development in the local economy (Nolan, 1983b). In well-located areas by the early 1980s a comprehensive system of technical services, from the *xian* down to the *cun* had become established (Nolan, 1983b). The *xian* level ran experimental stations, employed technicians to run village training courses, and published materials to help improve farm techniques. Both *xiang* and *cun* levels employed agricultural technicians and plant protection workers − in the case of an advanced *xian* in Sichuan province already by 1983 there were reported to be an average of two full-time agricultural technicians per *cun* (Nolan, 1983b). Pre-1978 the remuneration of technical service workers was unrelated to the quality of their work. By the early 1980s nearly all such workers had shifted to a 'contract' system with variable remuneration depending on how well work was done. A *cun*, for example, might pay an agricultural specialist under the 'floating wage' system, awarding graduated bonuses depending on how well the fields under their management had done (Nolan, 1983b).

Specialized households In the early 1980s the state encouraged the development of a group of 'specialized households' who could concentrate on a narrow range of farm or non-farm production and develop their efficiency in these lines. They could sit state-run exams and obtain formal registration as 'specialized households' and thereby gain access to various benefits (Nolan, 1983b; Oi, 1986a). The state laid down that the specialized households should be 'cherished and supported' and provided with the necessary social services and that their needs should be met in respect to information, supply and marketing, and technical progress (Central Committee, 1984, Article 3(iv)). By the end of 1984, around 14 per cent of China's peasant households were 'specialized households' (ZGJJNJ, 1985, II, 5). Their position as a rural elite group can be seen from the data in table 4.2.

Table 4.2 *Characteristics of 'specialized households' compared to ordinary peasants, 1984–1985*

Item	Unit	Specialized households	Ordinary peasants
Proportion possessing lower and middle school education	%	38.0	32.0
Proportion of workers with a high level of technical skill	%	18.0	8.0
Fixed capital per household	*yuan*	3020.0	629.0
Amount of machinery per household	horsepower	13.6	1.0
Business income per worker in 1984	*yuan*	2989.0	786.0
Net income per worker in 1984	*yuan*	1406.0	484.0
Proportion of household output marketed in 1984	%	83.1	59.4
Amount per worker of taxes in 1984 handed to state and 'collective retentions' handed to collective	*yuan*	199.9	42.4

Source: Rural Survey Group, 1986, 11

According to the criteria adopted in the 1984/5 national peasants survey, just 3.5 per cent of households surveyed were categorized as 'specialized households'. Their numbers were said to be greatest neither in 'areas which had formerly had a strong collective economy' nor in 'areas with a slowly developing commodity economy', but rather in 'areas in which the collective economy had formerly been weak, but where commodity production had grown fast in the previous few years' (Rural Survey Group, 1986, 11).

The rural non-agricultural economy   In the 1960s and 1970s, China's rural industries expanded quite rapidly. For example, production brigade and production team industries more than doubled their output (at constant prices) from 1971 to 1975 (ZGTJNJ, 1985, 239), and the number of commune-run industrial establishments rose from 12 000 in 1962, to almost 80 000 in 1975 (ZGTJNJ, 1985, 305). Though their share of total industrial output was small (in 1980, commune-run industry still produced just 7 per cent of China's total gross value of industrial output (SYC, 1982, 212), in certain sectors they produced a large share of total output, e.g. by the early 1970s almost half of China's cement, and over two-fifths of her nitrogenous fertilizer output, came from small rural plants (Byres and Nolan, 1976, 69).

Most observers considered that this was a sensible strategy to pursue.[9] Small rural plants had a short gestation period, they could make use of dispersed raw material deposits, they made use of local workers who could continue to live in the villages and, thereby, the economy saved on urban overhead costs, and, above all, they economized on transport costs — of materials, workers, food (to feed urban workers), and final products. Given that, in common with most less-developed countries, China's transport and distribution was extremely backward, and that in view, also, of the fact that this sector was neglected under Maoist policies of regional self-sufficiency, the quite rapid development of many types of rural small-scale industries made good sense.

As will be shown below, output of rural small-scale enterprises expanded dramatically in the 1980s. Few outside observers anticipated such an acceleration in the pace of growth of a sector that, from some standpoints, already appeared to be performing quite well. What factors explain this?

Major changes took place in respect to the collectively run (*xiangcun* — former commune and brigade) enterprises,[10] which, despite the massive expansion of non-collective rural enterprises in the 1980s, were still the dominant form of rural non-farm enterprise in the mid-1980s, in terms both of employment and total output, as shown in table 4.3.

Instead of being run directly by the collective authorities, virtually all such enterprises by the mid-1980s operated under some form of contract arrangement with the collective. A wide variety of contractors existed, ranging from individuals through groups of staff and workers or the whole enterprise's workforce, to the factory management (see table 4.4). A wide variety of production relationships existed in collective enterprises and the simple categories in the above table mask a great variety of contracting arrangements. However, certain generalizations can be made compared to pre-1978.

First, the position of managers altered. Instead of having a lifetime tenure, by the mid-1980s they were commonly appointed for a fixed term (say three years), often by the *xiang* authorities (see below) and the

Table 4.3 Structure of township (xiangzhen) enterprises in China in the mid-1980s

	Enterprises				Staff and workers				Gross value of output			
	m		%		m		%		100m yuan		%	
	1984	1985	1984	1985	1984	1985	1984	1985	1984	1985	1984	1985
Total	6.06	12.24	100	100	52.08	69.70	100	100	1709	2732	100	100
of which:												
1 xiang[a]-run	1.65	0.42	27.2	3.4	38.50	21.11	73.9	30.2	1433	1137	83.9	41.6
2 cun[b]-run		1.15		9.4		20.41		29.2		850		31.1
3 Peasants' jointly-run	0.90	1.12	14.8	9.2	5.22	7.71	10.0	11.1	126	245	7.4	9.0
4 Other co-operatively-run	0.21	0.28	3.5	2.3	1.34	1.75	2.6	2.5	33	62	1.9	2.3
5 Individual	3.30	9.25	54.5	75.7	7.02	18.81	13.5	27.0	117	438	6.8	16.0

[a] Formerly 'commune'; [b] formerly 'brigade'.
Sources: ZGJJNJ, 1985, v, 19; ZGJJNJ, 1986, v, 42

Table 4.4 *Proportion of* xiang-cun *collectively owned enterprises operating under different types of contract system, 1984—1985*

Type of contract	% of enterprises
1 *xiang* enterprises	
i Contracted to management	37
ii Contracted to staff and workers collectively	41
iii Contracted to individuals	17
iv Other forms	5
Total	100
2 *cun* enterprises	
i Contracted to management	19.4
ii Contracted to staff and workers collectively	32.4
iii Contracted to individuals	43.6
iv Other forms	4.6
Total	100.0

Source: Rural Survey Group, 1986, 9

criteria for appointing collective enterprise managers shifted decisively away from the political and towards the technical. Generally, managers had become solely responsible for their enterprise's profit and loss, thereby creating strong nagative pressures. On the other hand, there now were considerable financial incentives to succeed, unlike pre-1978 when there was a strict ceiling to incomes. The manager's income was now determined by the enterprise's economic performance, with a bonus depending on the degree to which the enterprise over-fulfilled contracted targets. Bonuses could be very high by the standards of rural China[11] (under-fulfilment of targets resulted in a financial penalty).

Within the enterprise, managers generally had much increased freedom to organize the production process without party intervention and profit seeking behaviour was strongly encouraged under the new ethos. Moreover, managers were still (as pre-1978) unencumbered by the necessity of having to deal with trade unions, since there generally still were none in *xiangcun* enterprises. In external relationships, there occurred a considerable increase in enterprise independence, so that managers came to behave in a manner much closer to genuine entrepreneurs.

For workers too there were dramatic changes post-1978. In the sixties and seventies workers in commune enterprises generally were paid in workpoints allocated through their production team. Though they might earn rather more than ordinary peasants, there was no relationship between their enterprise's performance and their income, and wages were paid as time rates (Nolan and White, 1980, 30−31). For most *xiangcun* enterprises, the 1980s saw a shift to piece rates, with basic rates and bonuses related to the enterprise's performance (in the medium and short term respectively). Work intensity increased sharply. The prospect of extra income for workers whose living standard was low and had been unchanged for many years, led them to accept greatly increased labour input for relatively small increases in personal income[12] (see table 4.5).

Table 4.5 *Growth of output per worker and average wages in* xiang- *and* cun-*run enterprises (at current prices)*

Year	Av. value of gross output per staff and worker, yuan	Av. wages per worker, yuan
1980	2190	379
1981	2455	438
1982	2740	491
1983	3144	544
1984	3724	621
1985	4788	729
% increase 1980−5	119	84

It is extremely difficult to estimate a real wage index for *xiangcun* enterprise staff and workers. The officially reported rate of inflation from 1980 to 1985 for all China's staff and workers' consumption was 22.6 per cent [ZGTJZY, 1986, 100].
Source: ZGJJNJ, 1986, v, 42

Reinforcing the pressure on wage rates was the huge army of under-employed workers in the Chinese countryside,[13] allowing expansion of the classic 'Lewis model' type (Lewis, 1954) as long as demand permitted. Unlike in state enterprises, if the rural collective enterprise's performance was poor, workers' wages could fall. Indeed, whereas in the public sector a state factory in 1986 went bankrupt for the first time since 1949, bankruptcy was already a real threat to *xiangcun* enterprises in the early 1980s, putting pressure on both workers and managers, though the pressure was eased by the fact that employees generally were found alternative employment by the *xiang* authorities.

The external setting of the former commune enterprises altered sharply too in the 1980s. Under the former system most material inputs were provided by the state and most of the final product sold to the state, both at state-fixed prices.[14] Relaxation of state controls in these areas began to take effect much earlier in the collective than in state enterprises. By the mid-1980s collective enterprises had greatly increased their freedom compared to pre-1978 to negotiate supply sources, prices and outlets. In the early/mid 1980s not only were rural non-farm enterprises given greatly increased freedom to purchase inputs, but they had much greater freedom than state enterprises to fix prices (Xue, 1985, 20). The reform of the pricing system for state enterprises only began to take serious effect in 1985 (Dong, 1986a).

Among other external forces assisting the expansion of *xiangcun* enterprises were (1) the sharp increase in average incomes (see below), fuelling demand for their products (most conspicuously, this stimulated a massive rural housing boom); (2) the rapid growth in output of 'economic' crops which are inputs for many of these enterprises; (3) the rapid rise in output from large-scale urban consumer durables enterprises, which frequently subcontract to local rural enterprises; (4) the continued backwardness of China's transport system which helped give many otherwise uncompetitive rural enterprises a cost advantage over urban enterprises.

It is a misnomer to call China's *xiangcun* enterprises of the mid-1980s collectives or co-operatives, since they were not generally owned and/or run by employees. Rather, they were owned by the *xiang* or the *cun*. Even where *xiangcun* enterprises had issued shares, these were more often owned by the subordinate collectives than by the employees. However, their success was very much dependent on co-operation. Standing above each enterprise was a multi-layered structure to assist the enterprises in whose success the higher structures had a strong financial stake (see below). Each province had a *xiangzhen* enterprise bureau which was linked to corresponding bureaux at the *xian* and *xiang* level. A *xian* bureau in an advanced area might have 1000 or more enterprises within its territory. It had important functions in providing credit, approving relatively large new projects, researching market opportunities, etc. However, the key level in strategic planning was the *xiang*. The relevant *xiang* department oversaw all the *xiangcun* enterprises owned by the *xiang* or *cun*. In advanced areas it usually had quite a large staff (up to 15–20 full-time workers). It often negotiated the purchase of inputs for enterprises; it took the decision about setting up new *xiang*-owned enterprises, held examinations for recruitment of new workers, raised capital for new *xiang* investments through issuing shares, re-arranged the employment of workers in enterprises which closed down, decided the level of 'basic wages' in different enterprises and determined the conditions under which bonuses were awarded, sought out new market opportunities and provided information on up-grading technical skills.[15]

In short, the deficiencies of the market were supplemented in a powerful way, with different levels above the enterprise undertaking critical 'strategic planning' functions that were beyond the scope of individual enterprises, in certain respects analogous to those functions undertaken by Italian *consorzi* to assist constituent small-scale enterprises (see, e.g., Best, 1986).

The changes in the 1980s in the way *xiangcun* enterprises operated clearly were extremely important. However, even more striking in qualitative terms (and, increasingly, in quantitative terms) was the rise of non-collective, non-farm enterprises in the mid-1980s. Under Mao, it was legally impossible for an individual or a group of co-operators to set up an independent enterprise. Indeed, anyone leaving agriculture to work in outside activity was liable to be seriously criticized. In the early 1980s such prohibitions were removed completely. Peasants were strongly encouraged to seek non-farm employment in the villages or small towns, so as to absorb some of the agricultural labour surplus and leave higher productivity, 'farming experts' to do the farming. Rural non-farm enterprises with a multiplicity of ownership and operating structures mushroomed. These included self-employed individuals, genuine self-employing co-operatives, small groups of owner-managers employing other workers, individual owner-operators employing workers, individuals and/or groups of peasants co-operating with *xiangcun* enterprises, individuals and/or groups of peasants leasing enterprises from the *xiang* or *cun*, and so on (see, especially, Watson, 1984−5). By 1985, these diverse forms of non-farm, non-collective enterprises were accounting for two-fifths of total employment and 27 per cent of the gross value of output in 'township' (i.e. rural non-farm) enterprises (ZGJJNJ, 1986, v, 42).

The regional pattern in terms of the relative importance of the collective sector in the non-farm rural economy in the mid-1980s was especially striking (and is discussed in more detail in chapter 6). The collectively owned sector generally was strong in areas where the rural non-farm economy was most advanced, especially those in close proximity to large urban centres such as Southern Jiangsu − indeed, by 1986−7 this was being referred to as the 'Sunan' (Southern Jiangsu) model. In less well-located areas. with less opportunities to undertake subcontracting from large factories, where technical skills were weaker, and where brigade and commune enterprises were weakly developed pre-1978, the private (and genuinely co-operatively) sector was relatively much more important. In some areas, such as Wenzhou in Southern Zhejiang province, the individual non-farm rural economy expanded very rapidly indeed in the mid-1980s. This alternative path of development was, by 1986/7, being referred to as the 'Wenzhou' model, and was becoming the characteristic form in poorer parts of the Chinese countryside.

To some degree the upsurge in rural non-farm enterprises in the 1980s was simply a return to the pre-1949 structure of employment. In the 1930s, it is estimated that the transport sector employed over 11 million people and handicrafts almost 16 million people (Feuerwerker, 1968, 7), a large number of whom were in villages or in the myriad small towns that dotted the rural landscape. Skinner estimates that in the 1890s there were over 38 000 'market towns' (Skinner, 1977a, 287). These probably formed the core of the majority of the 50 000 odd people's communes (SYC, 1982, 133) of the Chinese countryside in the 1960s and 1970s. Indeed, it was reported that in the mid-1980s there were 8000 'medium sized and small towns' in China, and a further 50 000 'rural market towns' (Lei, 1986, 18), a figure not greatly different from Skinner's for the 1890s. Under Maoist policies their economic function − centres of free market trade, petty manufacture, service provision (e.g. tea shops, restaurants, barbers shops, gambling houses), and information exchange − declined drastically. The rapid rise in this type of activity in the mid eighties reflected the fact that in a country at China's stage of development, in many (though far from all) economic activites, individual and small-scale rural enterprises are highly competitive: they use small amounts of capital per worker, are extremely flexible, employ a small number of very hardworking workers per enterprise, but produce a low value of output per worker (and, hence, provide low income) − see table 4.6.

Table 4.6 *Gross value of output per worker in township* (xiangzhen) *industry, in village* (xiangcun) *industry, and in state-run industry, 1984*

	yuan
1 State-run industry	14 070
2 *xiangcun* industry	5 244
3 *xiangzhen* enterprises	
of which:	3 281
xiangcun enterprises	3 722
Peasants' jointly-run enterprises	2 413
Other co-operative enterprises	2 462
Individual enterprises	1 666

Source: ZGJJNJ, 1985, v, 19; 1986, v, 44

The changes in the 1980s affecting the rural non-farm economy were dramatic. The role of market forces in this sector increased enormously, producing major changes in habits of thought. Dong Fureng commented in relation to the Wenzhou area: 'The market plays a more and more important role in people's life. ... People are concerned with changes in the market and pay great attention to market information. The slow and easy-going rhythm of rural life is being replaced by the intense rhythm of urban life. People are concerned with time, efficiency, results and business income' (Dong, 1986b, 2).

Hired labour Given the central role of the exploitation of wage labour in Marx's writings, this has been a delicate issue for the Chinese leadership. In the early 1980s private rural labour hiring started to re-emerge after a long prohibition. The party's response was a 1982 national regulation which limited a peasant to hiring two 'apprentices' and five hired labourers (Nolan, 1983b). However, this was followed shortly by Premier Zhao Ziyang's statement that if a person hired more than the regulations permitted, they should not be stopped: the appropriate policy was to 'wait and see' (Nolan, 1983b). After this, there was little direct restriction of individual labour hiring, and rural privately hired labour expanded rapidly (from a negligible base). This development has been of immense qualitative significance, and prompted a great deal of debate within the party.

However, given the huge extent of rural surplus labour, and the problems of labour supervision, there was quite limited expansion of hired labour in farming proper. In the rural non-farm sector the number of hired workers in individually run enterprises was growing rapidly in the mid-1980s, but the average enterprise size was minuscule. In 1985, they had an average of just two people (including the employer) per enterprise, compared to an average of 50 staff and workers per *xiang*-run and 18 per *cun*-run enterprise (ZGJJNJ, 1986, v, 42). However, the Chinese leadership is very sensitive about the issue of labour hiring by individuals. In 1985 the central authorities were reported to be on the verge of promulgating a law on the issue: 'The principle is, on the one hand, to turn hired labour into a co-operative effort, and on the other, to restrict the unfettered development of hired labour through policies and taxation' (Wang, 1985a, 4). Despite extensive discussion, by mid-1987 no regulation or law had been passed.

Income ceilings It was seen in chapter 3 that under Mao there were strict limits on income differentials both within any given village and at the spatial level. The change in approach after 1978 was dramatic. The idea that peasants should improve their income levels at a roughly similar pace ('the boat rises with the water level') was rejected firmly as inhibiting peasants' 'production enthusiasm'. Instead the key slogan became 'take the lead in getting rich':

It is only through people 'taking the lead in becoming rich' becoming examples of prosperity, creating experience of becoming well-off through hard labour, arousing other people's enthusiasm and

creativity, promoting human competition, that more and more
people can be led to take the path to common prosperity. If we
don't allow those people who possess the necessary conditions to
become well-off, but practise egalitarianism, 'advancing side by
side', we may subjectively hope for common prosperity, but will in
fact produce 'equal poverty', with everyone suffering hardship
together ... We must recognize that, unlike the natural economy,
development of the commodity economy inevitably leads to expansion of income differentials ... In the commodity economy's
competition of superior with inferior, whether people run things
well or badly naturally is reflected in their level of income. China's
villages are in the process of transformation from self-sufficient and
semi-self-sufficient production to relatively large-scale commodity
production; not only is it impossible to avoid differentials in peasants' income, but, moreover, for a certain period of time these
differentials may become wider. We cannot but conform to this
objective law of economic development, and, in the process of
allowing a portion of peasant households to 'take the lead in
getting rich', struggle to create the conditions for common prosperity.
[Hu and Yu, 1986]

Unlike in the past where the collective could directly control incomes,
individual households could now themselves decide on the degree to
which increments to income were ploughed back into production.

Continuities

The changes in the early/mid 1980s outlined on the preceding pages
amount to a revolution in daily life for China's vast peasant population.
However, not everything changed, and in the mid-1980s there still were
some important continuities with pre-1978.

China's leading policy makers and rural economists did not shift to
the view that market forces solve all economic problems. On the contrary,
they emphasised that many activities necessary to the success of the farm
economy exhibit 'lumpiness' and/or economies of scale. Intervention in
the market was recognized as being needed frequently to ensure that
such activities were provided (see, e.g., Lin, 1982; Du, 1983):

[T]he implementation of the household contract system has eliminated the drawbacks of the rural co-operative system, and only its
drawbacks, *not the system itself. China will hold fast to the co-operative
system*. Based on China's needs, the rural co-operatives should be

run under a two-level management system: one is individual house-hold management and the other unified management by the co-operative organisation ... Though some people maintain that the household contract responsibility system encourages individual farming, they are wrong, for this system represents a level in the co-operative organisation ... With the development of production and the transition from a rural natural economy to a commodity economy ... *many things cannot be accomplished by one family or a household alone.* [Dai, 1986, 4, my emphases − P.N.]

In the Chinese countryside after de-collectivization these were principally provided by the *hezuoshe* (former 'team'), *cun* (former 'brigade'), *xiang* (former 'commune') or *xian* (county), rather than by intervention through the price mechanism.

The most important such activity is irrigation and drainage. For a large part of Chinese agriculture this is 'the life-blood in the fight against frequently occurring drought, waterlogging, hail, wind and insect pest disaster' (Lin, 1982). In this area, too, important changes occurred post-1978. For example, in the past most rural water conservation was com-posed of collective projects built and/or repaired with labour directly conscripted and paid in 'labour days', the remainder being state projects. By the mid-1980s there was a much greater diversity of forms. Groups of households (or even individuals) could operate outside the collective structure to build water conservation projects for their own use or charge a fee for others to use them (Nolan, 1983b). Collectively organized water conservation projects were often subcontracted by the collective to specialist water-works construction teams − it was argued that the market was competitive and the specialized workers more skilled than ordinary peasants, so that water conservation work would be undertaken more efficiently (Nolan, 1983b). However, it was acknowledged explicitly that the free market would currently meet only a small portion of water conservation requirements, and the collectives remained massively the dominant organizer of this activity. Indeed, an important aspect of peasants' obligations to the collective was the requirement to pay either in labour time or in cash for collective water conservation (Sang, 1983, 137−9).

Another important aspect of farming in which the market often works imperfectly is in the provision of a wide variety of technical services, including accounting, seeds selection and supply, planting techniques and plant protection. As was seen earlier in this chapter, although the methods by which they were provided had changed, far from being dismantled, these vital activities had been greatly enhanced since 1978.

Other activities critical to the success of the rural economy, but beyond the scope of individual households, are power and road construction. In the countryside in the mid-1980s these activities were still primarily organised either by the *xiang* or by the *xian*. *Xiang* members were still required to provide contributions in cash or kind to ensure that these activities were undertaken (Nolan, 1983b; Hinton, 1983, 9); collectives also raised revenue for these activities with resources from the non-farm economy. In addition, the *xian* authorities contributed to these activities with revenues from the local economy.

We have seen that, while a bewildering array of new forms of ownership of rural farm and non-farm assets developed after 1978, there was still much that generally was beyond the scope of individuals or even small groups of co-operators. It was still the case in the mid-1980s that, for China's rural areas as a whole, a high (though declining) proportion of rural plant and equipment (including industrial enterprises, transport and spraying equipment, tractors, power stations, etc.) was owned by *xiang*, *cun*, and *she*, though, of course, with much altered methods of operation. Moreover, it must be stressed that this statement is not inconsistent with a sharp fall in the proportion of collectivity owned rural fixed assets over large areas of China, especially the poorer regions in which the collective non-farm economy had been weakly developed pre-1978 (for a full discussion see chapter 6). The income generated by the collective economy continued to play a vital role in subsidizing other collective activities. In 1984, for example, out of rural *xiangzhen* enterprises' total net profits[16] utilized in that year, 61 per cent was used for 'expanded reproduction', 16 per cent for collective welfare, 7 per cent for supporting agriculture, 6 per cent was distributed directly to co-op (*hezuoshe*) members, and 10 per cent was used for 'other purposes' (ZGTJNJ, 1985, 298). The continued importance of collective activity is shown by the fact that in the mid-1980s the collective was still the most important sector in total rural accumulation. In 1984, of the total funds invested in rural 'production' activities, just 1 per cent came from state support funds, compared to 6 per cent from the 'new economic associations' and 40 per cent from peasant households, while 54 per cent still came from collective investment (Present situation ... 1986, 2).[17]

An important issue in China's post-reform villages was the degree to which the local authorities could (or indeed, should) extract resources from the individual non-farm economy. There were many problems with taxing this sector, especially where the business had few workers and depended on trading, so that identifying business income was difficult. However, there were still plenty of channels through which resources could be extracted from this sector to support activities of use to the whole local community. These included business taxes, licence fees to start up businesses, rates, and fees for power supply. In the case of Wenzhou, where the private rural non-farm sector was especially highly developed, the total level of local authority income was much higher after than before the reform (Zhao, 1986).

Much-admired under Mao by many outside observers was the contribution made to rural living standards by collective welfare institutions (see chapter 3). Accident and old-age insurance is generally hard to operate in a poor, rural environment, so the collective has a potentially important role to play in this sphere. Education and health both often involve lumpy expenditures, are characterized by externalities, and are often beyond the incomes of poor people if the full cost-covering price is charged for services. Again, collectives played an important role in organising these activities under Mao. Post-1978 there were major changes in each of these areas, most strikingly in education (where teaching methods, exam methods, the balance between different sectors, etc., altered sharply) and in health (the incomes of doctors were related to 'success' indicators, and the subsidy element in the pricing of services was much reduced)[18] (Nolan, 1983b). Despite these changes national policy remained strongly committed to collective organization and provision of welfare activities. This was reflected in the contributions peasants in most areas were required to make to the 'collective welfare fund' (though in some extremely rich areas with exceptionally high income from collective enterprises, the contribution often was waived). In 1984, 'collective retentions' (including both welfare and some non-welfare purposes, e.g. payments to cadres) amounted to about 5 per cent of total 'village economic income' (or 8 per cent of villages' net income) (ZGTJNJ, 1985, 290).

THE VILLAGES' EXTERNAL ENVIRONMENT

Changes

Supply of industrial 'incentive' goods   For more than two decades in China the rate of growth of heavy industry was considerably faster than that of light industry. From 1957 to 1978 the average annual growth rate of heavy industrial gross output value at 'comparable' prices was 11.0 per cent, compared to 8.2 per cent for light industry (ZGTJZY, 1985, 309). After 1978 a sharp reversal occurred, with the corresponding figures for the 1978−1985 period being 8.2 per cent for heavy industry and 12.6 per cent for light industry (ZGTJZY, 1985, 309). For a wide range of industrial consumer goods (especially consumer durables) extremely high growth rates were achieved post-1978 as may be seen in table 4.7.

Table 4.7 *Output of selected light industrial products in China, 1979—1986*

	1979		1986
Cotton cloth (b. metres)[a]	12.2		15.8
Cigarettes (m. cases)	15.2	(1980)	25.9
Sugar (m tons)	2.5		5.2
Bicycles (m)	10.1		35.7
Sewing machines (m)	5.9		9.9
Wrist watches (m)	17.1		64.5
TV sets (m)	1.3		14.5
Cassette recorders (m)	3.5	(1982)	16.4
Cameras (m)	0.24		2.2
Washing machines (m)	1.3	(1981)	9.0
Refrigerators (m)	0.06	(1981)	2.2

[a] Here, and elsewhere in this book one billion is equal to 10^9.
Source: State Statistical Bureau, 1980, 1981, 1982, 1983, 1987

A number of new industries were set up (e.g. colour TVs, cassette recorders, household refrigerators) and grew rapidly to high levels of output. The range and quality of consumer goods increased quickly compared to pre-1978.

While the urban sector absorbed a disproportionately large share (relative to its population share) of the increased light industrial output, rural stocks of 'incentive goods' grew rapidly. In only a few years, the consumption of consumer durables attained high levels for the peasant population of a low income country (see table 4.8).

Table 4.8 *Stocks of industrial 'incentive' goods per 100 peasant households in China*

	1978		1985
Bicycles	30.7		80.6
Sewing machines	19.8		43.2
Radios	17.4		54.2
Clocks	51.8		163.6
of which: wrist watches	27.4		126.3
TV sets	0.4	(1980)	11.7

Source: ZGTJZY, 1986, 112

A number of factors helped produce this result. On the supply side, the intention of the central leaders to attempt to shift away from the 'steel blinkers' characteristic of administratively planned economies was signalled by the sharp switch in state investment away from heavy industry towards light industry in the late 1970s/early 1980s, though the shift could not be sustained,[19] for reasons discussed elsewhere in this book. Although state industrial reform by the mid-1980s had progressed much less rapidly than in agriculture (reform is a much more complex process in industry), important changes had occurred (especially after 1984) leading to somewhat greater responsiveness of Chinese state industry to market forces: state enterprises had greatly expanded their rights of profit retention[20] and their rights to pay out profits as bonuses[21] and welfare payments[22]; considerable relaxation of price control occurred after 1984;[23] the proportion of material supply allocated directly by the state fell, with state enterprises in this sector able to choose where they marketed production over and above the state plan (State Council, 1984). In the small-scale sector, as we have seen, there was an enormous increase in the independence of 'township' (*xiangzhen*) enterprises and in their responsiveness to market forces, with their production structure shifting away from the former narrow range of capital goods products (principally for agriculture) towards a wide array of wage goods (both directly and via sub-contracting). The independence of urban collectives also increased greatly in this period.[24] Moreover, the freedom of localities to determine the structure of production expanded considerably after 1979 (Wong, 1985) combined with much enhanced local financial independence. This led to a sharply increased incentive for local authorities to develop revenue- and employment-generating activities:

[I]n 1980 the state introduced revenue-sharing schemes that allowed most provinces to retain all or a fixed portion of profits from local enterprises. In many provinces, this system was extended downwards through revenue-sharing arrangements with counties. Rather than passing along profits and losses of their enterprises to the state budget, local governments are now more or less independent accounting units responsible for the financial health of these enterprises ... The effect of these changes has been to transform local governments into much more autonomous economic agents, with a strong incentive to maximise revenue and employment. [Wong, 1985, 268]

On the demand side, after 1978 major increases in urban real wages occurred following two decades of near stagnation.[25] In the countryside, the removal of consumption ceilings combined with the rapid increase in rural output and net income produced a massive surge in peasant demand in the 1980s.[26] There was a complex iterative relationship between peasant output and production of industrial 'incentive goods': increased output of incentive goods stimulated peasants' enthusiasm to work hard and acquire human and physical capital, which in turn helped stimulate farm output and income, and demand for industrial output. The stimulus effect was especially strong in the late 1970s/early 1980s, since there had been a long period of limited availability of such goods and there was a powerful impact from the demonstration effect of suddenly opening China up to the influence of international consumption habits.

The expansion of industrial consumer goods production was further stimulated by the price structure inherited from the Maoist era which had little relationship to either costs of production or demand. Under Mao, the prices of many industrial consumer goods were set relatively high in an attempt to influence indirectly the distribution of consumption, with tax rates only partially compensating for the differentials as illustrated in table 4.9.

Table 4.9 *Profit and industrial-commercial tax rates for selected industries, early 1980s*

	Profit rates[a]	Tax rates
Watchmaking	61.1	40
Bicycles	39.8	15
Daily utensils	30.0	–
Pharmaceuticals	33.1	5
Cotton textiles	32.3	5–18
Chemical fertilizer	1.4	3
Shipbuilding	2.8	–
Cement	4.4	15
Farm machinery	5.1	3

[a] Probably based on production costs.
Source: Wong, 1985, 270

In the new atmosphere of increased enterprise independence, but not, until the mid-1980s, significantly increased price flexibility, enterprises and localities eagerly responded by increasing output of those consumer goods with high post-tax profits. Indeed in a number of consumer goods industries, including watchmaking, bicycles, textiles and electrical appliances, output expanded far in excess of demand (Wong, 1985, 270). Lack of coordination of supply and demand remained a major problem throughout the mid-1980s,[27] which was most clearly manifested in the oversupply of unpopular commodities (State Statistical Bureau, 1987).
Farm marketing It was seen in chapter 3 that there was an almost

complete state monopoly of farm purchases (in 1978 a mere 4 per cent of farm sector marketing to the non-farm sector went through non-state channels (Duan, 1983)), and over 90 per cent of the non-farm sector's purchases of farm produce were one form or another of compulsory sale (ZGTJNJ, 1985, 479). At the prices paid by the state there was, for most farm products, a higher income to be earned by selling to the 'free' market. In 1984 the 'free' market price (urban plus rural) for grain was reported to be 102 per cent above the state list price, while for edible oil the comparable figure was 88 per cent, for fresh vegetables 61 per cent, for meat and eggs 30 per cent, aquatic products 65 per cent and fresh fruit 20 per cent (ZGTJNJ, 1985, 535). To stimulate farm output, after 1978 the state reduced the range of compulsorily purchased produce[28] and peasants were allowed to dispose of produce freely once they had fulfilled state sales targets (Nolan, 1983c). The proportion of farm output sold by peasants at state-fixed prices fell in the 1980s. Moreover, the state rapidly raised the proportion of compulsory purchases made at the higher 'premium' price for 'above quota' sales (in the early 1980s, the price for 'above quota' compulsory sales of grain, for example, was 50 per cent above the 'quota' price). Between 1978 and 1984 the proportions of agricultural and sideline produce purchased at 'list' (quota) price fell from 85 per cent to 34 per cent, while that purchased at 'above quota' prices rose from 8 per cent to 34 per cent, that purchased at 'discussion' price rose from 2 per cent to 14 per cent, and that bought at market prices rose from 6 per cent to 18 per cent (ZGTJNJ, 1985, 479).

A crisis in agricultural marketing quickly emerged in the mid-1980s. Serious storage and transport problems developed as output and sales rose at an unprecedented rate. The irrationalities of the state-fixed agricultural price system became increasingly criticized (see, e.g., Dong, 1986a): the relative price of grain was set too low, so that post-tax income per *mu* in 1981 was only 11 *yuan* for grain, compared to 68 *yuan* for cash crops (Dong, 1986a). However, the state could not afford to raise a lot further the purchase price of grain (see below) — much the most important item it bought from the peasantry. Indeed the state was caught in a vice that was tightening with the very success of the agricultural reform in stimulating output. The state was still the principal purchaser of farm output and the main seller to urban consumers, but in its desire to maintain urban price stability,[29] it allowed a gap to open up between the purchase and sale prices. For example, in 1984, the state bought grain (on average) at 395 *yuan* per ton and sold it at 359 *yuan* per ton (ZGTJNJ, 1985, 543 and 547). The state also sold pork and other non-staple foods at prices lower than those at which they were purchased from producers ('Price reform ...', 1986, 6). This contributed to the emergence of both local and national budgetary deficits. The losses involved meant that local state commercial enterprises were unwilling to handle agricultural produce (Dong, 1986a). The purchasing system had other problems. Multiple prices encouraged speculation, led to unfairness in that different areas had different political capacities to bargain for high 'above-quota' premium price sales, and produced the perverse result that prices fell in lean years and rose in bumper harvest years (due to a fall and rise respectively in 'above-quota' sales) (Dong, 1986a).

Following the cautious measures to reform the agricultural marketing set-up in the early 1980s, the state responded to the crisis by announcing drastic changes to the compulsory procurement which had been in operation since the early 1950s (Central Committee, 1985). The old system of state compulsory purchase[30] of grain and cotton was to be abolished and replaced by contracts[31] and open market purchases.[32] The contract was to be concluded between the peasants and the commercial departments 'after discussion prior to the planting season' (Central Committee, 1985). The state undertook to provide a guarantee for the peasants in the shape of a commitment to purchase without limit at the former 'quota' price any grain the peasants wished to sell them, even if the market price fell below the former 'quota' price. For products other than grain and cotton which still were compulsorily procured in one form or another, the old system was to be 'gradually abolished' at different speeds for different products and in different areas, and replaced by a system under which products were 'freely brought to the market, freely exchanged and quality is reflected in price'. It was declared emphatically: 'No unit is any longer permitted to send mandatory production plans down to the peasants' (Central Committee, 1985).

In the urban areas state control of prices of farm produce was relaxed drastically in 1985, with only 'grain, cooking oil and a few other products' apparently still having their prices set by the state (Dong, 1986a).

In the past, state commercial departments were, in practice, indistinguishable from 'supply and marketing co-operatives'. An important development in farm marketing in the mid-1980s was the beginnings of a return to genuinely co-operative forms of operation in the 'supply and marketing co-operatives' with the state's encouragement (Han, 1987a): 'The supply and marketing co-operatives must be fully independent units of account, with self-responsibility for profit and loss, independent management, and democratically run by the masses' (Central Committee, 1985). In the case of model supply and marketing co-operatives, constituent peasants and collectives were share owners who were issued with dividends out of the annual profits, and who were technically able to determine the co-op's policy through attendance and voting at shareholders' meeting (Nolan, 1983b).

Agricultural—industrial terms of trade   In its attempt to stimulate the growth of agricultural production after 1978, the government substantially raised the purchase price of farm produce: the state purchase price index increased by no less than two-fifths from 1978 to 1981 (see table 4.10).[33] At the same time the price at which the state sold industrial products to the villages rose very little. Consequently, this period saw a sharp improvement for the peasants in the relative prices they encountered (see table 4.10).

Table 4.10 *Index of agricultural and sideline products' purchase price relative to retail price of industrial products in the villages*

	1957	1978	1981	1984	1985
1 Purchase price of agricultural and sideline products[a]	67	100	139	154	167
2 Retail price of industrial products in the villages	102	100	102	108	111
Index of relative prices of agricultural and industrial products ($\frac{2}{1} \times 100$)	152	100	73	70	66

[a] Includes list ('quota') prices, discussion price and 'above-quota' price.
Source: ZGJJNJ, 1986, III, 62

In simple statistical terms, an important part of the massive increase in farm sector purchases from the non-farm sector in the late 1970s/early 1980s was made possible by the sharp rise in farm sector purchasing prices. However, after a long period of stagnation or slow increase in living standards the sudden sharp improvement in the peasants' terms of trade and the extra opportunities opened up for purchasing newly available industrial goods may have stimulated peasant incentives to produce and market farm produce.

Continuities

Taxation   Despite much discussion, by mid-1987 no moves had been made to introduce a progressive personal income tax in China's villages. The agricultural tax, levied on the output of farmland, in the early 1950s took a substantial portion of agricultural output (around 12 per cent of the value of crop output in 1952 (Byres and Nolan, 1976, 621)) and made a major contribution to the national budget (29 per cent in 1950 and 15 per cent in 1952 (ZGTJNJ, 1985, 524)). However, despite the rise in farm output and prices, it hardly changed over the long term (2.7 b. *yuan* in

1952; 3.3 b. *yuan* in 1983 (ZGTJNJ, 1985, 523). By the early 1980s, the agricultural tax accounted for only about 1 per cent of the gross value of agricultural output and less than 3 per cent of national budgetary income (ZGTJNJ, 1985, 238 and 523).

Among the policies to encourage the rural, non-farm sector were generous tax allowances to new enterprises (Central Committee, 1985). However, there were heavy taxes on established enterprises. Tax rates on local enterprises varied according to the type of product. For example, in Guanghan *xian* in 1983 there were 20 different rates, ranging from the lowest of 10 per cent of profits in the construction industry to the highest rate of 55 per cent in the textile industry (Nolan, 1983b). In 1984, *xiangzhen* (township) enterprises reportedly paid over 38 per cent of their gross profits in state taxes of one type or another (ZGTJNJ, 1985, 298). Even the 'new economic associations' (different forms of non-collective co-operation), a large proportion of which would have been entitled to tax exemption, reportedly paid 9.2 per cent of their gross profits in tax (including renumeration for the operators of the 'new economic associations').[34]

As well as providing funds for higher levels, under the new revenue-sharing arrangements (see above), taxes from constituent enterprises formed a key element in expanding the financial capacities of *xian* (county) authorities. For example, in the model Guanghan *xian* (Sichuan province), in which *xiangzhen* enterprises were very advanced,[35] these enterprises' tax payments amounted to 28 per cent of the *xian*'s total tax income and its share was expanding rapidly (Nolan, 1983b). Accordingly, *xian* authorities had a strong interest in ensuring that the mid-1980s' rates of taxation on non-farm enterprises were maintained.

Compulsory procurement and state price fixing   Despite the massive shift in policy which began in the early 1980s and accelerated rapidly in 1985, it remained the case that the state would continue to purchase a large part of agricultural marketings. Even after the reforms, in 1985, 83 per cent of agricultural and sideline sales were to state departments of one kind or another (ZGTJZY, 1986, 93). Moreover, there is ample evidence that a large portion of state grain purchase contracts after the reform retained their compulsory character. For example, the Canton Daily (*Guangzhou Ribao*) in May 1985, shortly after the announcement that compulsory grain procurement had been abolished, commented: 'Some people have a mistaken view of the purchase contracts, saying that they would sign if they thought they were suitable and refuse if they were not. *This simply will not do*' (my italics — P.N.) (quoted in Fewsmith 1985, 50). Oi's careful analysis of the 'new' grain purchase system concludes: 'The methods cadres use and the process by which they guide the peasants to their decisions are similar to the system of compulsory sales, which the contract system is supposed to replace' (Oi, 1986b, 285). My own discussions in China confirm this.

While the purchase prices of a large number of farm products, indeed, were allowed to fluctuate freely with market forces, this was not true in practice for the most important ones. The state contract purchases not only of grain and cotton, but also of 'several other important products' still had 'state-fixed prices' (ZGJJNJ, 1986, v, 49). By 1987, the number of farm products purchased by the state at state-fixed ('unified') prices, had fallen from 113 to 25, and were reported to account for 30 per cent of the total value of farm sales (Gao, 1987). Moreover, a considerable proportion of remaining sales was at 'floating' prices with the state fixing the (often very narrow) limits of the float.

While ration tickets were abolished for all types of food products except grain and edible oil, the vast bulk of urban food produce continued to be sold through state outlets[36] with either basically state-fixed prices or floating prices. Even in the free markets, in large cities the prices of 'several important subsidiary foodstuffs' had a state-fixed price ceiling (ZGJJNJ, 1986, v, 49).

The Chinese leadership in the mid-1980s was deeply concerned to maintain grain marketings at an adequate level and to control food prices in cities. It was reluctant to allow market forces to become the principal determinant of farm output and urban food prices for fear of the political de-stabilization that might follow from accompanying price rises[37] — the 'Polish problem' was never far from their minds. Even the relatively small urban food price rises for 1985 (14.4 per cent) and 1986 (7.4 per cent) (State Statistical Bureau, 1987) caused great popular dissatisfaction in a society used to a long period of price stability (see chapter 6 for further discussion).

The system of supply of industrial inputs to agriculture Changes took place in the early/mid 1980s in the nature of the supply of agricultural inputs. The factories producing them (both state and collective) were affected by the industrial reforms, so that they became more responsive to market pressure. A free market in farm inputs also was allowed to develop, legitimating much former black market activity.

However, a large part of the supply of agricultural inputs continued to be through state channels at state-fixed prices. Access to these was strictly rationed. A three-tiered market for certain key inputs such as chemical fertilizers and gasoline developed. The state supplied a large portion of these inputs at relatively low prices. At these prices demand in most areas still greatly exceeded supply. A second portion was supplied by the state at higher, market-influenced prices. A third, still higher price existed on the free market, to which supplies came from a variety of channels.[38]

Indeed an integral part of the state's post-reform capacity to influence peasants to sign contracts voluntarily was its position as supplier of priority-priced farm inputs (Oi, 1986a, 240):

> In order to safeguard and encourage the peasants' enthusiasm for producing and marketing grain, we will suitably reduce the amount in the contract fixed purchase, expanding the proportion procured at market negotiated prices; the peasants who conclude the contract will be supplied with a definite amount of priority-price chemical fertilizer, and given preferential treatment in credit allocation.
> [Central Committee, 1986, 3]

We have seen also that the state used its dominant position in the supply of farm inputs to give priority access to the 'specialized households'.

There are major problems with this system. For example a multiple price structure encourages illegal activity. It makes it likely that personal ties and corruption will affect the way local officials allocate the scarce inputs. Moreover, the system provides an important remaining item of power in the hands of local cadres.[39]

Inter-sectoral resource flow   Looking at inter-sectoral flows from a simple balance of trade perspective, the post-1978 period saw an acceleration of previous trends. As the volume of inter-sectoral trade rapidly expanded (rising by almost 80 per cent in real terms from 1978 to 1983), 'imports' rose by a much greater extent than 'exports', leading to a substantial rise in the farm sector's import surplus at current prices and an extremely sharp rise in the import surplus at constant prices – see table 4.11.

Table 4.11 *Farm sector*[a] *trade with the non-farm sector (billion* yuan*)*

		1952	1957	1970	1978	1983
Farm exports	(a)[b]	14.1	21.8	34.8	55.8	126.5
	(b)[b]	16.8	21.8	26.0	38.7	69.6
Farm imports	(a)	15.8	24.9	48.4	86.4	170.6
	(b)	17.0	24.9	46.3	85.4	150.6
Imports minus	(a)	1.7	3.1	13.7	30.6	44.1
exports	(b)	0.2	3.1	20.2	46.7	81.1

[a] Excluding rural small-scale non-farm enterprises.
[b] (a) current prices; (b) 1957 prices.
Source: Sheng, 1986

I have noted already the shortcomings of this approach in analysing inter-sectoral flows. First, there is the vexed question of 'unequal exchange' between sectors. We have seen that many Chinese economists argued that, despite the improvement for the farm sector in its terms of trade from the 1950s through to the late 1970s, these still existed 'unequal exchange': the 'value' (in terms of a crude proxy for 'socially necessary labour time' embodied in the products) of industrial products sold to agriculture was argued to be much less than their 'price', while the reverse was true for agricultural products sold to industry (Chen, 1982). After 1978, the relative position of agriculture improved. The 'embodied labour' per unit of agricultural product fell as farm labour productivity rose, and the price per unit of farm produce rose; both labour productivity and prices rose less rapidly in industry than in agriculture. Despite this, it was argued that 'unequal exchange' still existed in the exchange between agriculture and the non-agricultural sector.[40]

A second problem in analysing inter-sectoral relations in the mid-1980s was the rapid change in the structure of the rural economy. As will be shown in chapter 5, the rural non-farm economy in the mid-1980s was growing at an extremely high rate and could be expected to outpace the growth rate of farm output for the foreseeable future. Already, by 1984 the share of agriculture stood at only around three-fifths of the gross value of rural output, and the proportions were changing quickly (see table 4.12).

Table 4.12 *Share of different sectors in the gross value of social product in the countryside (%) (at current prices)*

	1984[1]		1985[2]	1986[2]
Total village output	100.0		100.0	100.0
Agriculture	63.2		57.7	53.1
Rural industry	23.1			
Rural construction	7.4	36.8	42.3	46.9
Rural transport	2.6			
Rural commerce, and food and drink	3.7			

Sources: [1] ZGTJNJ, 1985, 241
[2] State Statistical Bureau, 1987, 21

The rural non-farm economy is intimately related to the farm economy, and it makes less and less sense to exclude it from one's analysis of 'inter-sectoral' relations.

CONCLUSION

This chapter has suggested that there were more continuities in the Chinese countryside through to the mid-1980s than many western accounts allow. Although in relative decline and greatly changed in form, the collective non-farm economy remained very important. China's policy makers had not shifted to the view that a completely individualistic, free market rural economy was desirable either for distribution or growth. Collective institutions remained centrally important in welfare provision. Moreover, without collective and local state agencies such as the *she, cun, xiang* and *xian*, many activities vital to the prosperity of the rural economy (e.g. irrigation, communications, research) probably would not have occurred at as high a level as they did in the mid-1980s.

There were some important continuities, too, in the villages' external environment. Although levels of personal and agricultural taxation remained low, rural non-farm enterprises (much the most dynamic element in the rural economy in the mid-1980s) continued to pay over part of their profits for use by the *xiang* for collective purposes, and to pay a relatively high proportion of their profits in taxation, much of which was used by the *xian* authorities for purposes beneficial to the whole (largely rural) area under its jurisdiction. The compulsory purchase of farm produce at state-fixed prices remained important. The supply of industrial farm inputs continued to be channelled largely through the state system with both the advantages (e.g. ability to direct inputs towards priority needs) and disadvantages (e.g. incentive to corruption) that this entailed. Moreover, despite the shift in the agricultural—industrial terms of trade, Chinese economists still argued that 'unequal exchange' operated in respect to exchange between the two sectors.

Beyond these elements of continuity, a revolution took place in the rural micro-economic setting, amounting to a thoroughgoing de-collectivization: contracting out collective land, selling collective means of production, contracting out many of those non-land assets still collectively owned, removing income ceilings, allowing unfettered development of individual and genuinely co-operative non-farm enterprises, permitting a real rural market in hired labour, etc. The texture of daily life in the villages was transformed in a way unimaginable in the mid-1970s. A vast array of economic decisions formerly in the hands of collective cadres was now taken individually by almost 200 million peasant households. The political and social implications of such a change were profound. The CCP still had important channels of control over China's peasants, and many people have underestimated these. However, it will be impossible to prevent the development of new forms of peasant socio-political independence alongside their increased independence in economic decision-making. By allowing such a massive change in the rural setting, China's leaders emphatically turned their backs on the Stalinist approach towards the peasantry, and returned to the 'Bukharinist' path of the Chinese countryside which characterized part of the period between land reform and collectivization.

Chinese policy-makers and theoreticians hoped that de-collectivization would eliminate the inefficiencies of collective farms and encourage individual households' enthusiasm to work hard and diligently, and to improve their human and physical capital. The optimal micro-economic setting was considered to be a combination of the individual household economy supplemented by appropriate collective and state actions.

The difficulty in assessing the factors contributing to China's rural economic performance since the late 1970s (examined in the following chapter) is the fact that such important changes occurred too in the external environment: major reforms took place in the marketing system (though the most important of these did not occur until 1985), a major improvement (for agriculture) took place in the internal terms of trade, and a dramatic increase took place in the supply of industrial 'incentive' goods.

It is extremely difficult to assess what effects might have resulted from trying to reform the external environment without making major changes at the micro-economic level. The arguments in chapters 2 and 3 suggest that while this might have done much to improve the rural sector's performance the more fundamental problems were those at the micro-level. This view receives support from the Soviet Union's agricultural experience. In the post-Stalin period there were massive changes in the rural sector's external environment including a huge rise in supplies of both industrial farm inputs and incentive goods, and a big shift in the inter-sectoral terms of trade (in favour of agriculture). However, despite some important changes at the micro-level (e.g. a shift away from 'collective' towards 'state' farms), the fundamentals of agricultural organization remained unchanged. While this produced considerable long-term growth of farm output, the inefficiency of large-scale production units was a major factor in the extremely high capital requirements of Soviet agriculture, with over 25 per cent of total national investment in the 1970s allocated to the sector. This suggests that while constructing an appropriate external environment for the farm sector obviously is a necessary for good farm performance, it is for from sufficient.[41]

5

Performance of the Rural Sector since 1978

'[China's post-1978 rural economic reforms have led to] the market playing a more and more important role in production and in people's lives. In some villages the mutual economic relationships of each and every household have come to be mediated through exchange. People are concerned with changes in the market and pay a great deal of attention to market information. The slow and easy-going village life is being replaced by the quick and intense urban life. People have begun to be concerned about time, efficiency, results, and business income.

Dong, 1986b

The preceding chapter outlined the dramatic changes in China's rural institutions after 1978 with the triumph of the 'Bukharinist' segment of the Chinese leadership. From early on in this reform a fairly clear reform model could be perceived, in sharp contrast to reforms in the large-scale industrial sector, where the problems were much more complex and the reform model was not clear.[1] The essence of the rural reform model was individual operation of farmland supplemented by extensive co-operation and state action to provide an effective framework for households' productive endeavours. This still left a wide array of important issues in rural policy about which there could be dispute (e.g. the degree of state intervention in farm marketing, farm price policy, hired labour, the permitted dimensions of income inequality, international trade in food products) but at the core of the reforms there was a solid base upon which virtually all Chinese leaders and most Chinese people were in agreement, insofar as one can tell.

This book has stressed that important non-institutional changes also occurred after 1978, including major changes in the relative prices of farm and non-farm products, urban demand for farm produce and the supply of industrial incentive goods to peasants. However, I have argued that these would have been insufficient to produce a dramatic improvement in the performance of the rural economy. Moreover, these changes were not unconnected with the transformation in rural institutions. For example, growth of output of industrial incentive goods was assisted greatly by the rapid expansion of the rural non-farm sector both in relation to sub-contracting and direct supply of finished products.

This chapter outlines the extraordinary progress in China's rural economy after 1978 in relation to farm output, farm productivity, the non-farm sector, living standards and the decline in poverty. This immense change, affecting a vast number of people, was of the greatest historical importance, and one that provokes deep reflection in anyone concerned with rural policy in developing countries.

FARM OUTPUT

There are few (if any) examples in modern economic history of such a sustained break in trend growth rates of agricultural output as that achieved in China from the late 1970s to the mid-1980s. The gross value of farm output at 'comparable' prices[2] reportedly increased its compound annual average growth rate from 2.8 per cent from 1955–5 to 1975–7, to no less than 8.4 per cent from 1975–7 to 1983–5 (ZGTJNJ, 1985, 238; ZGTJZY, 1986, 32).[3] The acceleration was broad-based, with a wide range of farm products reportedly experiencing unprecedentedly rapid growth as shown in table 5.1. The reported increases in output per caput were equally striking — table 5.2.

It is openly admitted in China that there were difficulties in obtaining accurate comparable figures for the rural economy pre- and post-1978. Prior to the 1980s the number of professionally trained statisticians was small for a country China's size. Also, peasants had a strong incentive to conceal private sector activity. After 1978 this latter became legitimate and, hence, it could have artificially inflated the post-reform output data. Moreover, the return to individual farming meant that most farm output was not now publicly recorded (under the commune system most farm output went 'across the scales'). Therefore, it might be argued, the Chinese government has little idea of the real level of output. A sceptical view of the reliability of the apparent contrast in performance might conclude by noting that China's policy makers naturally wish to paint as bright a picture as possible of the post-1978 performance.

On the other hand, there are the following points to consider. The number and quality of professional statisticians increased sharply in the

Table 5.1 *Chinese agricultural output, 1950s—1980s*

	Average annual output (m metric tons)			Compound annual growth rate (%)	
	1955—7	1975—7	1984—6	1955—7 to 1975—7	1975—7 to 1984—6
Grain	191.00	285.00	392.00	2.0	3.6
Cotton	1.54	2.16	4.65	1.7	8.9
Oilseeds	4.71	4.18	14.14	−0.6	14.5
Jute and hemp	0.279	0.764	2.11	5.2	12.0
Sugar cane	9.05	17.02	47.09	3.2	12.0
Beetroots	1.58	2.61	8.50	2.5	14.0
Silk cocoons	0.126	0.201	0.366	2.4	6.9
Tea	0.114	0.232	0.439	3.6	7.3
Cured tobacco	0.256[a]	0.836	1.668	6.1	8.0
Fruits	2.79	5.49	11.63	3.1	8.7
Meat (pork, beef, mutton)	3.99[a]	7.86	17.38	3.5	9.2
Aquatic products[b]	2.76	4.53	7.1	2.5	5.1

[a] 1957 only.
[b] It is hard to disentangle the proportion included in farm production.
Sources: Luo, 1985, 186, 190, 194; ZGTJNJ, 1985, 255—6, 267, 270; State Statistical Bureau, 1986; ZGTJZY, 1986, 38; State Statistical Bureau, 1987

Table 5.2 *Output per caput of major farm products in China (kg)*

	1952	1957	1975—7	1983—5
Grain	288.0	306.0	306.0	380.0
Cotton	2.3	2.6	2.3	4.9
Oilseeds	7.4	6.6	4.5	12.4
Meat (beef, pork, mutton)	6.0	6.3	8.5	15.2
Aquatic products	3.0	4.9	4.9	6.1

Sources: ZGTJNJ, 1985, 273; ZGTJZY, 1986, 40

1980s. In estimating pre-1978 levels of output, the extensive local collective records are of immense help. To cope with the statistical problems of the break-up of collective farming the 1980s saw a rapid extension of rural sample surveys. Moreover, output figures can be checked against steadily improving sample surveys of income and consumption.[4] Unlike pre-1978 there now existed a wide array of channels through which outsiders could assess the rough extent of the reliability of Chinese data ranging from high level professional contacts with policy makers and statisticians[5] to numerous informal contacts. Although there were shortcomings in Chinese data, these mostly were readily acknowledged by Chinese statisticians, and there is general agreement among Western experts that the data were as good as one was likely to encounter in a country at China's stage of development. Accordingly, it seems safe to assume that 'most of the apparent growth (in China's farm output post-1978) is real' (Stone, 1985, 114).[6]

Fluctuations in weather naturally can have an important influence on agricultural output. However, the modernization of Chinese agriculture in the 1960s and 1970s meant that the effect of weather instability was much reduced (Kueh, 1984b, 82). Moreover, although 1982 and 1983 were unusually good years for weather (World Bank, 1985, 9), the period after 1978 was not one of exceptionally few natural disasters (ZGTJNJ, 1985, 302).[7] It is likely that most of the increase of farm ouput can be explained by factors other than the weather (Stone, 1985, 114).

FARM SECTOR PRODUCTIVITY

The sown area reportedly fell sharply in the 1980s,[8] from 150 million hectares in 1978 to 144 million hectares in 1985 (ZGTJZY, 1986, 35), as China's farmers concentrated their efforts on higher-yielding fields. The total sown to grain fell especially sharply, from 121 million hectares in 1978 to 109 million hectares in 1985, and its share of total sown area accordingly contracted from 80 per cent in 1978 to 76 per cent in 1985 (ZGTJZY, 1986, 35).[9] The improvement in yields post-1978 was dramatic. Virtually all crops recorded exceptionally rapid rates of growth over the period (table 5.3).

After accelerating in the mid-1960s, China's population growth rate began to slow down in the late 1960s[10] (table 5.4). This began to feed through into a declining growth rate of labour supply in the late 1970s and early 1980s. In addition, the reforms allowed households to determine their own pattern of labour allocation. Large numbers of family members left agriculture (at least, for a large part of the year) to work in non-farm occupations, leaving the remaining members to intensify their agricultural labour input. These factors were reflected in the slow rate of growth of the agricultural labour force post-1978, reportedly increasing by just 6 per cent from 1978 to 1985 (ZGTJZY, 1986, 29).

The sharp acceleration in farm output in the late 1970s and early 1980s was produced by a farm labour force growing much more slowly

Table 5.3 *Output per sown hectare of principal crops (metric tons)*

	1957	1975	1978	1984	1975 as % of 1957	1984 as % of 1978
Grain	1.46	2.35	2.53	3.61	161	143
Cotton	0.28	0.48	0.44	0.90	171	205
Peanuts	1.01	1.21	1.34	1.99	120	149
Rapeseed	0.38	0.67	0.72	1.23	176	171
Sesame	0.33	0.39	0.50	0.56	118	112
Hemp	2.11	2.36	2.64	4.66	112	177
Sugarcane	38.93	31.87	38.50	54.28	82	141
Sugarbeet	9.44	8.18	8.17	16.50	87	202
Cured tobacco	0.72	1.52	1.72	2.16	211	126

Source: ZGJJNJ, 1981, VI, 11; ZGTJNJ, 1985, 263−4

Table 5.4 *Natural growth rate of population[a] (number per 1000)*

1952	20.0
1957	23.2
1965	28.4
1970	25.8
1975	15.7
1981	14.5
1984	10.8
1986	14.1

[a] Birth rates minus death rate.
Sources: ZGTJZY, 1986, 21; ZGTJNJ, 1985, 186; State Statistical Bureau, 1987

than in the preceding period and than the total work force. The reported growth of farm labour productivity is perhaps the most striking of all the data on the farm sector after 1978. After long years of stagnation under Maoist policies (see chapter 3) farm output per worker (in real terms) reportedly grew by almost 60 per cent from 1978 to 1984, and by almost 80 per cent from 1975 to 1984[11] (see table 5.5).

Some Western analysts expressed the fear that de-collectivization would lead to a collapse of rural capital formation in Chinese agriculture. As tables 5.6 and 5.7 show, this was not the case.[12] In the mid-1980s total purchases of industrial producer goods by the farm sector were, in fact, much larger than pre−1978.

Table 5.5 *Farm labour productivity*

	1952	1957	1965	1970	1975	1978	1979	1980	1981	1982	1983	1984	1985
GVAO [a] **(b. yuan)**													
1970 prices[1]	63.6	79.3	87.1	105.8	128.5	145.9	158.4	164.6	–	–	–	–	–
1980 prices[2]	–	–	–	–	–	–	–	196.4	209.1	232.7	250.8	281.6	291.2
Agricultural labour force million[3]	173.2	193.1	234.0	278.1	294.6	294.3	294.3	302.1	311.7	320.1	325.1	325.4	311.9
GVAO per worker (yuan)													
1970 prices	367.0	411.0	372.0	462.0	436.0	496.0	538.0	545.0	–	–	–	–	–
1980 prices	–	–	–	–	–	–	–	650.0	671.0	727.0	771.0	866.0	934.0
Index of GVAO per worker													
1970 prices	74.0	83.0	75.0	93.0	88.0	100.0	108.0	110.0	–	–	–	–	–
1980 prices	–	–	–	–	–	–	–	100.0	103.0	112.0	119.0	133.0	144.0
'linked' index	74.0	83.0	75.0	93.0	88.0	100.0	108.0	113.0	123.0	123.0	131.0	146.0	158.0

[a] GVAO = gross value of agricultural output. Data at 1970 prices (1952–80) include brigade and production team industries, but exclude commune enterprises' output. Data at 1980 prices (1980–5) exclude both *cun* (former brigade) and *xiang* (former commune) output.

Sources: [1] ZGNYJJGY, 1982, 28
[2] ZGTJZY, 1986, 232
[3] ZGTJNJ, 1985, 213, and ZGTJZY, 1986, 29

Table 5.6 *Sales of agricultural means of production, 1957—1986 (billion yuan)*

	1957	1965	1970	1975	1978	1980	1983	1985	1986
At current prices	3.3	8.0	12.9	22.5	29.4	34.6	42.3	50.4	57.6
At 1957 prices	3.3	7.7	13.8	24.9	29.4	34.1	43.3	40.8	—

Sources: ZGTJZY, 1986, 88; ZGTJNJ, 1985, 464; State Statistical Bureau, 1987

Given that by the late 1970s China had already established an extremely high level of irrigation (the leading 'input' in the Asian 'Green Revolution'), the most important single agricultural input for increasing farm output was chemical fertilizer. Far from stagnating, the consumption of chemical fertilizer more than doubled from 1978 to 1986 (see table 5.7). Moreover, the quality of chemical fertilizers improved due to (1) a reduction in the proportion supplied by low quality small plants, (2) improvement in quality in large plants, and (3) more sophisticated fertilizer handling and application (Stone, 1985, 118).

Table 5.7 *Changes in supply of farm inputs, 1978—1986*

	Unit	1978[1]	1980[1]	1983[1]	1984[1]	1985[1]	1986[2]
Stocks of:							
1 Total motive power of machinery	m h.p.	159.8	200.5	245.0	265.1	284.3	(310)[a]
2 Large and medium sized tractors used in agriculture	m	0.56	0.74	0.84	0.85	0.85	0.87
3 Small-sized and walking tractors used in agriculture[1]	m	1.37	1.87	2.75	3.30	3.82	—
4 Large and medium sized tractor-pulled agricultural implements[1]	m	1.19	1.37	1.31	1.24	1.13	—
5 Motors for drainage and irrigation in agriculture[1]	m h.p.	65.6	74.6	78.5	78.5	78.2	(82)[a]

Table 5.7 *continued*

6	Combine harvesters	thousand	19.0	27.0	35.7	35.9	34.6	–
7	Trucks for agricultural use	thousand	73.8	137.7	274.8	349.3	427.6	494.0
8	Animal-drawn carts with rubber tyres							
	1 Large	m	2.49	2.40	2.59	2.85	2.88	–
	2 small	m	29.6	35.2	55.6	59.5	61.1	–
9	Motorized fishing boats	m h.p.	2.91	3.51	4.44	4.56	4.99	–
	Mechanically ploughed area	m ha.	40.7	41.0	33.6	34.9	34.4	–
	Irrigated area of which:	m ha.	45.0	44.9	44.6	44.5	44.0	–
	power-irrigated area	m ha.	24.9	25.3	25.3	25.1	24.6	–
	Chemical fertilizers (nutrient weight)[2]	m tons	8.8	12.7	16.6	17.4	17.8	19.5
	Electricity consumed in the rural areas	billion kwh	25.3	32.1	42.8	46.4	50.9	57.5

[a] Approximate figures.
Sources:[1] ZGTJZY, 1986, 43–4
[2] State Statistical Bureau, 1987

The data on agricultural machinery in the table 5.7 superficially show the same story, with the total horsepower used in 'agriculture' almost doubling from 1978 to 1986. However, although technically categorized for 'agricultural' use, much of this was used either wholly or partly for non-agricultural purposes. A truck might carry grain to market at harvest time, but carry other products during the rest of the year. Large and small tractors are commonly used only part of the time in the fields; for much of the time they transport goods on the roads. In fact, in certain important respects, mechanized inputs into agriculture proper stagnated or declined. From 1978 to 1985, the power-irrigated area hardly altered and the mechanically ploughed area fell by over 15 per cent (despite a large increase in tractor stocks).

The remarkable growth of farm output after 1978 was achieved with a relatively small addition to the stock of fixed capital for use in agriculture proper,[13] so that there must have been a sharp fall in the agricultural fixed-capital-to-output ratio. The main technical basis for the growth of output was the huge increase in the quantity of chemical fertilizer together with the improvements in its quality (Stone, 1985, 118).

THE RURAL NON-FARM ECONOMY

Impressive as the growth of farm output was, growth of the non-farm rural economy was even more dramatic. The total value of output of this sector at current prices rose more than fourfold from 1979 to 1985 (the gross value of output of the rural non-farm economy rose from 49.3 billion *yuan* in 1979 to 201.1 billion *yuan* in 1985) (Research department, 1986, 13) and the increase in 'real' terms was not far removed from this figure.[14] Employment also grew very quickly. The numbers employed in the rural non-farm economy reportedly rose from 24 million in 1979 to 46 million in 1985 (Research department, 1986, 13). By 1986 the 12.2 billion 'rural enterprises' were reportedly employing 76 million workers, amounting to 20 per cent of the rural workforce (Han, 1987 c). By 1985 the structure of the village labour force was as shown in table 5.8.

Table 5.8 *Distribution of villages' labour force in 1985*

	Workers (m)	%
Total	371.0	100.0
of which:		
1 Agriculture, forestry, animal husbandry, sidelines, fishing	303.5	81.9
2 Industry	27.4	7.4
3 Construction	11.3	3.0
4 Transport, postal services	4.3	1.3
5 Commerce, food and drink	4.6	1.2
6 Other	19.9	5.2

Source: ZGJJNJ, 1986, III, 13

The sharp rise in the importance of the rural non-farm sector employment in the mid-1980s is reflected in the rapidly changing composition of total rural production. As was noted in chapter 4, the reported share of the rural non-farm economy (at current prices) in total rural social product rose from 37 per cent in 1984 to 47 per cent in 1986 (ZGTJZY, 1986, 33; State Statistical Bureau, 1987). By 1985 *xiang* and *cun*-run industry was producing over 18 per cent of national industrial output value (ZGTJZY, 1986, 50). In certain sectors of the economy its contribution by the mid-1980s had become extremely important. In 1985, *xiangzhen* (township) enterprises produced 29 per cent of China's coal, 50 per cent of its clothes, and 53 per cent by value of building materials (Han, 1987 c).

INCOMES AND LIVING STANDARDS

The rapid growth of farm output after 1978 brought about a revolution in the diet of the whole Chinese population as shown in table 5.9.

Table 5.9 *Food intake of the Chinese population (average per person per day)*

	1952	*1978*	*1983*
Calories (no.)			
Whole population	2270.0	2311.0	2877.0
of whom:			
1 Urban dwellers	—	2715.0	3183.0
2 Rural dwellers	—	2224.0	2806.0
Protein (g)			
Whole population	69.6	70.8	82.5
of whom:			
1 Urban dwellers	—	81.6	87.5
2 Rural dwellers	—	68.5	81.7
Fats (g)			
Whole population	28.3	29.9	47.2
of whom:			
1 Urban dwellers	—	49.0	74.9
2 Rural dwellers	—	25.7	40.7

Source: ZGTJNJ, 1985, 480

In just a few years the Chinese population pulled sharply away from average levels of food intake that had probably changed little over many centuries, as Chinese farm output expanded with ever more intensive applications of 'traditional' technology at more or less constant returns to extra labour input (Perkins, 1969). Indeed, Ishikawa (1967b, 78—9) speaks graphically of Asian countries' agricultural systems under traditional technology moving along a 'subsistence parabola': increases in population associated with a fall in cultivated land per person, increasing intensity of cultivation and yields per acre, and more or less constant output per person at around subsistence level. China in the early 1980s at last decisively broke away from this 'subsistence parabola'.

Sample survey data (see table 5.10) reveal a dramatic and broad based transformation of peasant living standards from 1978 to 1985.

Table 5.10 *Changes in peasant living standards as revealed by sample surveys*[a]

Average per caput consumption of	1978	1985	1985 as % of 1978
Grain (unhusked) (kg)	248.0	257.0	104
of which: fine grain (kg)	123.0	209.0	170
Vegetables (kg)	141.0	131.0	93
Edible oil (kg)	1.96	4.04	206
Meat (beef, pork, mutton) (kg)	5.76	10.97	190
Poultry (kg)	0.25	1.03	412
Eggs (kg)	0.80	2.05	256
Fish and shrimps (kg)	0.84	1.64	195
Sugar (kg)	0.73	1.46	200
Alcoholic drink (kg)	1.22	4.37	358
Cotton cloth (m)	5.63	2.54	45
Cotton (kg)	0.40	0.43	108
Synthetic fibre cloth (m)	0.41	2.50	610
Silk and satin (m)	0.02	0.07	350
Shoes (rubber, leather and canvas (pairs)	0.32	0.55	172
Average area of housing space per caput:			
Total (m^2)	10.2	17.34	170
of which: living space (m^2)	8.1	14.70	181
Stocks of consumer durables per 100 households:			
Bicycles	30.7	80.6	263
Sewing machines	19.8	43.2	218
Radios	17.4	54.2	311
Clocks and watches	51.8	163.6	316
of which: watches	27.4	126.3	461
Television sets	negligible	11.7	—

[a] The number of peasant households surveyed was 6095 in 1978 and 66642 in 1985.
Source: ZGTJZY, 1986, 110–12

The proportion of superior 'fine' grains in the peasants' diet rose from 50 per cent to around 80 per cent. Large increases (of 100 per cent or more) were registered in per caput consumption of the principal foodstuffs apart from grain and vegetables. The quality of vegetables rose as vegetable markets became increasingly competitive. Big increases were recorded in non-traditional textiles as the peasants increased the variety of their clothing. A rural housing boom of enormous dimensions took place: average per caput peasant expenditure on housing rose from less than 4 *yuan* in 1978 to over 39 *yuan* in 1985 (ZGTJZY, 1986, 111). In just seven years peasants' living space per caput rose no less than 80 per cent, and, of course, a large amount of reconstruction work to improve the quality of existing rural housing space went on in this period. At least as striking as these improvements was the extraordinarily rapid rise in stocks of basic consumer durables. By the mid-1980s, most peasant households had a radio; almost half had a sewing machine, and, on average, there was almost one bicycle per household. TV sets had been almost unknown in the countryside in 1978, except as a collective good in some prosperous areas: by the mid-1980s more than one in ten peasant households owned one.

A sign of the growing level of real income in China's villages was the shift in the pattern of consumption that began to appear in the 1980s, away from the traditional massive dominance of food. Sample survey data showed that the share of food in peasants' expenditure fell from 68 per cent in 1978 to 58 per cent in 1985, while that of housing rose from 3 per cent to 12 per cent and that of daily use goods etc. from 7 per cent to 11 per cent in the same period (ZGTJZY, 1986, 111).

POVERTY

Much attention was paid in the economic development literature in the 1970s to aspects of inequality.[15] However, the relationship between the diverse measures of inequality and poverty is extremely complex.[16] Fields' (1980) study makes a powerful case in relation to the dangers of looking only at measures of inequality to the neglect of measures of poverty. It is quite possible for inequality to become greater at the same time as poverty declines. Whether such a situation constitutes an improvement is a matter of opinion. This author is persuaded of the case for poor countries that absolute poverty measures generally are more important than inequality measures.

After 1978 new possibilities opened up for improving the lot of poor peasants. The relatively small number of them who lived in advanced areas generally benefited from the extremely rapid growth of output in those areas: new possibilities occurred for earning income on land sub-contracted to them, and non-farm employment opportunities expanded quickly. Moreover, the rapid increase in funds available to collectives and local state authorities in well-located areas created the opportunity to tackle the problems of local poverty effectively (Nolan, 1983a, 70–1). Well-organised areas set up special organizations at the *xian* (county), *xiang* and *cun* level to help poor households and units. The *xian* used its resources to help poor peasants by, for example, giving them priority supply of chemical fertilizer, loans on favourable terms, granting free medical care, waiving or reducing education fees, and providing technical advice.[17] Within the *she*, well-organised areas still maintained intact the 'five guarantee' system for the poorest households, and provided pensions for the retired peasants (Nolan, 1983, b). However, the 'poor' people receiving assistance at the local level in rich areas were often well-off by the standards of poor areas (Nolan, 1983a, 70–1).

Much more important is the question of broader geographical concentrations of poverty of the kind discussed in chapter 3. The issue of large spatial concentrations of poverty has been taken seriously by theoreticians and by the central and provincial leaderships: 'all localities and departments' were instructed to 'regard helping poor areas to overcome backwardness as an important item on their agenda' (Song, 1986). As early as 1979 the State Council decided to remit the agricultural tax on poor areas for three successive years (Nolan, 1983a, 72). In 1984 it was decided that poor areas would be exempted from both the agricultural tax and the enterprise income tax (Lu, 1984, 26). Poor areas were permitted to introduce 'contracting to the household' well before other areas (Watson, 1983), and from 1984 were allowed to practise free market pricing of previously planned goods (e.g. grain and other agricultural products, sideline products, native products) (Lu, 1984, 26). Under the new policies, the poor areas were free to develop lines of production in which they had a comparative advantage rather than having to produce products (notably grain) determined by the state.

Although in the mid-1980s there still were tight controls on peasants' formal place of residence, poor localities often benefited from the enormously increased freedom granted to peasants to do 'outside work' (Nolan, 1983a). The end of rationing for most foodstuffs and the easy availability of grain coupons (and grain outside the ration) made it easy for peasants to leave their technical place of residence (where their *hukou* (household registration) is) to work and live elsewhere. The degree of labour mobility increased dramatically compared to the 1970s. Two easily observable, but striking examples of this were the burgeoning markets in large cities for female domestic helps and craftsmen (especially carpenters) often coming from poor areas. In Beijing, casual estimates suggest that by 1986 there were at least 10 000 rural girls who were working as domestic helps. Indeed, the demand for domestic helps was rising so fast that their real wages increased quite quickly in the mid-1980s.[18] There is plenty of evidence that rich areas with agricultural labour shortages were attracting workers from distant parts (Kung, 1986, 25; Kung and Chan, 1987; Dong, 1986b) and there were many press reports of peasants coming from poor areas to take over contracts on land in suburban areas of big cities in the east of China. Through the return of remittances this 'trickle down' mechanism almost certainly was helping poor areas, though the net benefits of migration for any particular region are complex and one should be wary of drawing over-simplistic conclusions.

In addition to migration occurring through the workings of market forces, the state attempted for some exceptionally poor areas to assist rural migration. For example, in the mid-1980s the Ningxia Hui Minority People's Autonomous Region government assisted over 110000 impoverished peasants to move to better areas within the Region. These moves appear to have been voluntary and relatively sensitively organized. For example, one of the schemes involved assisting one or two workers from each family to settle in a new area (often opening up wasteland for cultivation). Only if the pioneer efforts were successful were the other members of the family helped to move.[19]

The dynamism of the rural economy increased the funds available to the state which might be used to assist poor areas. The sharp rise in total tax payments from rural non-farm enterprises, has already been noted, a part of which was passed on to authorities above the *xian* level. Detailed data for 1984 on public finance at the *xian* level in Anhui province show this vividly (see table 5.11). The richest *xian* in the province generated much higher public financial incomes per person than poor and middle-income *xian*. However, they handed over much larger amounts to the central and provincial governments. Despite this they retained much larger financial incomes than middle and poor *xian*. However, assistance from the provincial budget was much greater for poor *xian* than for rich *xian*. The net outcome was that there was very little difference in the average per caput revenues available to rich, middle and low income *xian* — in other words, this was a very egalitarian system.

Striking too was the rise in voluntary peasant savings alongside the rise in incomes in the 1980s. Average per caput rural savings rose from roughly 7 *yuan* in 1978 to over 60 *yuan* in 1984 (ZGTJNJ, 1985, 185 and 580), often providing resources for the state to channel towards poor areas via the credit systems.

A variety of measures were taken in the 1980s by special state organizations at different levels to help poor areas. For example, special low

Table 5.11 *Public financial income and expenditure in Anhui province, 1984, yuan*

	Average net income per peasant	Average per caput public income				Financial subsidies from the province	Total financial outlay
		total financial	handed to central government	handed to provincial government	retained by the xian		
1 Average for the five *xian* with the highest average peasant incomes[a]	428	26.8	6.6	2.0	18.3	5.5	26.6
2 Average for five *xian* with middle level average peasant incomes	273	20.4	5.1	0.3	14.9	8.7	24.8
3 Average for the five *xian* with the lowest average peasant incomes	171	11.7	2.9	0.2	8.7	16.7	26.9
1 as % of 2	157	131	159		123	63	107
1 as % of 3	250	229	284		210	33	99

[a] Excluding suburban areas of cities.
Source: Calculated from AHJJNJ, 1985, 325–555

interest and interest-free funds were allocated to help poor areas expand profitable lines of production. Special funds were established to help road-building in poor areas (Central Committee, 1985).[20] Purchasing departments were set up to purchase special mountainous areas' products, such as medicinal materials, which might otherwise be hard to market (Central Committee, 1985). Relevant departments formed 'volunteer service brigades' to go to the poor areas to supply scientific, educational and medical services, with special state bonuses given to those who volunteer (Central Committee, 1985).[21] Poor areas were encouraged to 'take the initiative in establishing lateral ties with economically and technologically advanced areas and regions, so as to import financial and human resources from other areas to develop their own' (Song, 1986).

A great variety of sources, both Chinese and Western, suggest that the absolute numbers and the proportion of the rural population in poverty fell sharply after 1978 (though, it must be stressed the numbers in poverty in the mid-1980s were still very large). The World Bank (1986 (a), 30) concludes: '[Using] a poverty line based on food intake requirements of 2185 kilocalories per day, it is estimated that the proportion of the rural population in poverty declined from 31 per cent in 1979 to 13 per cent in 1982'...'; *the speed and scale of the improvement is probably unprecedented in human history'* (my emphasis — P.N.) It seems most unlikely, in view of the range of measures taken, and the seriousness with which they were pursued, that the dimensions of poverty did not decline further after 1982. This view is reinforced strongly by evidence on regional inequality and poverty presented in chapter 6.

CONCLUSION

The period from 1978 to the mid-1980s was an extraordinary one in China's history. Exceptionally rapid growth of farm output laid the foundation for a transformation of the Chinese people's diet. The growth of agricultural output was not due to a sudden surge in the supply of capital inputs. Rather it occurred because of an extremely rapid growth of farm labour productivity, which suggests tremendous 'slack' in the pre-1978 rural economy. China's package of agricultural reforms unleashed an extraordinary change in the intensity and quality of rural labour (though not necessarily in the number of hours per worker).[22] The rapid growth of rural labour productivity was increasingly assisted by the sharp acceleration in output in the rural non-farm economy. The growth of rural productivity in turn underpinned the extremely rapid growth of average incomes. Perhaps the most striking accompaniment of the acceleration in the growth of the rural economy was the quick decline in the numbers in poverty.

6

Problems

Shichang yu jihua de guanxi jiu shi niao yu longzi de guanxi: 'The relationship between market and plan is like the relationship between a bird and its cage' (if the cage is too small, the bird cannot spread its wings; if the cage is too large, the bird will escape through the bars and fly away).

Description of China's reforms in the 1980s,
attributed to Chen Yun

The story in chapter 5 is one of almost unmitigated success for the Chinese post-1978 rural reforms. In fact, a wide array of new problems emerged. Collective farms have serious shortcomings but they have the virtue of simplifying life for planners and policymakers. Trying to cope with hundreds of millions of independent decision makers and accepting a substantial measure of market forces makes their life vastly more complex. It is undoubtedly much easier in most respects to plan 'parametrically' (i.e. control the main economic parameters within which enterprises operate) for a small number of large enterprises than for a myriad small ones.

A wide array of criticisms has been levelled at China's rural reforms of the 1980s. They range from dire predictions of an imminent collapse of agricultural production to concerns that 'capitalism' has been 'restored' in China's villages. If one is to criticize the Maoist system and argue in favour of the principal features of the post-Mao rural reforms (as this book does) it is vital to do so with one's eyes open, recognizing frankly the difficulties and problems that were emerging in the wake of the reforms. Accordingly, this chapter examines a number of the most important criticisms that have been made. It concludes that many of the problems have been exaggerated but that some important difficulties do exist. Nevertheless, it is quite possible to argue strongly, as this book does, in favour of the reforms on balance, and to hope that the Chinese leadership will take steps to tackle the most serious of the new problems.

FALTERING AGRICULTURAL GROWTH RATES

As was seen in the preceding chapter, from the late 1970s to the mid-1980s, the reported real growth rate in Chinese agriculture was over 8 per cent per annum. This was extremely fast, both by the standards of China pre−1978 and in comparison with other developing countries.[1] Indeed, most unusually for a large, poor economy, over the course of several years, the growth rate in agriculture was faster than in industry. However, by 1984−86 there were signs that the agricultural growth rate was beginning to decline − see table 6.1.

Table 6.1   *Year-to-year change in gross value of agricultural output (excluding* cun-*run industry (%) (at 1980 prices, except for 1985−1986)*

1980−1	6.5
1981−2	11.3
1982−3	7.8
1983−4	12.2
1984−5	3.5
1985−6	3.5[a]

[a] Current prices.
Source: ZGTJZY, 1986, 32; State Statistical Bureau, 1987

While the 1984−5 figure is partially explicable in terms of natural disasters, little of the 1985−6 figure can be explained in this way. Does this constitute cause for serious concern?

Unlike many developing countries where agriculture has to keep pace with rapid population growth, the fact that China's population growth by the mid−1980s had fallen to less than 1.5 per cent per annum greatly reduced the pressure on agriculture. Even after the upward shift in the population growth rate in China in 1986, the annual growth rate still stood at just 1.4 per cent (State Statistical Bureau, 1987), compared to 2.6 per cent for low income countries (excluding China and India) (World Bank, 1986b, 228). Even in 1985−6, China's agricultural growth rate was more than double the rate of population growth.

China's huge size (plus strategic considerations) makes it unlikely that imports will play a major role in meeting domestic demand for agricultural products.[2] Moreover, its size makes it impossible for agricultural growth to be sustained at high levels through international trade, especially given present international trading arrangements whereby the advanced capitalist countries' farm sectors are highly protected. Although agricultural exports provide an important source of foreign exchange and are extremely important to certain regions in China, they are, and will probably continue to be, of relatively small importance for the whole country's agricultural economy.[3] It is true that exports of light industrial products using agricultural raw materials grew rapidly in value in the early/mid 1980s. Much the most important were textiles, which more than doubled in value (excluding man-made textiles) from 1981 to 1984.[4] However, their growth rate was limited by protection in the advanced capitalist countries. Moreover, the share of man-made fibres in China's textile production was increasing quickly. Even on generous assumptions about future growth rates, it was unlikely that natural fibre exports would make a major contribution to sustaining the extremely rapid post-Mao growth of farm output.

If agriculture were to continue to expand at the rate of the late 1970s/early 1980s the fundamental influences would be domestic demand, pricing policy and the supply response from agriculture. A number of features are striking in respect to the pattern of demand. First, the income elasticity of demand for grain for direct consumption (as opposed to animal feed) is low, probably around 0.2 (ZGTJNJ, 1985, 566−7), which is hardly surprising given that the average national consumption level in the mid-1980s was around 250 kilograms (ZGTJNJ, 1985, 576). Secondly, the income elasticity of demand for housing, consumer durables and goods for recreation is relatively high:[5] 'the current consumption wave is moving towards household electrical appliances; with this swift change in China's consumption pattern, the percentage of spending on non-daily necessities is rapidly on the rise' (China Rural Development Research Group, 1986, 16).

The biggest question mark hangs over the income elasticity of demand for subsidiary foodstuffs. The income elasticity of demand for these is much greater than for grain, probably around 0.9−1.0 (ZGTJNJ, 1985, 566−7), and at relatively high levels of urban income, consumption of these foodstuffs continues to rise fairly steadily, while direct consumption of grain increases very little − see table 6.2.

Overall, then, the combination of slow (albeit faster than in the immediate past) population growth and a low income elasticity of demand for grain, alone makes it likely that Chinese agricultural output will grow less rapidly in the period ahead than in the period from the late 1970s to the mid-1980s. This was an exceptional adjustment phase during which China passed rapidly from quite low to quite acceptable average levels of

Table 6.2 *Average per caput consumption in urban staff and workers' families at different levels of average per caput income (kilograms per caput, 1984)*

yuan *per caput per month*	< 25	35−50	> 70
Grain	128.0	140.0	156.0
Fresh vegetables	99.0	143.0	174.0
Edible oil	5.0	6.2	9.2
Pork	7.3	15.5	23.2
Beef, mutton	3.6	2.5	3.9
Poultry	0.8	2.3	5.8
Fresh eggs	2.4	6.8	11.1
Fish, shrimps	2.0	6.3	14.3
Sugar	1.5	2.5	4.7

Data are drawn from sample survey of 12 500 urban households.
Source: ZGTJNJ, 1985, 56

food intake. How far and how fast the dietary transition will continue is unpredictable. The price question is of central importance in determining this. A key issue is the degree to which the prices of farm produce reflect costs of production. If the share of animal products in the Chinese diet is to rise substantially a lot of resources will have to be devoted to the process. Ash, for example, argues that to increase the share of meat in Chinese diet by 10 per cent will require a 35 to 40 per cent rise in China's grain consumption (Ash, 1987). He argues that in the already high-yield areas, with good irrigation facilities, the incremental capital−output ratio is high (see, also, Nolan, 1983a), while in the poorly located areas in Northern China, a great deal of investment in irrigation needs to be undertaken if grain yields are to increase in such a way as to provide the basis of a substantial rise in output of animal products by around the year 2000. If prices are allowed to reflect changing costs, then it is hard to predict the way in which demand will respond, especially at a time when income distribution is altering quickly and a wide range of new consumption possibilities is opening up for China's population.

Although the role of market forces in agricultural price formation increased greatly in the 1980s, it was seen in the previous chapter that the state still had (in 1986−7) a great deal of control (through direct price setting and determining the limits of floating prices) over both agricultural purchase prices and urban food retail prices. The state could not greatly increase the prices it paid for farm produce without either sacrificing other goals or causing a substantial budget deficit, neither of which it wished to do. Accordingly, after rising by 39 per cent in the three years 1978–81 (ZGTJNJ, 1985, 530), the state's purchasing price index for farm purchases rose more slowly in the 1980s, increasing 28 per cent in the five-year period 1981–86 (ZGTJZY, 1986, 100; State Statistical Bureau, 1987). If the state wished to raise purchasing prices sufficiently to help sustain a faster growth of agricultural output than in 1984–86 (though, it should be stressed, these growth rates were not slow, especially in relation to population growth) then it could do so without undesirable budgetary consequences by simultaneously raising state food prices in the cities. Alternatively, it could allow market forces to become the fundamental determinant of both farm purchase prices and urban retail food prices: given the present (1986–7) gap between state and free market prices, a greater role for market prices surely would result in a short-term rise in both? However, the regime is acutely inflation-conscious. Even a 14 per cent reported rise in retail food prices in 1985 (State Statistical Bureau, 1987), negligible by Latin American standards, caused great discontent among an urban population long used to price stability, and the 'Polish problem' (food price increases leading to urban riots) is never far from the leadership's mind.

Price alone does not determine farm output, and future farm sector growth prospects depend, too, on establishing the right rural institutions in the post-collective-farm epoch.[6] Problems relating to these will be examined later in this chapter. However, price surely is extremely important in determining the future growth of farm output?[7] This is made even more important by the increasing availability in the countryside in the 1980s (especially in advanced areas) of opportunities to earn income in the non-farm sector (discussed further below). A major economic issue for China in the period ahead is the degree to which rural resources are devoted to the farm and the non-farm sector, and, in the absence of administrative measures, price will be of central importance in determining the outcome.

The Chinese leadership may well be more concerned than it need be about urban retail food prices. Simply looking at the question of political stability, China in the mid-1980s is very different from Poland. Her urban working class lacks the organizing traditions of Polish workers and is isolated from the international working class movement. Moreover, the massive rise in popular living standards in the 1980s provides a solid basis for continued price reform. However, it is obviously highly desirable to protect the poorest segments of the urban population from the effects of food price rises.[8] These groups spend much less per caput on food than richer urban dwellers[9] and the effect on them of a sharp increase in food prices would be extremely serious. Given the close monitoring of people's lives in China it should be possible there (unlike in most developing countries) to provide targeted, means-tested subsidies or food at subsidised prices to compensate the poorest urban groups for food price rises. If the government did fail to protect these groups it would deserve fierce criticism.

THE STRUCTURE OF THE RURAL ECONOMY

The structure of China's rural economy altered fast in the 1980s. First there was a substantial shift away from agriculture towards non-agricultural activities.

The rapid rise in the share of non-farm employment within total rural employment was noted in chapters 4 and 5. While the value of total rural fixed assets more than doubled from 1978 to 1984,[10] the value of fixed assets in agriculture alone rose less rapidly,[11] with agriculture in some areas basically 'living off past gains' (Rural Survey Group, 1986). Detailed data from 1983−4 show clearly the stagnation in the accumulation of agricultural fixed assets compared to other rural activities (table 6.3).

Table 6.3   *Stocks of fixed assets (original value) in China's villages (year-end)*

	1983 (100 m yuan)	1984 (100 m yuan)	1984 as % of 1983
Total	1632	1892	116
of which:			
1 Housing and building materials for 'productive use'	471	577	123
2 Livestock	490	560	114
3 Agricultural, forestry, livestock and fishing machinery	238	241	101
4 Industrial and sideline machinery	267	283	106
5 Transport equipment	165	231	140

Source: ZGNCTJNJ, 1986, 249−50

The structure of rural output and income also was altering quickly in the 1980s. While real agricultural output from 1980 to 1985 increased by 48 per cent, *cun* (village)-run industrial output increased (in real terms) by 271 per cent (ZGTJZY, 1986, 32). From 1984 to 1986 the share of the non-agricultural sector in total rural social product (at current prices) rose from 37 per cent (ZGTJZY, 1986, 33) to 47 per cent (State Statistical Bureau, 1987). Within peasant households' net income, income from the non-agricultural sector rose from 15 per cent in 1978 to 30 per cent in 1984 (ZGTJNJ, 1985, 571).

This rapid shift in the structure of the rural economy reflected in part the sizeable pool of rural 'surplus' labour for much of the year, prepared to work for small additions to household income. Under the Maoist system, the inefficiency of collective labour had necessitated tight control of rural labour allocation so as to ensure priority for the agricultural sector. The sharp rise in agricultural labour productivity in the 1980s greatly increased the size of the surplus labour and was accompanied by a new freedom to allocate rural labour. Moreover, given the structure of state prices and the pent-up excess demand for many non-agricultural goods and services, in the mid—1980s the returns to labour from rural non-agricultural work frequently were above those from agriculture. A 1985 national survey reported the average income per labour day to be 4.9 *yuan* for crop production and 4.4 *yuan* for animal husbandry, compared to 8.6 *yuan* for commerce and food and drink enterprises, and 15 *yuan* for transport and industrial production (Hu and Yu, 1986). In Cangnan *xian* in Wenzhou in 1985 the average per worker annual income of those engaged in agriculture was reported to be around 600 *yuan*, compared to about 3000 *yuan* for those engaged in industry, and around 7000 *yuan* for those engaged in buying and selling (Zhao, 1986).

Is it a matter of concern that such a rapid change in the structure of the rural economy was occurring?

A number of points should be borne in mind when considering this question. In the first place, the extraordinarily rapid growth of the rural non-farm economy in part reflects the fact that small, non-state rural enterprises in the mid-1980s were, in general, much freer than state enterprises to make independent decisions. If the reform of large-scale enterprises continued in the late 1980s, then many of the activities in the rural, small-scale sector might cease to be profitable.[12] Secondly, growth in the rural non-farm sector often has beneficial feedback effects upon agriculture, by drawing labour off the land (and allowing farm labour productivity to rise), by providing resources for improvements in peasants' human capital (via better education, health, etc.), and by stimulating exchange (via better transport and market information). Thirdly, it has been demonstrated that enormous slack existed in China's pre-1978 collective farms: the stagnation in agricultural fixed capital was accompanied by a rapid growth of farm output from the late 1970s to the mid-1980s. Fourth, it should not be forgotten that while agricultural fixed capital stagnated, supplies of current inputs to agriculture (e.g. chemical fertilizers, electricity) rose quickly. When this is taken into account the performance of agricultural investment in the 1980s appears much better. Finally, as discussed in the previous section, it would be surprising if Chinese agricultural output were to sustain its extremely rapid growth rate of the early 1980s. Given reasonable expectations about the income elasticity of demand, one would expect that as incomes rose the rural non-farm sector grew more rapidly than the farm sector.

This is not to deny that there were problems in respect to the balance between the rural farm and non-farm sector. The two key elements ensuring that too rapid a shift in resource allocation did not take place are those discussed elsewhere in this chapter: first, the state's price policy, and second, the degree to which rural collective and state institutions are able to intervene when the market 'fails'.

The second major change in the structure of China's rural economy in the early and mid-1980s was the shift within agriculture proper away from crop production in general, and especially away from grain production.

It was noted in chapter 5 that a big shift occurred in the structure of China's sown area in the early/mid-1980s. From 1978 to 1984 the area sown to non-grain crops rose by over six per cent while that sown to grain fell by over six per cent (ZGTJZY, 1986, 35). In 1985, an even sharper reorganization of the sown area took place. The area sown to grain fell by a further 4.0 million hectares (3.5 per cent), and that sown to non-grain crops rose by a further 3.4 million hectares (10.9 per cent) (ZGTJZY, 1986, 35). The long-term shift in the structure of sown area was a response to the relative profitabilities of different types of production under the new conditions of greatly increased independence for farmers. In the late 1970s/early 1980s, the net income per hectare from grain was generally much below that for other activities (Dong, 1986b; Nolan, 1983a, 25). A 1985 national survey showed the average net income per *mu* from grain production to be only 85 *yuan*, but 172 *yuan* from economic crops (Hu and Yu, 1986). In the new circumstances of increased freedom of resource allocation, peasants shifted resources to more profitable lines of agricultural production. From 1980 to 1985 the real increase in the gross value of crops output was 36 per cent (for grain, the figure was 18 per cent), while for forestry the increase was 54 per cent, for animal husbandry 65 per cent, for fishing 77 per cent, and household sidelines 176 per cent (ZGTJZY, 1986, 32 and 37).[13]

Many people both inside and outside China viewed the relative shift away from grain as extremely disturbing and argued that it justified a return to comprehensive administrative controls over agriculture. In fact, the shift away from grain was less of a problem than was feared. By the early 1980s, China's average per caput grain output had climbed rapidly to relatively high levels for a poor country, from 319 kilograms in 1978 to 396 kilograms in 1984 (ZGTJNJ, 1985, 273). China's average per caput personal (direct) consumption of grain in 1984,250 kilograms, (ZGTJNJ, 1985, 576), came close to the world average (Tian, 1986). As has been noted already, unless China wished to undertake a rapid, sustained expansion of meat production, there would appear little point in raising grain output much beyond the mid-1980s level of around 400 kilograms per caput.

The Chinese state in the mid-1980s was unwilling either to allow market forces to determine fully the price of grain or to increase substantially the price it paid to peasants for grain. Moreover, there were several reasons for the state to intervene to keep grain output above the levels that would have resulted from the free operation of peasant households in response to the given array of relative prices. First, most obviously, was the international dimension. In the mid-1980s, despite some increase, China still had a relatively small net import of grain.[14] Her policy makers were determined to keep things that way, considering it 'unrealistic for a large country like China to rely on imports to solve the country's food problem'. (Wang, 1985b). Accordingly, grain imports were strictly controlled. Second, as we have seen, although the numbers in poverty declined sharply in the early 1980s there were still large numbers of poor peasants reliant on the state to supply them with grain (Wang, 1985b). Third, the state needed to sustain a high level of grain reserves in case of severe national disasters (Tian, 1986).

For these reasons, China's policy makers decided that it would be unwise to allow peasants to determine freely how much grain to produce: 'Since agriculture is the foundation of the national economy and grain is the foundation of agriculture, *we must not take grain production lightly*. Measures should be adopted to ensure the steady growth of our grain production, with the average annual level of 400 million tons as the basis' (Tian, 1986) (my emphasis — P.N.). It has already been seen that in the mid-1980s the state was giving special bonuses (e.g. priority supplies of cheap chemical fertilizer and petrol) to households that signed contracts for grain sales to the state. Furthermore, in the allocation of state capital construction outlays for agriculture, priority was given to grain-growing areas selling a lot of commodity grain to the state (Song, 1986). In 1982 China began to set up a group of 50 commodity grain-producing *xian*. These 50 *xian* alone (amounting to 2.3 per cent of the total number of *xian* in China) produced 83.35 million tons of grain in 1983—5 (about 7.5 per cent of China's total grain output), of which 39 million tons was sold to the state (about 11 per cent of total grain sales to the state) (He, 1986, 24; ZGTJNJ, 1985, 255 and 481). The state also introduced special assistance (e.g. better prices) to households who specialized in grain (Wang, 1985b). Localities were instructed to 'use industry to support agriculture' by setting aside a portion of *xiangzhen* enterprises' profits to subsidize grain growing farmers (Questions and answers . . ., 1986, 5). Finally, it has been shown that, although the new grain contracts (post-1984) were supposed to be concluded voluntarily, this was by no means always the case, and local authorities continued to use direct administrative measures to maintain the required level of grain sown area, output and marketings.

CLASS RELATIONS[15]

Information problems

Only a few commentators outside China have been concerned with the implications of China's rural reform package for intra-village class relations, yet this is a central criterion by which to judge rural developments. It is possible that even if class relations had become more unequal and exploitative one might still judge the reforms to have been an overall success if the achievement of other goals (e.g. reducing poverty, raising average living standards) was considered to outweigh the alteration in class relations. However, to concentrate on the macro indicators to the neglect of intra-village relations is curiously blinkered, not only for someone who considers that economics is better understood by analysing political as well as narrowly economic influences, but also for anyone trying to make a judgement about wider aspects of the direction in which China is travelling.

Unfortunately, it is extremely difficult to draw clear conclusions about this vital question. In the first place, on this issue the Chinese government releases negligible information and there is virtually no published research from within China. One can search in vain through the pages of relevant journals,[16] or for publications in Chinese bookshops. The sort of detailed village surveys which appear in large numbers in other Asian countries just do not exist in China. Instead, the focus is on technical and organizational questions. The closest one gets to proper village surveys is information on income distribution at an aggregate level, articles on the dimensions of and policies to deal with rural poverty, detailed studies of specialized households, and surveys of differentiation across quite large geographical areas.

For foreigners in China it is now easy to obtain a superficial picture of village life, through personal observation or discussion with Chinese. However, it is still impossible for foreign researchers to undertake field-work of the kind that is undertaken over a large part of the rest of Asia. One can visit villages, talk to peasants and rural officials, but not undertake the sort of detailed investigations necessary to draw firm conclusions about village class structure.

Regional differences in class relations

It is extremely dangerous to make generalizations about intra-village class structure for the whole of China. Careful surveys in the mid-1970s of two Philippines villages just 15 or so kilometres apart showed vividly that apparently similar forces can, in a different setting, produce a quite different outcome for village socioeconomic structure: 'Comparison of the ways in which the two village communities adjust their institutions in response to population pressure, technological change and the land reform program sheds light on the process by which *the same economic forces can produce different institutions, depending on different social environments created through different ecologies and histories*' (Hayami and Kikuchi, 1981, 142, my emphasis — P.N.).

Even in technologically stagnant pre-1949 China there were massive regional differences in the nature and degree of intra-village inequality. Take, for example, the distribution of farmland. Perkins (1969, 90—1) shows the massive variation in the incidence of landlordism across the broad regions of China. Local evidence is even more impressive. Ash (1976, ch. 2) presents data for 56 *xian* (counties) in pre-1949 Jiangsu province showing huge variations in the degree of tenancy. Some of these variations are systematic and can be easily explained, but many cannot; 'Until more evidence becomes available, it seems best to treat such apparent anomalies as examples of *the wide variation in rural socioeconomic conditions that could exist within an otherwise integral economic and geographical region*' (Ash, 1976, 14, my emphasis — P.N.).

If such variations in class structure existed under relatively stable technology, one should be even more cautious about generalization in a time of rapid, regionally differentiated technical progress. Among the most important factors bearing upon intra-village class relations which are regionally differentiated are the following:

1 Extended family relations. The most notable example is the clan system in South China. In the main Pearl River Delta *xian* (Guangdong province) in the 1930s, clans owned upward of 50 per cent of cultivated land (Chen, 1973, ch. 2). While the degree to which traditional clan

relations revived in the 1980s is hard to assess, in some areas kin relationships again formed an important component of the new forms of economic and social co-operation: 'The new and emerging family form is ... made up of a number of peasant households related by close kin ties, which have developed new forms of association or co-operation based on economic and socio-political links and exchanges' (Croll, 1986, 28).[17] In some areas intra-village class divisions in the 1980s may have become closely related to kin divisions.

2   Development of the non-farm economy. I have shown (and will explore further below) the enormous regional variations in the extent of the non-farm economy. In areas where the rural non-farm economy is hghly developed, the village class structure is very different from other areas. First, village class relations, instead of being mainly agriculture-based, come to be based both on agriculture and industry. Second, by drawing off large numbers of agricultural workers for non-farm work the possibility is opened up for farms to expand in area and become more mechanised. Third the extra employment opportunities tend to increase the employment of women outside the home which, in turn, tend to reduce the birth rate. Fourth, the higher income level in these districts has multiple implications for class structure e.g. it increases the availability of credit compared to other areas; it increases the resource base from which the local collective and state apparatus can benefit, enabling the public infrastructure to be more developed than in other areas.

3   Collective economy. Not only is the non-farm economy unevenly developed between regions, but, as has been seen (and is further discussed below), the collective element in the non-farm economy is much stronger in some areas than in others. This, also, has many implications for class structure. Working for a 'collective' undertaking may be different from working for a private employer in terms of the degree of influence the worker has on the decisions taken within the enterprise. More relevantly, the collective enterprise directly provides funds for a variety of local purposes (e.g. health, education, support of poor households, infrastructure) which have implications for class structure.

Just a few important spatial contrasts have been mentioned here. They serve, hopefully, to caution against simplistic generalizations about the outcome of China's reforms for village class relations. Even the briefest acquaintance with the enormous regional variations in class relations in India in the 1970s and 1980s would serve as a further warning: 'Given the very uneven nature of capitalist development in India, superimposed upon the uneven impact of colonialism on an already highly varied and immense subcontinent, it is not surprising that there should be tremendous regional variations in agrarian relations and the development of production.' (Omvedt, 1981, A—153). The evidence on which one can base statements about rural class relations in China in the 1980s is flimsy. Moreover, the complexities of regional variations should not be forgotten. With these substantial qualifications in mind, this section now attempts to make a cautious assessment of the situation in the mid-1980s.

Proletarianization

The extent of agricultural hired labour in the mid-1980s was quite limited (see, e.g., Wang, 1985a). This is not surprising. First, there was still some fear about the openness of hired labour in fieldwork (Nolan, 1983b). Second, traditional forms of peasant labour exchange to cope with peak period labour shortages re-appeared soon after the reforms. In central Sichuan in 1983 I was surprised (though I ought not to have been) to observe groups of households harvesting crops together on individual plots in order to gather in the crops quickly at the optimal time. Third, given the high degree of rural 'surplus' labour (even with the increased non-farm employment) most farms still only needed extra labour (if at all) in the peak season. A large proportion of workers in the rural non-farm sector still lived in the villages, and at the peak season these workers typically returned to work on the family farm.

As I have noted already, the Chinese government in the mid-1980s was for some time said to be preparing to introduce a law to restrict rural hired labour (Wang, 1985a). Whether this is necessary in agriculture is debatable. Also, it could have perverse results. Insofar as extra labour power is, indeed, needed on farms, such a law (if effective) would tend to encourage richer peasants to meet labour power shortages by expanding employment of machines rather than people.[18]

Employment in the rural non-farm sector rose rapidly in the 1980s. However, it was only in very advanced areas that by the mid-1980s the proportion outside farming approached (and, occasionally, exceeded), that employed in the farm sector. For example, in the suburban *xian* of Wuxi municipality (Jiangsu province) by 1985, 'rural industry' employed about 40 per cent of total rural labour power (Xue, 1985, 18).

Within the rural non-farm sector in the mid-1980s, relations of production varied enormously from one type of operation to another. The number of peasants running individual non-farm businesses had expanded rapidly,[19] though still a small proportion of the total rural workforce. A large number of new non-farm rural enterprises were run on co-operative principles with a group of peasants as the joint shareholders, or with a group of peasants pooling their capital with other institutions (the forms

were numerous).[20] Many apparently 'co-operative' ventures turned out
to be less co-operative on close analysis: workers often had no sharehold-
ings or owned very few shares, with correspondingly few rights (Nolan,
1983b); sometimes the 'co-operators' were simply a small group of rich
peasants with rights proportional to their capital contribution who hired
a number of non-shareholding workers.[21] The net effect of these sorts of
relationships is that despite the 'co-operative' title the position of workers
often was little different from that of workers in small capitalist enterprises
in other developing countries.

Much the largest segment of employment in the rural non-farm sector
was in 'collective' *xiang* or *cun*-run enterprises.[22] As was pointed out in
chapter 4, it is a misnomer to call these 'co-operative' enterprises, since
the owners normally are not the workers themselves, but rather the
larger collective unit (*cun* or *xiang*). Although the authority of individual
collective enterprises expanded in the 1980s, and most of these operated
under some form of contract system, there was still generally tight
control by the *xiang* or *cun* over their conditions of operation (e.g. appoint-
ment of managers, wage system, allocation of profits) (Nolan, 1983b): 'A
widespread phenomenon in the *xiang* and *cun* enterprises at present is
that the basic rights reside in the hands of the *xiang* and *cun* party and
government organs, so that they have not become truly the masses' co-
operative enterprises' (Rural Survey Group, 1986, 6). Even though individual workers sometimes had shares in their 'collective' enterprises, the
major shareholders in such cases frequently were the constituent *cun* and
she (Nolan, 1983b). Workers were, typically, non-unionized. while the
relationship of the *xiangzhen* enterprises to the *xiang* greatly reduced their
independence compared to small rural 'capitalist' industries in other
developing countries, the position of workers in these enterprises was not
much different. Ultimate authority resided with the enterprise manager
who was not, typically, responsible to the enterprise's workers, but
rather to the *xiang* or even *xian* authorities (Nolan, 1983b).

Assets

'Human capital'[23]   An important element in intra-village stratification is
the balance between workers and dependants in different households.[24]
As was shown in chapter 3, this was the principal reason for the differences
in average per caput income between households within a given production
team under the Maoist commune system. Under the commune system,
due to the collective ownership of most rural assets, the distribution of a
large proportion of grain 'according to need' and fairly equal access to
welfare facilities, it is likely that there was a high degree of mobility of

families between different average per caput income positions corresponding to changes in worker—dependant ratios. An important issue in
the post-reform rural economy is whether the initial differences in worker—
dependant ratios will combine with the changes in access to assets to
produce increasing inequality with more rigid class divisions, as opposed
to the high degree of mobility in incomes that characterized the previous
system.

Post-1978 changes in the provision of rural health and education are
analysed in detail later in this chapter. The main changes were these: in
many poorly-located areas, the collective welfare system declined after
the reforms. In such areas, it is possible that this led to widening class
differences in human capital, since access to welfare facilities became
more strongly dependent on income. In the many areas where collective
welfare was still intact and often, indeed, greatly enhanced, the results of
changes in the provision of welfare facilities were more complex in terms
of their class impact. The average level of provision was much higher
than in poor areas, but one would expect the new differentials in intra-
village incomes (see table 6.4) to be reflected in some inequality in
human capital (e.g. ability to pay for attendance at secondary school,
ability to buy books, papers and other educational material). The close
connection between educational level and rural income can be gauged
from a 1985 national peasant survey, on which table 6.4 is based.

Table 6.4   *Relationship between peasant income and educational level, 1985*[25]

Average per caput net income of household (yuan)	Educational level of household members
284	'illiterate'
385	'primary school education'
466	'lower middle school education'
556	'higher middle school education'
756	'higher level specialized education'

From a 1985 survey of 36 668 households in 28 provinces, cities and autonomous regions.
Unfortunately, from the limited data provided, it is impossible to tell the degree to which
the differences in education are regionally rather than class based.
Source: Hu and Yu, 1986

However, as I have stressed elsewhere in this book, while a basic
minimum level of literacy and numeracy is essential to the acquisition of
knowledge,[26] formal education is far from being the only contribution to

the 'knowledge' segment of human capital. Much of the information useful to 'petty commodity producers' in China in the mid-1980s was available fairly equally to all peasants in a given area, either through the revival of traditional forms of spreading information or through the rapid spread of new forms (e.g. people travelling on buses, tractors and bicycles; provision of information by the *xian* or *xiang* authorities; increased ownership of radios and TVs).

In a poor society where both farm and non-farm work are heavily reliant on physical strength, diet is an important aspect of human capital. The system whereby a large proportion of grain in the villages was allocated 'according to need' disappeared with the de-collectivization of agriculture, and village rationing[27] disappeared for most other major food products. While average levels of food consumption in the 1980s rose strikingly, and beyond a certain point the income elasticity of demand for food in general declines, it is certain that the widening of the range of income differentials between village strata was accompanied by a widening of the range of food consumption. Just how this relates to class differences in work capacity is virtually impossible to say.

Land While land allocation practices varied greatly when *bao gan dao hu* was introduced in the early 1980s, it was seen in chapter 4 that the most commonly adopted practice (in 70 per cent of cases) was to allocate the collective land in accordance with family size (Rural Survey Group, 1986). In other words, the 'land reform' was highly egalitarian, putting equity ahead of efficiency. Although contracted out to households, the collective technically still remained the owner of the farmland: 'Under the household responsibility system, the land is still owned by the collective. Peasant households have the right to use the farmland for a contracted period, *but the land cannot be let, bought, or sold by the peasants*' (Lu, 1984, 23) (my emphasis − P.N.). For land contracts to be transferred from one household to another was supposed to require the collective's approval (Central Committee, 1984). It was visualised that as families' worker−dependant ratios altered, so land would be reallocated among members of the village. Indeed, instead of having to wait until the end of the contract, the collectives frequently set aside 5 to 10 per cent of collective land ('flexible land'), contracted out on short term contracts, to be used to meet needs for land arising in the short term from changes in worker−dependant ratios which could not be met by voluntary land contract to transfers. In its idealized form, before the extension of land contracts to 50 years, the system had a lot in common with the periodic repartition of land in the idealized version of the late-nineteenth-century Russian *mir* (Volin, 1970, 78−80). In theory, there can be no concentration of land ownership and no exploitation via land rent accruing to individuals.

In fact, the situation was more complex than this. The state encouraged the 'gradual concentration of farmland in the hands of farming experts' (Central Committee, 1984), and in some highly developed areas where there was a rapid exodus of peasants into non-farm work, a high degree of concentration in land operation emerged. In practice, the transfer of land use from one household to another was often not organized by the collective, but, rather, was directly negotiated between the households concerned: '"Leasehold markets", akin to property transactions in the distant past, have begun to mushroom, despite constant appeals from the authorities for surrendering redundant or unused land parcels for non-compensatory reallocation by the collectives' (Kueh, 1984a, 128). It was reported in late 1984 that one-eighth of the rural population in Zhongshan city (Guangdong province) had contracted for 40 per cent of the total area of farmlands and fishponds in the city. The report of this on the front page of People's Daily was hailed as 'an objective trend and a progressive step', stating that through such concentration, skilled farmers would be better able 'to develop the potential of the land through inputs of science and technology' (quoted in Fewsmith, 1985, 53). In such areas, the degree of mechanization of farmwork was high (Kung, 1986, 20). In districts where the opportunities for off-farm employment were less, the processes were more complex and concentration of holdings was hardly developing at all. Across the whole country, the proportion of farmland subcontracted from one household to another was, probably, quite small — perhaps as little as 1 per cent by 1986−7 (though precise estimation is extremely difficult owing to the fact that many sub-letting arrangements must be unreported).[28] Because land is the basic form of rural security, even in areas with plenty of non-farm employment, some peasants were reluctant to sub−let land, afraid that this might be the first step to losing control over it completely. One estimate is that in 1986−7 as much as 2−3 per cent of farmland was being left idle by families who preferred not to farm but were unwilling to subcontract.[29] The extension in 1987 of the contract period on land (probably to 50 years) should help to reassure peasants of their long-term rights to the usufruct of the land allocated to them under *bao gan dao hu* and so enable the land rent market to become even more active than it already was in 1986−7.

Although the CCP's authority in the villages declined after 1978, it still enabled the state to influence local affairs in a fashion unmatched in possibly any other developing country (see, e.g., Bernstein, 1986).[30] The party could still exercise control over village economic life via such mechanisms as the allocation of grain purchase quotas, permission to set up non-farm enterprises, the distribution of electricity supplies, petrol and chemical fertilizers, the allocation of credit, rights to have children under the 'birth plan' and so on. The Chinese government is deeply opposed to the development of a pure *rentier* class in the countryside and the emergence of a parasitic landlord class living solely off rental and other 'non-labour' income seems most unlikely in the foreseeable future. A situation may well be developing not too dissimilar from that in some parts of pre-1949 China, whereby the 'ownership' (or 'bottom right' pre-1949) is vested in the collective[31] (i.e. land cannot be bought or sold), but the individual occupier (as of the time of land distribution in the 1980s) has a permanent right either to cultivate directly or sub-let (the 'surface right' pre-1949) (See, Ash, 1976, 41, for a discussion of pre-1949). The probable granting in 1987 of a 50-year contract period in farmland was tantamount to giving peasants permanent rights to cultivate or sub-let. If the party could prevent the extensive illegal acquisition of land ownership or of rights to sub-let rented land, the outcome of such a situation would be that ownership rights and rights to obtain rental incomes were distributed widely within the peasant community, while operational holdings could, in principle, become much more concentrated.

Farm assets other than land The most important easily divisible assets apart from land are seeds and fertilizers. The application of chemical fertilizers massively increased post-1978, more than doubling from 1978 to 1985 (ZGJJNJ, 1986, III, 17). Evidence from other Asian countries suggests that in a relatively free market situation, there tends not to be a great difference in the application of chemical fertilizer per hectare across farm sizes in a modernizing area (see, especially, Bhalla and Chadha, 1982). In China the marketing of farm inputs is rather complex, and in the case of chemical fertilizers, the major part is administratively allocated rather than entering the free market. Quite how this affects the distribution of this key input between strata is hard to say in the absence of detailed information.

Evidence from elsewhere in Asia indicates that in the early stages of the 'Green Revolution' the larger farmers tend to adopt new seed strains earliest, mainly because they are best able to bear the risk (see, e.g. Dasgupta, 1977). However, in modernizing areas, smaller farmers have tended soon afterwards to adopt new high-yielding varieties (Dasgupta, 1977; Bhalla and Chadha, 1982; Hayami and Kikuchi, 1981). In China too, it tends to be the larger farmers who adopt new seed strains earlier, often operating under direct contract with the *xian* seed experimentation centres (Nolan, 1983b). There is no reason to think that in China too, successful new seeds would not be quickly adopted by other strata.

In the mid-1980s an important portion of the key 'lumpy' inputs still were organized and supplied collectively or by the local state authorities-irrigation, power supply and crop spraying being the most notable examples. In some areas there were problems with the continued provision of these critical facilities. However, in the large part of China where these facilities were still maintained, it seems unlikely that economically stronger households would be able to monopolize them. Indeed, it was often the case that all households in a given area had to participate in (and pay fees for) the provision of a particular collective service. Crop spraying, for example, often has to be carried out on all the lands in a given area or not at all. In the mid-1980s many collectively owned 'lumpy' assets were subcontracted to individuals or groups of operators, the most important example being transport equipment. Increasingly, too, such assets were purchased privately. There appeared to be considerable competition between operators. Activities such as rural transport have relatively low start-up costs, ease of entry and few economies of scale.

Credit Access to credit is centrally important in understanding rural class relations both in 'traditional' and modernizing agriculture. Under the pre-1978 Maoist system the state (agricultural banks) and quasistate (credit co-operatives) exercised an almost complete monopoly over rural credit. In the 1980s a wide variety of unofficial forms of rural credit emerged, as demand for credit grew rapidly and government policy relaxed. These forms of credit included direct loans between individuals, credit 'associations' and old-style private banks (*qian zhuang*) (Dong, 1986b). These generally lent at much higher interest rates than state or quasi-state credit institutions, which provided loans at extremely low nominal rates of interest (indeed, during the inflation of the 1980s they were often negligible in real terms).

The state responded to this situation in two ways. First, a more flexible approach began to be adopted towards the interest rate charged by state and quasi-state institutions. Second, it passed legislation making it illegal for individuals to run financial institutions; the various credit 'associations' and traditional Chinese-style banks (*qian zhuang*) were banned (Dong, 1986b). Given the excess of demand over supply for rural credit in China in the 1980s, it is doubtful if such administrative measures could be wholly successful in controlling non-individual private credit. Moreover, even if the state was successful in maintaining for itself and for co-operative credit institutions a dominant position in the rural credit system, there is no guarantee that different rural strata would have equal access to credit. In the mid-1980s these institutions were increasingly urged to make profits, and the tendency to lend to those with the best business prospects was a logical consequence.

There is plenty of evidence that in China in the 1980s official credit tended to go to those who were in the best position to repay loans. The national survey of peasant households in 1985 (Hu and Yu, 1986), found that rural credit provision exhibited the characteristic of 'the richer one is, the more credit one gets'. According to the survey, peasant households with average net per caput incomes of over 1000 *yuan* obtained credit levels 22 times those of average peasant households, and 2.88 times that which the average 'specialized household' obtained. Hu and Yu comment soberly:

> The demands for funds from those who are expanding their production scale rises, while some low income households relying on their own funds find it difficult even to support simple reproduction, so that their need for funds is increasingly urgent. The practice of showing favouritism towards 'big households' not only fails to produce the required economic effectiveness but also has undesirable social consequences. [Hu and Yu, 1986]

While the state does provide loans to poor households, often at preferential rates, Hu and Yu's findings show clearly that more could be done in this direction.

Rural non-farm enterprises   What were the possibilities in the post-reform Chinese countryside for the development of a powerful class of capitalist owners in the rural non-farm sector?

A useful starting point to begin analysis of this question is to make a distinction between different types of enterprise in this sector. First, one can distinguish between enterprises which produce directly for the rural market, and those that subcontract from large urban firms. Generally, the closer one moves to big cities, the higher is the proportion of rural enterprises in the latter category. Second, one can distinguish between collectively-owned enterprises and those owned by individuals or groups of voluntarily co-operating peasants. Here it bears reiterating that despite the rapid growth rate in the mid-1980s of the individual and co-operative sector, the 'collective' sector (i.e. *xiang* plus *cun*-run enterprises) remained dominant in the rural non-farm economy, producing almost 60 per cent of the value of output from that sector in 1985 and accounting for 73 per cent of that sector's workforce in the same year (ZGJJNJ, 1986, v, 42). Third, despite some growth post-1978, the average size of rural non-farm enterprises in the mid-1980s still was very small. In 1985, China's *xiangzhen* (township) enterprises contained an average of just 26 workers (ZGJNJ, 1986, v, 43−4). Moreover, the average size of collective enterprises greatly exceeded that of individual and co-operative enterprise (see table 6.5).

In sum, the situation in the mid-1980s was not one in which large-scale individual rural capitalist non-farm enterprises were emerging. In subcontracting with the urban sector, collectively run enterprises massively

Table 6.5   *Average size of different types of* xiangzhen *enterprises in China, 1985*

	Workers per enterprise	Gross value of output per enterprise (yuan)
xiang-run enterprises	50.3	270 700
cun-run enterprises	17.7	73 900
A part of peasants' jointly managed enterprises	6.9	21 900
Other co-operative enterprises	6.3	22 100
Individual enterprises	2.0	4 700

Source: ZGJJNJ, 1986, v, 42

dominated, and all rural enterprises engaging in these activities faced relatively monopsonistic conditions, which were not conducive to the emergence of large subcontracting firms. The rural individual sector employed a large, and rapidly growing, number of people, but the scale was, on average, extremely small, and market conditions were very competitive. The part of China where individual hiring labour in non-farm enterprises was almost certainly most advanced was Wenzhou city in Zhejiang province, with a population of 6.2 million, including over 5 million peasants living in the suburban area under the city's administration (Wenzhou Rural Research Group, 1986, 4). In early 1986 in Wenzhou's villages, there were reportedly 13 000 individual households, hiring labour (almost entirely in the non-farm sector); they hired a total of 40 000 workers, i.e. there was an average of just 3.1 workers per enterprise (Zhao, 1986, 37). Just 120 'big hiring households' hired over 30 workers per enterprise, with an average of just 50 workers in each (Zhao, 1986, 37). It is true that the different forms of co-operative enterprises may sometimes conceal 'capitalist' production relations, but the average enterprise size in this sector was still relatively small, and, either producing under subcontract for urban enterprises or for the rural market, conditions were highly competitive. It is true that in the collective sector a large proportion of enterprises had been leased out. However, as has been seen, in contrast to a pure capitalist enterprise, the collective was able to determine the conditions of the contract under which the enterprise was run, and did, ultimately, own the productive assets.

Intra-village income inequality   Were the post-1978 reforms accompanied by polarization of incomes within any given village?

Serious analysis of this issue by non-Chinese is frustrated almost completely by the lack of published information of a type that is readily available in most other developing countries, even ones with extremely authoritarian governments. Aggregate data on income differentials for a region, such as the Chinese authorities frequently provide, is of only limited value for helping to understand class relations within villages.

After the removal of income ceilings in the late 1970s, the range of income in any given village certainly widened. Already in the early 1980s there were reports of '10 000 *yuan*' households, with average per caput net incomes many times the village average, let alone that of the poorest members of the village. Of course, such extremely rich households (often, initially, 'specialized households') probably constituted a small fraction of the village population, as is indicated in table 6.6.

Table 6.6 *Distribution of Chinese peasant households at different levels of average per caput net income, 1984*[a]

Average per caput net income (yuan)	No. of households	% of households
< 100	2656	7.24
100−150	3310	9.03
150−200	3666	10.00
200−300	7585	20.69
300−400	6054	16.51
400−500	4114	11.22
500−600	2758	7.52
600−700	1875	5.11
700−800	1231	3.36
800−900	812	2.21
900−1000	592	1.61
1000−10 000	1729	4.70
>10 000	285	0.77

[a] These data are from a national sample survey of over 37 000 households in 28 provinces, autonomous regions and directly administered cities.
Sources: Rural Survey Group, 1986, 6

These data are, of course, for the whole country, and one would not expect them to be replicated in each village. However, in the extreme case of Wenzhou city, where the non-farm economy and private business activity advanced at an extraordinarily rapid pace in the mid-1980s, the differentials were of an astonishing dimension − in the order of at least 500:1 as between the highest and the lowest income in the city's rural areas, and at least 100:1 as between the highest and the average (see table 6.7).[33]

Table 6.7   *Income differentials among rural residents in Wenzhou city in 1985*[a]

	yuan
Average per caput income of rural residents in the city	417
within which: Cangnan *xian*, Yishan *qu*	552
: 30-odd *xiang* in 3 *xian*	200
: Mocheng *xiang*, Pingyang *xian* (1984)	137
within which: Wuyi *cun* (1984)	105
Average income of individuals hiring labour:	35 000
of which: highest	150 000
Average wages of workers hired by individuals	800
of which: highest	5 400
: lowest	540

Distribution of income among 147 traders ('buyers and sellers') in rural markets
in Wenzhou's 9 *xian*:

Net income	Numbers of traders	% of traders
1 000−2 000	32	22
2 100−5 000	31	21
11 000−20 000	18	12
21 000−50 000	25	17
51 000−100 000	2	2
'just cover costs or make a loss'	39	27

[a] In 1985 Wenzhou city had a total population of 6.2 million [Wenzhou Rural Research
  Group, 1986, 4], living in 9 *xian* and 2 *qu*, of whom over 5 million were rural dwellers
  (Zhao, 1986, 36).
Source: Zhao, 1986

Within the individually run non-farm sector in Wenzhou there were
large differentials between owners and workers. A survey of 38 'big
hiring households' (an average size of 50 workers per enterprise) showed
that in 1985−6 the average annual wages of hired workers were around
800 *yuan*, compared to an average income of 35 000 *yuan* for their
employers, amongst whom the highest income was around 100 000 *yuan*
(Zhao, 1986). Not surprisingly, the Wenzhou situation prompted a great
deal of discussion.[34]

China's rural tax system in the early 1980s was quite unprepared for
the sudden emergence of a relatively small number of extremely rich
peasants such as those in Wenzhou. 'Red eye disease', the envy of rich
neighbours, spread rapidly as the rural reforms got under way. China

lacked a system of effective direct taxation of peasant income. China's personal income tax law (Fifth National People's Congress, 1980) was designed for wage incomes of over 500 *yuan* per month[35] (a progressive tax ranging from 5 to 45 per cent) and income from shares, bonuses, rents, etc. (a tax of 20 per cent of all such income). It was not intended to apply to peasants for whom there was no formal system of personal income tax. It is true that peasants were supposed to pay the 'agricultural tax' but, as has been seen, this had been unchanged for many years, and of course was of no relevance to the rapidly growing non-farm sector.

Collective enterprises, as I have shown, were required to hand over part of their profits to the *xiang* authorities and to pay part over to higher authorities in business 'income tax', unless given exemptions for special reasons. By and large, this system seem to have worked well, with reasonably effective monitoring of enterprise accounts by local authorities.

The biggest problem was individual businesses. It is true that many richer villages made substantial 'voluntary' contributions to the local community. There were innumerable reports in the mid−1980s of rich peasants financing banquets, and building roads, schools, hospitals, etc., for their local community. Sometimes these contributions were extracted illegally by local cadres as a form of *ad hoc* taxation. Sometimes they represented a wise 'insurance policy' for local rich people−memories of Maoist days had far from gone. Often, they occurred because rich people wished to be well-regarded by their local community. It is unlikely that this form of activity had a big effect on local differentials.

In the mid-1980s increasing concern was discernible at all levels about the very high incomes of a tiny minority of individual peasant businesses. As I shall argue later, there is good reason to believe that market forces might eventually reduce these incomes, but there was, clearly, great resentment that some extremely rich people (by Chinese standards) should be virtually free of taxation. The government responded by introducing a set of temporary regulations to deal with this situation (Lin, 1986). These regulations concerned 'income tax' payable by both urban and rural individual industrial and commercial households. The rates were steeply progressive. Households with net annual incomes of 4000 to 6000 *yuan* paid a rate of 30 per cent on that portion of their income. The rate rose to 45 per cent for that portion of income between 12 000 and 18 000 *yuan*, and to 60 per cent between 30 000 and 50 000 *yuan*, while for incomes over 50 000 *yuan*, the rate rose to around 80 per cent.

The new system was far from perfect. Under this rather crude system, some serious anomalies could arise. For example, an individual business with a net annual income of 500 *yuan* was supposed to pay just 7 per cent (35 *yuan*) in business income tax, while a co-operative or jointly-run business with ten workers, and a net annual income per worker also of 500 *yuan* paid at a 30 per cent rate (i.e. 102 *yuan* per person); if the co-operative business expanded to 20 workers, again with a net annual income per worker of 500 *yuan*, then the tax payment would rise to 40 per cent, or 141 *yuan* per worker (Zhao, 1986, 42). However, correcting the principles of taxing rural non-farm businesses was less of a problem than identifying the enterprises' income. The problems with collective enterprises where the collective owned the productive assets and where the local authorities generally worked closely with the enterprises, were, clearly, much less than with the myriad small enterprises, where there were admitted to be serious difficulties. For example, in Wenzhou (in 1985/6) it was acknowledged that 'the great majority of individual enterprises have no account records, so that some business households have inadequate tax levies, and some basically pay no tax at all' (Zhao, 1986). However, generally speaking, the larger the individual undertaking, the easier it should be for the local authorities to obtain estimates of business income. Moreover, even an imperfect (though, hopefully, improving) business tax system can raise more revenue in an expanding economy than a perfectly effective one in a stagnant economy.

It is worth reiterating that, while there were serious deficiencies in China's rural tax system in the mid-1980s, the local authorities in most areas were more successful than in other low-income economies in generating revenue to provide public goods. These sources included taxes on both collective and non-collective non-farm enterprises, licences for a wide array of economic activities, public utility charges, rates on private and commercial buildings, as well as voluntary savings in a variety of public or quasi-public financial institutions (see, e.g., Pei, 1986).

The extension of the range of intra-village income differences dramatically altered the texture of village life compared to the Maoist period. A small proportion of the population of most villages was now able to lead a much better life than ordinary villagers, and a vastly better life than the poorest stratum. Many households which had 'taken the lead in getting rich' in the mid-1980s quickly accumulated relatively large savings. This may well be a symptom of the considerable shortage in the supply of some highly desired consumer durables: one can only expect inequalities in the consumption of these items to have widened in the late 1980s. The data in tables 6.7 and 6.8 provide a more concrete idea of the real meaning of intra-village income differentials in the mid-1980s.

Table 6.7 *Consumption level of Ningxia peasant households grouped according to households' average per caput net income, sample survey data, 1983 (yuan)*

	Whole region	<100	100– 49	150– 99	200– 99	300– 99	400– 99	500– 799	800– 999	>999
Total number of households surveyed	480	15	43	70	137	110	66	35	3	1
Percentage of households	100.0	3.1	9.0	14.6	28.5	22.9	13.8	7.3	0.6	0.2
Value of consumption for different items (average per caput)										
1 Livelihood products:	205.3	77.1	108.9	141.9	187.9	242.4	296.3	349.9	585.9	709.0
Food	126.5	56.7	77.5	97.9	118.3	144.8	170.1	198.6	239.6	549.7
of which:										
grain	80.9	45.8	58.4	69.4	78.6	91.2	97.5	105.6	125.1	179.0
subsidiary foodstuffs	34.1	8.7	15.1	23.2	30.6	40.3	47.8	69.6	104.1	213.0
other foodstuffs	9.9	2.1	3.3	4.2	7.4	11.6	21.4	20.0	9.9	157.7
food eaten outside the home	1.7	0.1	0.7	1.1	1.6	1.7	3.5	3.4	1.5	–
Clothing	28.8	11.7	13.3	18.5	27.2	36.4	39.1	50.3	36.9	62.7
Daily use goods	15.7	2.7	4.0	5.4	14.7	20.3	27.3	31.3	94.3	21.7
Cultural and service goods	5.7	0.1	1.7	2.2	2.2	6.9	12.2	18.4	151.3	1.7
Books, papers, magazines	0.5	–	0.2	0.3	0.6	0.6	0.9	0.4	1.4	–
Medical and health products	3.8	0.9	2.4	3.0	3.1	3.9	7.6	4.6	6.3	8.0
Housing	12.6	1.3	3.6	4.5	12.2	14.6	24.0	25.8	38.0	3.3
of which: electricity fees	1.5	0.2	0.5	0.9	1.4	2.0	2.4	2.9	3.6	3.3
Fuel	10.7	3.0	5.7	9.1	9.4	12.7	14.4	19.0	13.4	62.0
Other goods	1.0	0.7	0.6	1.0	0.2	2.3	0.7	1.7	4.9	–

2 Culture and services of which:	3.5	2.3	2.2	2.6	3.1	3.8	5.1	6.5	7.9	1.0
educational expenses	0.7	0.3	0.4	0.4	0.7	0.8	0.8	1.3	0.4	–
medical expenses	1.1	1.9	0.9	1.2	1.0	0.7	2.0	1.1	5.3	0.7
3 Other non-loan outlays	15.8	5.8	4.3	7.7	14.9	18.6	21.5	42.9	36.3	137.0
of which: gifts to relatives and friends	9.3	5.1	2.0	5.1	8.8	10.9	12.5	23.5	28.3	116.3

Source: Ningxia Hui Nationality, 1985, 148

Table 6.8 Consumption level of Ningxia peasant households grouped according to households' average per caput net income, sample survey data, 1983 (physical terms)

	Unit	Whole region	<100 yuan	100–49 yuan	150–99 yuan	200–99 yuan	300–99 yuan	400–99 yuan	500–799 yuan	800–999 yuan	>999 yuan
Average per caput consumption of:											
Vegetables	jin	204	71	91	112	205	259	275	348	556	286
Vegetable oil	jin	6.1	2.5	2.9	4.4	5.3	7.1	8.9	11.8	20.3	25.7
Animal oil	jin	1.6	0.4	0.9	1.4	1.6	1.9	2.1	2.9	1.3	5.7
Pork	jin	9.2	3.0	4.9	6.8	7.7	10.9	12.4	19.0	44.8	67.7
Beef, mutton	jin	4.7	0.4	1.7	3.3	4.4	5.3	6.3	10.4	5.8	37.0
Milk	jin	0.1	–	–	–	–	–	0.3	1.5	2.5	–
Poultry	jin	0.6	0.1	0.2	0.3	0.4	0.5	1.0	1.8	1.9	18.0
Eggs	jin	1.2	0.5	0.6	1.0	1.1	1.4	1.4	2.4	0.6	–
Fish and shrimps	jin	0.1	–	–	–	–	0.1	0.2	0.2	1.3	–
Sugar	jin	1.9	0.2	0.4	0.7	1.6	2.1	3.5	5.5	1.3	11.3
Cigarettes	packs	13.1	2.4	4.3	5.5	10.0	17.6	24.2	27.7	54.0	140.3
Alcoholic drink	jin	0.8	0.4	0.4	0.4	0.5	0.9	1.4	1.7	4.4	15.7
Tea	jin	0.6	0.3	0.5	0.4	0.6	0.6	1.0	1.2	1.0	1.0
Candy	jin	0.7	0.1	0.4	0.6	0.7	0.8	0.8	1.2	0.6	3.3
Fruits	jin	3.0	1.5	2.1	1.8	3.6	3.1	3.1	5.6	6.9	6.7
Cotton	jin	0.7	0.6	0.7	0.7	0.7	0.6	0.5	0.9	0.5	–
Fuel (wood & stubble)	dan	4.4	2.0	3.3	5.0	3.8	4.8	5.1	6.1	5.0	5.0
Coal	jin	448	120	193	186	422	572	718	843	1175	1333

Year-end stocks of consumer durables (per 100 people):

Bicycles	no.	17	6	8	9	15	21	30	32	50	33
Sewing machines	no.	9	3	5	7	9	10	13	11	13	–
Radios	no.	11	4	3	8	10	14	15	14	38	33
Clocks	no.	22	8	9	12	21	27	34	41	63	33
of which: watches	no.	17	5	5	9	17	20	26	33	50	33
TV sets	no.	1.6	–	0.3	0.2	1.0	1.6	4.0	6.3	12.5	–
Tape recorders	no.	0.4	–	–	0.2	0.5	0.8	0.3	1.1	–	–
Large pieces of household furniture	no.	33	9	15	12	33	43	52	57	75	100
of which: writing desk	no.	9	2	2	–	10	13	15	15	38	38

One kg = two *jin*.
Source: Ningxia Hui Nationality, 1985, 174–5

It must be reiterated that the data presented in tables 6.7 and 6.8 are for a whole region (Ningxia's population in the mid-1980s was over three million) rather than for individual villages, and it is impossible to disentangle local from regional inequality in such data. However, a vast amount of qualitative and anecdotal evidence suggests a rapid widening of the range of intra-village income differentials post-1978. As these data show, the gaps in income that exist in China's villages today are accompanied by wide differences in real living standards between the top few per cent and the village average, and extremely wide differences between the top and bottom few per cent.

What of the long term? Is it likely that intra-village income differentials will, as many Western critics fear, and as Stalin in the late 1920s and Mao in the mid-1950s both predicted, become progressively wider? Making due allowance for massive regional variations, there are certain factors that are likely to inhibit this process:

First, despite considerable problems, it does appear that as modernization proceeds smaller farms have a reasonable chance of gaining access to scarce inputs — both divisible and lumpy. As in many other modernizing parts of Asia, it is likely that all strata of farmers in modernizing areas will be able to utilize new technology even though the benefits will be unequal.

Second, studies of other Asian countries where rural industrialization has proceeded rapidly have found that the process tends to have an equalizing effect on intra-village differences. Incomes in these activities are often higher than in agriculture, and the workers tend not to be drawn disproportionately from higher income village strata (Saith, 1986]. The rapid growth of China's rural non-farm sector in the 1980s and its expected future rapid growth have a strong equalizing effect on intra-village income differences.

Third, there is likely to be considerable fluidity over time in the rural class structure. It was argued in chapter 3 that in the Maoist communities there was a high degree of inter-temporal movement in peasant households' positions in the village income hierarchy, though average income changed very little over time. By the mid-1980s, a much larger proportion of rural productive assets were privately inheritable and access to human capital formation had become more unequal between different strata. Moreover, local economic and political power had begun to interact in new ways that might help the better-off to maintain their superior positions. Despite this, there still existed forces which would help to retain a certain degree of fluidity in the village class structure. Land was still collectively owned, and though sub-renting was developing, there appeared to be a competitive market for farm land with reasonable

Table 6.9 *The relationship between average per caput net income and family structure for peasant households in Ningxia Hui Nationality Autonomous Region, 1983 (sample survey data)*

	Whole region	<100 yuan	100–49 yuan	150–99 yuan	200–99 yuan	300–99 yuan	400–99 yuan	500–799 yuan	800–999 yuan	>999 yuan
Average number of persons resident in each household	6.2	7.2	6.7	6.9	6.5	5.9	5.7	5.0	2.7	3.0
Average number of full and part time workers per household	3.0	2.6	2.7	3.0	3.0	3.0	3.0	2.8	2.0	3.0
of which: full time	2.5	2.3	2.3	2.6	2.5	2.4	2.4	2.3	1.3	1.0
: part time	0.5	0.3	0.4	0.4	0.5	0.6	0.7	0.5	0.7	2.0
Full and part time workers as % of the household's permanent residents	47	36	41	44	47	50	52	56	75	100
Number of household's permanent residents of less than middle school age (i.e. under 12) per 100 permanent residents	17	34	23	20	17	14	14	2	–	–

Source: Ningxia Hui Nationality, 1985, 176–7

access for those who wished to farm it. A large proportion of capital in the rural non-farm economy was collectively owned and non-inheritable. Despite important new problems with the rural welfare system there still was, in most areas, a more robust system, with more equal access for different strata, than in most, if not all, developing countries. Moreover, there were, indeed, 'Chayanovian' elements still at work in China's intra-village differentiation. As the data in table 6.9 suggest, there was still a relationship between family structure (i.e. the stage in the lifetime cycle at which a household finds itself) and a household's position in the village income structure. As has been noted, access to human and physical capital was not equal as between peasant classes, and one can expect reduced inter-generational class mobility within China's villages compared to pre-1978. However, over large parts of rural China in the mid/late 1980s access still appeared to be equal enough to ensure that changes in families' demographic structure over the course of the family life cycle did facilitate a relatively large amount of movement between income positions.

Fourth, despite the problems encountered, the Chinese leadership is devoting serious attention to trying to construct an effective system of progressive taxation in the villages.

SPATIAL INEQUALITY

I have stressed throughout this book that China is a huge country with a wide diversity of economic conditions. Even within a single province there is, typically, a wide variety of circumstances (see, e.g., Nolan, 1983 a). In analysing countries of the size of China or India one is, effectively, looking at an amalgam of many different 'countries' in an economic sense. Despite certain important uniformities in political and economic relationships, even in a socialist country like China powerful regional processes operate. The overall performance of such subcontinental-sized economies is a combination of favourably positioned 'economies' (e.g. coastal Guangdong, Jiangsu and Hebei provinces in China's case) and unfavourably-placed ones (e.g. Xinjiang, Ningxia and Gansu provinces). It is not surprising that most very large economies perform neither very well nor very badly. The four economies in East Asia (Hong Kong, Singapore, Taiwan and South Korea) upon which such attention was focused in the development literature of the early 1980s had a combined population around 62 million, the same as a single one of China's medium-sized provinces and considerably smaller than that of China's most populous province Sichuan (99.7 million in 1982). The problems in analysing massive economies (in terms of area and population) and comparing them with small economies was well illustrated by Lewis (1978): 'If India was carved into countries of Latin America's size, we would find several regions that matched Latin American or South-East Asian performance; what holds down the India average is the large population that continues to live at subsistence level on inadequately watered marginal lands, without profitable cashcrops' (Lewis, 1978, 216−17, quoted in Chakravarty, 1987, 14).

It was shown (in chapter 3) that at the end of the Maoist period there were still important regional inequalities in the Chinese countryside. Spatial differences in rural labour productivity inherited from pre-1949 had probably not narrowed, and, indeed, may have widened. There remained wide imbalances between labour and natural resources, accentuated by the tight controls on labour migration and perhaps also by inequalities in the natural rate of population growth. The relationship of population growth to rural economic development is complex. In the Maoist period population growth rates began to fall spontaneously in the most advanced areas. In intermediate areas the growth rate was high, but in the very poorest (often national minority) areas conditions were so bad that population growth sometimes was very slow. In the words of a modern Chinese proverb, 'illness and poverty go together'.[36] Unequal access to large urban markets was only slowly resolved owing to the low priority given to transport expansion (hence, in part, the high returns to rural transport in the mid-1980s) and the isolation of backward areas remained an important fact of economic life. Modern farm inputs tended to be allocated disproportionately to certain areas, those with greater capacity to use the new inputs effectively and with more financial capital with which to purchase the inputs. It was seen too, that the rural small-scale industries which grew quite rapidly in certain lines of production in the 1960s and 1970s, tended to be concentrated spatially in areas to large cities, which possessed large investible surpluses per person.

However, it was seen, too, that under Mao there were factors at work that tended to prevent regional rural inequalities growing as rapidly as they might have done. Strict ceilings were placed on the level of income and consumption. Factors such as the slow growth of demand (both urban and rural), prohibitions on many types of non-farm activity and the lack of incentives for local authorities or enterprises, combined to slow the growth of the rural non-farm economy, which prevented well-located areas from capitalizing fully on their advantages.

The post-1978 reforms dramatically transformed this situation. Well-located areas close to large population centres and transportation links

Table 6.10 *Selected economic indicators for different Chinese provinces, 1980–1984*

Area	Average per peasant net income, current prices				Gross value of total rural social product per rural worker, current prices			
	1980 (yuan)	1984 (yuan)	Increase, 1980–4 yuan	%	1980 (yuan)	1984 (yuan)	Increase, 1980–4 yuan	%
Beijing	290	664	374	129	1810	3360	1550	86
Tianjin	278	505	227	82	1318	2920	1602	122
Hebei	176	505	122	69	857	1298	441	51
Shanxi	156	351	195	125	935	1623	688	74
Inner Mongolia	181	336	155	86	871	1451	580	67
Liaoning	273	477	204	25	1639	2548	909	55
Jilin	236	487	251	106	1852	2774	922	50
Heilongjiang	206	443	237	115	1927	2741	814	42
Shanghai	397	785	388	98	1789	3509	1720	96
Jiangsu	218	448	230	106	1202	2214	1012	84
Zhejiang	219	446	227	104	1031	1783	752	73
Anhui	185	323	138	75	665	1178	513	77
Fujian	172	345	173	101	867	1499	632	73
Jiangxi	181	334	153	85	860	1217	357	42
Shandong	194	404	210	108	981	1723	742	76
Henan	161	301	140	87	775	1084	309	40
Hubei	170	392	222	131	816	1532	716	88
Hunan	220	348	128	58	706	1088	382	54
Guangdong	274	425	151	55	891	1447	556	62
Guangxi	174	267	93	53	601	781	180	30

Sichuan	188	287	99	53	621	914	293	47
Guizhou	161	261	100	62	473	785	312	66
Yunnan	150	310	160	107	503	708	205	41
Tibet	–	–	–	–	676	945	269	40
Shenxi	142	263	121	85	643	1015	372	58
Gansu	153	221	68	44	579	701	122	21
Qinghai	–	294	–	–	928	1135	207	22
Ningxia	178	313	135	76	786	1202	416	53
Xinjiang	198	363	165	83	1011	1595	584	58
All China	191	355	164	86	870	1399	529	61

Source: ZGNCTJNJ, 1985, 173 and 202

(domestic and international), with better human capital (in the formal sense of better education, and the informal sense of greater skill in production and trade), and larger investible surpluses per person, grew especially rapidly after the constraints on incomes and production structure were removed and market forces sharply increased their role in the rural economy.

Already in the late 1970s there were wide differences between provinces in rural output per worker (see table 6.10), with much higher levels in most of the well located coastal and north-eastern provinces, and especially high levels in the suburban areas of the large municipalities under direct central control. From the late 1970s through to the mid-1980s these same areas generally experienced faster than average growth rates of rural labour productivity and much larger than average increases in the absolute level of total rural output per worker. The differences in the growth of output per worker were accompanied by wide differences in the growth of peasants' personal incomes, as table 6.11 and map 6.1 show. In just a few years in the early 1980s the range of provincial average peasant incomes widened appreciably, the standard deviation of provinces' average peasant incomes widened sharply, and the coefficient of variation also increased substantially:

Table 6.11   *Chinese provinces, cities, and autonomous regions: average per caput net income of peasants (*yuan*) (current prices)*

	1980	1984
1 Range:		
Highest-average	206	430
Highest-lowest	258	564
Highest as % of average	208	221
Highest as % of lowest	280	355
2 Standard deviation	54	124
3 Coefficient of variation (%)	29.8	34.9

Source: Calculated from ZGNCTJNJ, 1985, 202

This kind of broad analysis needs to be supplemented by an examination of intra-provincial processes. If we look at the case of Anhui province (see maps 6.2 and 6.3 and table A.3 in the Appendix), it can be seen that there were wide differences in the growth of output per person and average peasant incomes in different *xian* and *shi* from 1978 to 1984.

The range of incomes between *xian* in absolute terms widened considerably as did the standard deviation − see table 6.12.

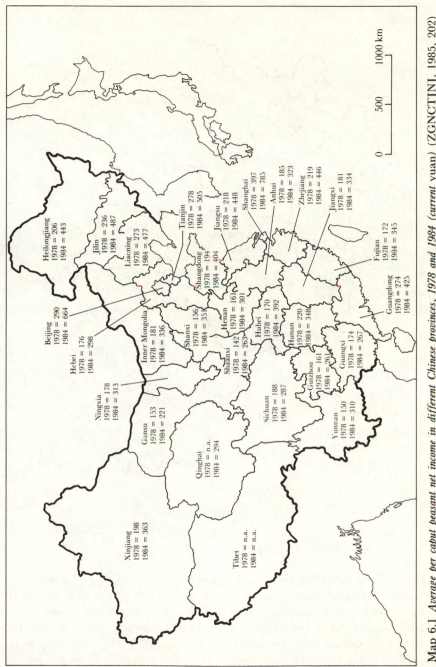

Map 6.1 *Average per caput peasant net income in different Chinese provinces, 1978 and 1984 (current yuan)* (ZGNCTJNJ, 1985, 202)

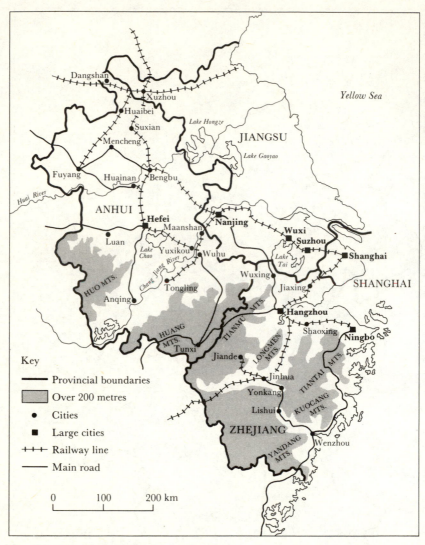

Map 6.2 *Anhui and neighbouring provinces*

However, it should be noted that the picture at the intra-provincial level
was less straightforward than at the inter-provincial level, as is indicated
by the fall in inter-*xian* inequality in Anhui province when examined in
proportional terms. For a large range of middle income *xian* there was no
clear relationship between growth of per caput income and output in
1978−84 and their original (1978) per caput income and output level.

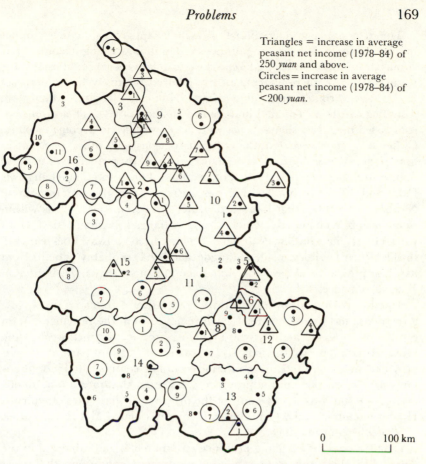

Triangles = increase in average peasant net income (1978–84) of 250 *yuan* and above.
Circles = increase in average peasant net income (1978–84) of <200 *yuan*.

0   100 km

Map 6.3 *Average per caput output and income in different parts of Anhui province, 1978–1984 (all data at current prices) (Appendix)*

Table 6.12 *Anhui province: average per caput peasant income* (yuan) *by xian/shi*

	1978	1984
Range		
Highest-average	100	194
Highest-lowest	149	325
Highest as % of average	220	159
Highest as % of lowest	538	289
Standard deviation	25.7	83.4
Coefficient of variation (%)	31.0	26.6

Source: Calculated from AHTJNJ, 1985, 325–525

The regional characteristic of growth is apparent if one examines maps 6.2 and 6.3. Certain points stand out in striking fashion. The suburban areas of cities, and *xian* close to relatively large cities (by the standards of Anhui province), mostly enjoyed relatively large increases in average incomes (including Hefei, Huaibei, Bengbu, Maanshan, Tongling, Suzhou, Tunxi, Linan, and Chuzhou cities). This group encompassed the major share of *xian* with large increases in average incomes. Closer inspection reveals rather obvious reasons why other *xian*, not at first glance so well located, experience relatively large increases in rural output and incomes post-1978. For example, Laian and Tianchang *xian* (10.2 and 10.3) are both within easy reach of the great metropolis of Nanjing in neighbouring Jiangsu province, and Xiao *xian* (9.3) is within easy reach of Xuzhou city, which also is in Jiangsu; Jiashan (10.7), Guoyang (16.4) and Guding (9.8) each benefits from railway lines running through their territory; while Guangde *xian* (12.4) probably benefits from its close proximity to resource-rich Lake Hu, just across the border in Jiangsu province.

Equally striking is the concentration of most of Anhui's relatively low growth *xian* in three large areas, each removed from the province's main centres of economic activity: the low-lying area in the northwest of the province adjacent to the relatively backward eastern part of Henan province, in which there are no major economic centres; the Huo mountains area in the west of the province and the much larger mountainous area in the south-west and south of the province at the centre of which is Huang mountain and which abuts an equally isolated and mountainous part of Zhejiang province.

Detailed data for Zhejiang province (see map 6.4, and table A.2 in the Appendix) show the wide range of production conditions that exist within a single province. Again, as with the Anhui data, the regional pattern is striking. The *xian* with high output per person were nearly all concentrated in the coastal plain area in the north of the province, close to the cities of Ningbo, Shaoxing and Hangzhou, and adjacent to the rich area of southern Jiangsu (Jiangnan) and, of course, the great metropolis of Shanghai. Particularly striking is the very high level of output per person from rural industries in these areas, ranging from around 1300 *yuan* in Yin and Shaoxing *xian* to less than 50 *yuan* in Songyang, Jingning, Yunhe, Qinngyuan, Wencheng, and Taishun *xian* (see table A.2 in the Appendix). The *xian* with low levels of output per person were all concentrated in the mountainous areas in the south and west of the province. If one takes the whole Anhui-Zhejiang area, then the local dimensions of inequality in the rural 'productive forces' are even more strikingly revealed — table 6.13.

Places of high output per caput *xian*
(>1000 *yuan*) are marked with triangles;
low output per caput *xian* (<500 *yuan*)
are marked with circles

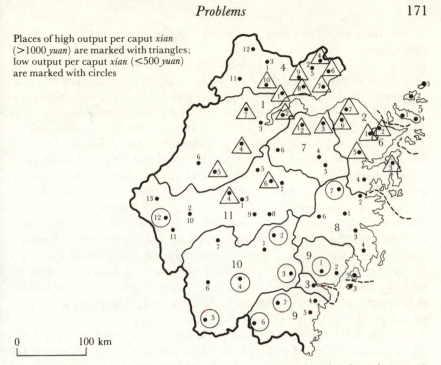

0   100 km

Map 6.4 *Zhejiang province: average per caput agricultural and industrial output in different* xian, *1984 (yuan) (Appendix)*

Table 6.13   *Gross value of agricultural and industrial output (GVAIO) per caput in Zhejiang and Anhui provinces, 1984 (yuan)*

	Number of xian	
GVAIO per caput (yuan)	*Zhejiang province*	*Anhui province*
> 2000	2 (highest: 2180)	0
1500−999	10	0
1000−499	10	0
500−999	32	22 (highest: 886)
< 500	13 (lowest: 239)	53 (lowest: 241)

Source: Derived from ZJJJNJ, 1985, and AHTJNJ, 1985

In the mid-1980s, then, there were wide spatial income inequalities in the Chinese countryside. Table 4.1 (Appendix) reveals clearly the spatial concentration of rich and poor *xian*, across the whole country. If we look firstly at the very poorest *xian*, that is, those with an average per caput net income of less than 100 *yuan*, then we can see that although over the whole country in 1984 they embraced just 2.6 per cent of the peasant population, in Yunnan the figure was 16 per cent, in Ningxia 21 per cent and in Gansu 44 per cent. Indeed, Gansu and Yunnan between them contained 56 per cent of the total national peasant population living in such *xian* — a very high degree of spatial concentration of poverty. At the other end of the scale, just 2.6 per cent of the peasant population lived in 1984 in *xian* with an average per caput income of over 600 *yuan*, but 81 per cent of these were in the three provinces of Guangdong, Jiangsu, and Liaoning, and in the suburban areas of Beijing and Shanghai, indicating a high degree of spatial concentration of rural affluence. It should, of course, be noted that only a small proportion of the peasant population lived in *xian* with very high and very low average per caput incomes: in 1984 over half lived in *xian* within the narrow band of 100−300 *yuan*.

Corresponding to the wide range of average per caput incomes between provinces is a wide range of average consumption, as Tables A.4 and A.5 in the Appendix show. For a number of important foodstuffs, and especially, for many consumer durables, average levels of consumption in rich coastal provinces in 1984 were considerably higher than in poor inland provinces.

There is a big difference between 'uneven growth' and 'polarization'. The evidence presented so far in this section strongly suggests that rural growth of labour productivity and incomes in the 1980s was quite uneven between different areas, but that most parts of the countryside experienced at least some real growth. If we look at the fairly robust evidence on average levels of physical consumption in different provinces (see tables A.4 and A.5 in the Appendix) it can be seen that there were major advances even in the poorest provinces with the smallest increases in average per caput net income (at current prices). Gansu is the worst − placed province in these respects, yet even here it is reported that large increases took place in the early 1980s in average peasant consumption of superior food grain, vegetables, edible oil, fresh eggs, and alcoholic drinks, and in average stocks of bicycles, sewing machines, radios and wristwatches.

The intra−provincial evidence is generally less robust. It is too often in monetary terms or concerns 'poor' areas that on close inspection turn out not to be very poor.[37] However, if we look at the evidence from, for example, Anhui province, then, on the basis of the figures reported (see table 4.3 in Appendix) it must be concluded that every single *xian* in the province experienced some real income growth in 1978−84. The worst placed *xian* is probably Huoshan, located in the mountainous, remote area of the same name in the west of the province. In 1978 it had quite a low average per caput income and it experienced the smallest growth of output and income of any *xian* in the province in 1978—84. However, making rough assumptions about the proportion of output marketed and market prices, it seems likely that average real incomes in Huoshan *xian* increased by at least one-third over this period.[38] The 1984—5 National Sample Survey found that just 3.9 per cent of peasant households had experienced a decline in income in 1978—84 (Rural Survey Group, 1986, 7).[39]

The institutional reforms released untapped production potential in poor as well as advanced areas. The increase in peasant freedom to determine the production structure also helped poor areas, enabling them to diversify into local specializations. The increase in state purchase prices may have been more beneficial for areas with larger per caput marketings, but poorer areas also derived some benefit. The rapid growth of output and incomes in advanced areas probably also brought net benefits via the normal workings of the market for poorer areas by, for example, increasing demand for specialized products (e.g. mountain herbs, fungi, timber products), and increasing demand for labour from poorer areas (which, in turn, generally results in a flow of remittances and, sometimes, of skills to poor areas). The rapid expansion of non-farm employment in well—located areas opened up possibilities for farm employment in these areas for migrants from poor regions. In addition, as we have seen, the rapid growth of incomes in advanced areas provided extra income for the state (at different levels) with which to attempt to raise the level of labour productivity and income in poorer areas.

WELFARE AND HUMAN CAPITAL

One of the most admired aspects of China's pre-1978 collective system was its ability to mobilize resources for welfare purposes — education, health and provision for the poorest members of the local community (see chapter 3). Many observers have been sceptical of the capacity of local state and collective institutions to sustain these facilities under the rural contract system of the mid-1980s. Under the collective system, it is argued, local leaders were able to extract resources directly from collective income, but with a large proportion of income in private hands, the resources for such activities had to be handed over by individual households, creating a number of problems, e.g. the community's assessment of these activities' importance might differ from that of the cadres; some members of the community might object to such payments on the grounds that they would currently be likely to make little use of them (e.g. they have no school-age children and are in good health); with the privatization of much of the economy and the widening of local income differentials, better—off members of the community might (e.g. by bribing cadres) be able to avoid making payments or make relatively small payments for such activities. Moreover, in many parts of China, the collective non-farm economy, from which resources could be most easily extracted, was extremely weak.

Welfare funding

At first glance, it does appear as if a deterioration occurred from the late 1970s to the mid-1980s. The absolute level of rural 'collective retentions' rose by only a small amount (from 18.9 billion *yuan* in 1978 to 22.3 billion *yuan* in 1984),[40] and declined sharply as a proportion of total village income from 16.7 per cent in 1978 to 7.2 per cent in 1984) (ZGNCTJNJ, 1985, 189; ZGTJNJ, 1985, 185).

However, these data provide a misleading picture of the funds available for rural welfare. First, the collective retentions under the old collective system were required to perform a much wider range of functions than under the reformed system. Formerly, the retentions had to fulfil a wide range of both accumulation and welfare needs. After the reforms, many of the accumulation functions were devolved to the household, allowing the proportion of collective retentions devoted to welfare to rise. Second, as I have noted, the charges for rural welfare services rose in the 1980s,[41] so that a larger contribution to welfare units' income was derived from fees rather than direct payments by the collective (which had implications for class relations). Third, a considerable proportion of financial support for rural welfare services has always (post-1949) come from the state, and is not included in the collective retentions figure. In the early 1980s, for example, only about one—half of China's rural hospital beds were in collectively owned hospitals (ZGNCTJNJ, 1985, 275), and only around one-half of village primary schools were owned and run collectively.[42] There was a considerable increase in funds generated for local authorities in most areas after the reforms, and it is likely that this helped to boost the total funding available for rural welfare.

Education

It is this aspect of rural welfare in the mid-1980s, where the biggest problems existed. Irrespective of the ability of the state and the collective to provide education, there were serious demand problems (especially in poor areas), exacerbated by the increased short-run opportunity costs of schooling owing to the post-reform increase in real income per labour

day over most of rural China, and owing to the privatization of the
benefits from education. In very advanced areas where a wide range of
non-agricultural employment was available the problem was less severe,
since a relatively high level of education was often a pathway to higher
income as discussed earlier. However, for a wide range of areas, there
was little economic advantage in peasants attending school for more
than 4—5 years, after which time they hopefully had acquired basic
numeracy and literacy skills. Equally, there were widely admitted to be
big differences in the capacity of different areas to supply education. In
the richest areas (following the 'Southern Jiangsu' as opposed to the
'Wenzhou' path), a high level of funding was available not just from
individual levies, but also from direct levies from a rich collective economy. Indeed, in some areas both the individual contribution to collective
retentions and primary school fees were abolished in the 1980s.[43]

Across the whole of rural China in the 1980s, there was a sharp
decline in the numbers attending school. However, owing to the reported
decline in rural population over the same period,[44] the fall in the proportion of the rural population attending school was not so serious — table
6.14.

Table 6.14   *Changes in numbers in China's rural schools, 1978—1984*

	1978 (m)	1984 (m)	Changes 1978—84	
			m	%
1 Higher middle[1]	9.5	2.0	−7.5	−79
2 Lower middle[1]	38.7	26.7	−12.0	−31
3 Primary[1]	128.8	114.5	−14.3	−11
4 Total[1]	177.0	143.2	−33.8	−19
5 Rural population[2]	790.1	704.7	−	−
4 as % of 5	22.4	20.3	−	−

[a] The fall in the rural population from 1978 to 1984 is, reportedly, due to the change in the
criterion for setting up *zhen* (small towns) leading to a relatively fast increase in newly-
established *zhen* (ZGTJZY, 1986, 21).
Sources: [1] ZGNCTJNJ, 1985, 270
            [2] ZGTJZY, 1986, 21

The proportion of primary-school-age children attending school in
China after the rural reforms was still high by the standards of other
low-income countries, despite some probable decline in the proportion
in the 1980s.[45] In China in 1983, it was reported that for children aged 8

to 12 years, over 87 per cent attended school (ZGNCTJNJ, 1985, 271),[46] compared to 74 per cent of school-age children reportedly attending primary school in 1983 in low-income countries other than China and India (World Bank, 1986b, 236).[47] Although, as the data in table 6.15 show, the proportion attending school fell of quickly after the age of 12, there is reason to believed that over a large part of rural China there was a strong incentive to acquire a minimum of education, and the evidence presented suggests that the state and collectives between them were able to meet this need. The question of quality of educational provision is, of course, another matter. There is plenty of evidence to show that there are problems with the quality of rural teachers (Watson, 1986, 11), but it would be a bold person who would claim that the quality of rural education in general had fallen in the 1980s.

Table 6.15 *Proportion of school-age children reported to be attending school in China's villages, 1983 (year end)*

Age (years)	%
7	58
8	82
9	89
10	91
11	89
12	85
13	75
14	60
Total	79

These data are drawn from sample survey statistics of over 146 000 children.
Source: ZGNCTJNJ, 1985, 271

Education is not simply a matter of school attendance. It is also possible to raise one's educational level by discussion, watching TV and listening to the radio, and private study of books, magazines and newspapers. Even the most casual observer of life in China in the 1980s could not fail to see over much of the countryside a sharp rise in individual peasants' desire to acquire knowledge. Attendance at school for many years is not always (beyond a certain point) the most efficient way for the individual household to acquire the kind of knowledge likely to be useful in the rural economy. As I have shown, stocks of radios and TVs rose sharply in the 1980s (even in poor areas), broadcasting a mass of material of both formal and informal value for the rural economy.[48] Publications of books, magazines and newspapers rose very quickly too in the 1980s (see, e.g., the data in ZGTJNJ, 1985, 597−8). A large part of the increase was absorbed by the rural population (though, of course, urban consumption levels still were, generally, much above those in the countryside). Moreover, the intensity with which practically useful materials were used almost certainly increased in comparison to pre-1978, when the personal (as opposed to collective) advantage in improving one's human capital was relatively small. The contribution to technical progress of a book on chicken rearing is likely to be much greater if it is avidly passed from peasant to peasant than if it sits unused on the shelf of the production brigade's library.

Health

At first glance it appears as if the de-collectivization in the Chinese countryside was accompanied by a serious decline in rural health care. Perhaps the strongest symbol of rural health care under Mao was the part-time 'barefoot doctor' (and other part-time rural health workers). The number of part-time rural health workers fell seriously in the 1980s: the number of rural 'barefoot doctors' declined from 1.40 million in 1981 to 1.25 million in 1984 and the number of 'medical workers in rural production teams' fell from 2.01 million in 1981 to 1.16 million in 1984 (SYC, 1982, 479; ZGTJNJ, 1985, 613). In addition, the number of collectively owned keypoint hospitals and collective hospital beds fell in the early 1980s (see tables 6.15 and 6.16).

The real picture was much more complex. Firstly, the collectives' capacity to mobilize resources for health purposes far from disintegrated. The number of peasants per barefoot doctor had hardly altered by the mid-1980s; the total number of collectively owned *xiang* hospitals (as opposed to 'keypoint' hospitals) actually increased; the number of collectively owned hospital beds only fell by a small proportion; while the number of part-time collective medical workers declined, the number of full-time collective medical personnel rose. Second, rural state-run medical facilities expanded in most respects, often quite substantially, frequently using resources generated by the rapidly expanding rural economy (the relationship is clearest at the *xian* level). Third, the rural population declined over this period, so that, overall, there was a considerable improvement in the per caput availability of rural health facilities (see table 6.15). Fourth, peasants near urban areas had access also to urban health facilities, which expanded rapidly in the early 1980s.[49] Fifth, even in backward areas the commitment to rural health was often sufficiently

strong to often produce some improvement in access (despite conditions
falling far short of those in advanced areas):

Table 6.16   *Rural health facilities*

	Hospital beds per 10 000 peasants		Rural medical personnel per 10 000 peasants	
	1980	*1984*	*1980*	*1984*
All China	9.0	10.4	12.1	14.4
Shanghai	15.3	14.4	24.2	24.2
Jilin	11.6	18.9	15.2	23.2
Jiangsu	11.5	12.6	14.2	15.3
Fujian	8.4	9.9	12.3	15.5
Guangxi	5.2	7.2	7.1	10.7
Gansu	5.3	5.7	8.0	8.3
Tibet	2.8	3.7	4.0	3.2

Source: ZJNCTJNJ, 1985, 278; SYC, 1982, 90; ZGTJNJ, 1985, 185

Table 6.17   *Rural health facilities, 1978–1984*

	1978		1984		Change,	1978–84
	000	*%*	*000*	*%*	*000*	*%*
1 Hospitals	55.0		55.5		+0.5	+0.9
of which:						
(1) 'key' hospitals	11.2		10.6		−0.6	−5.4
of which: collectively owned	1.8	16.5	1.6	15.1	−0.2	−11.1
(2) *xiang* hospitals	43.9		44.4		+1.1	+2.5
of which: collectively owned	34.8	79.4	35.5	79.0	+0.7	+2.0
2 Hospital beds	747.4		731.4		−16.0	−2.1
of which:						
(1) 'key' hospitals	295.0		297.4		+2.4	+0.8
of which: collectively owned	56.7	19.2	51.9	17.4	−4.8	−8.5

Table 6.17 *continued*

(2) *xiang* hospitals	452.3	434.0	−18.3	−4.0
of which: collec-				
tively owned	314.3 69.8	305.6 70.4	−8.7	−2.8
3 Medical personnel	963.3	1 012.9	+49.6	+5.2
of which:				
(1) 'key' hospitals	312.5	354.8	+42.3	+13.5
of which: collec-				
tively owned	72.9 23.3	71.9 20.3	+1.0	+1.4
(2) *xiang* hospitals	650.8	658.2	+7.4	+1.1
of which: collec-				
tively owned	470.7 72.3	479.7 72.9	+9.0	+1.9
4 Technically skilled medical personnel	837.9	884.51	+46.6	+5.6
5 No. of peasants per:				
(1) hospital	14 362	12 686	−1676	−11.7
(2) hospital bed	1 057	963	−94	−8.9
(3) technically skilled medical worker	820	696	−124	−15.1

Source: ZGNCTJNJ, 1985, 275; ZGTJZY, 1986, 21

Local help for poor households

It was seen in chapter 3 that Chinese collectives under Mao established a quite effective system of local poverty relief, given the low average income level. Western observers have feared for the decline of this system just as they have for other collective activities:

> I don't think there is anyone looking after [poor peasants] in an organised way now ... But what I am more concerned about is who is going to take care of people if there are floods, droughts, or famines, or if the rural economy suddenly turns sour. If any of these things happen − which is not impossible − there are going to be a lot of people back out on the roads begging, with no place to go and nothing to eat ... If you ask me, a situation like that would

put China back pretty close to the way it was before 1949. [Hinton, quoted in Schell, 1984]

Farmland was provided to all rural households in the land redistribution post-1978, but the problem of labour poor households remained. Far from declining, the system of collective support for 'five guarantee' households became more robust as income levels rose in the 1980s. The total number of people supported under this hardly altered (around three million in both 1980 and 1984). Of these, the number directly provided for in retirement homes more than doubled (112 000 in 1980, 241 000 in 1984), and the amount of assistance per caput for those outside retirement homes rose from 64 *yuan* in 1980 to 142 *yuan* in 1984 (ZGNCTJNJ, 1985, 282). A system of collective and state assistance for a much broader category of poor people, the 'impoverished households' (*pinku hu*), was begun after 1979. By 1984 38 million peasants were receiving help from this source, though the amount of assistance averaged just 4.5 *yuan* per person (ZGNCTJNJ, 1985, 289). Finally, state assistance to areas stricken by natural disasters rose substantially after 1978 (from 419 million *yuan* in 1978 to 691 million *yuan* in 1984, at current prices (ZGNCTJNJ, 1985, 291)).

Unsurprisingly, there still were in the mid-1980s wide regional variations in the level of support for locally poor people, directly related to the prosperity of both the individual and the collective economy. Villages in the richest parts of China had already established an old-age pension system by the early/mid 1980s (Nolan, 1983b). For example, in a very rich part of Shandong province in 1985, retired peasants received a monthly stipend of 70 *yuan* per person from the collective,[50] which was around the same level as the average per caput income level of urban workers in state enterprises.[51] By 1984, villages containing just 664 000 peasants had set up such a system: about half of these were in the Shanghai suburbs alone, and outside Shanghai, Beijing, Tianjin, Liaoning, Jiangsu, Zhejiang and Guangdong, there were virtually none (Sichuan had just three *cun* (villages) with such a system, while Shenxi had only seven) (ZGNCTJNJ, 1985, 288). Rural retirement homes were highly spatially concentrated: in 1984, Beijing, Tianjin, Shanghai and eleven provinces between them contained almost nine-tenths of the total (ZGNCTJNJ, 1985, 282). The capacity of the local collective structure to support 'impoverished households' also was extremely uneven: average funds per caput for 'impoverished households' in 1984 ranged from 12.4 *yuan* in Heilongjiang, 11.5 in Shandong, and 10.2 in Jiangsu, to less than one *yuan* in Guangxi, Guizhou, Gansu, and Yunnan (ZGNCTJNJ, 1985, 282).

ACCUMULATION AND PHYSICAL CAPITAL

Many people outside China expressed concern at the possible impact of China's de-collectivization on rural capital accumulation.[52] The anxious range from those who recognized the inefficiency with which capital was used in collectives pre-1978 but who were worried about the ability of the post-reform system to sustain lumpy investments (notably irrigation), to those who considered that there was likely to be a general rural investment crisis after de-collectivization.[53]

In fact, generalized fears of the latter sort were not fulfilled. Average per village (*cun*) stocks of fixed assets (at original value, excluding land) rose from 244 000 *yuan* in 1978, to 574 000 *yuan* in 1984 (Rural Survey Group, 1986), i.e. an increase of 135 per cent[54] — hardly a 'collapse' of rural accumulation! Moreover, as might be expected in a situation where, for much of the year, there was substantial surplus labour, in the mid-1980s investment in current inputs greatly exceeded investment in fixed assets. Of total self-financed village investment in 1984, just 20 per cent was used to purchase fixed assets and 80 per cent for the purchase of current inputs (Rural Survey Group, 1986).[55] Clearly, focusing only on fixed capital provides an extremely misleading picture of the rural accumulation process. Rural consumption of some important current inputs rose very rapidly in the early 1980s. The tonnage of chemical fertilizers used rose from nine million in 1978 to 18 million in 1985, and the consumption of electricity in the rural areas increased from 25.3 billion kwh in 1978 to 50.9 billion kwh in 1985 (ZGJJNJ, 1986, III, 7) These are huge increases.

However, important changes took place in the structure of village investment. The issues of farm versus non-farm investment, and grain versus non-grain investment were discussed earlier in this chapter. Another important change in the composition of village investment was the distribution between the collective and non-collective sectors. Naturally, following China's rural reforms, the share of the collective sector in rural investment declined. However, even after the main reforms, the collective system still accounted for over one—half of new self-funded village investment.[56] and its share of total village fixed assets in 1984 still stood at 47 per cent (ZGNCTJNJ, 1985, 249). Not surprisingly, following the sale of many collectively owned agricultural capital goods, the collective sector's stock of agricultural fixed assets fell (by 11 per cent—at original value— from 1978 to 1984 (Rural Survey Group, 1986)). However, the great dynamism of the collective non-farm economy in the 1980s is indicated by the fact that collectively owned non-farm rural fixed assets rose by 160 per cent from 1978 to 1984 (Rural Survey Group, 1986).

As always, the country-wide figures masked striking regional differences. The 1984/5 national sample survey showed that total collective fixed assets (at original value) had increased by 53 per cent from 1978 to 1984 (Rural Survey Group, 1986). However, increases in total collective assets were confined to just 34 per cent of the villages surveyed, mainly located in Beijing, Tianjin, Heilongjiang, Shanghai, Jiangsu, Zhejiang and Shandong (Rural Survey Group, 1986). It should be noted too that to increase total collective assets simultaneously with selling a large amount of collective agricultural assets shows just how dynamic the collective economy was in these areas. In 1984, collective investment was above 55 per cent of total village investment only in Beijing, Tianjin, Shanghai, Liaoning, Shangdong and Henan. In eight provinces and autonomous regions collective investment was less than 10 per cent of the total; in Jiangxi and Hunan the proportion was less than 1 per cent, while in Qinghai and Yunnan there was 'no collective investment at all' (Rural Survey Group, 1986).

The Chinese rural non-farm economy is strikingly unevenly developed as between regions, with a small number of coastal provinces vastly more developed than most of the rest of the country (see map 6.5). Indeed, the five coastal provinces of Guangdong, Zhejiang, Jiangsu, Hebei and Liaoning, plus the major cities within them (Beijing, Tianjin and Shanghai) alone accounted for 61 per cent of all rural industrial output value in China in 1984 (ZGNCTJNJ, 1985, 14). In areas with weekly developed non-farm economies, in which there also were often relatively few 'lumpy' farm assets, de-collectivization of most collective animals and small and medium farm implements meant that an extraordinarily rapid expansion of the collectively owned non-farm economy would have been required to sustain growth of total collective investment.

In fact, what appeared to be happening was a division of the rural economy into two broadly different types of area (with, of course, many sub-variants). Generally densely populated areas (the exception being the north-east) with highly developed rural non-farm economies (accounting for a large share of the national total) maintained the collective sector in a massively dominant position in the non-farm economy frequently with rapid advance of collective accumulation in this sector; this was the 'Southern Jiangsu' model. In many areas, generally those that were more sparsely populated and backward, the individual and genuinely co-operative non−farm sector expanded more rapidly than the collective non-farm sector. The most successful example of this was in Wenzhou (Zhejiang province). By mid-1987 the 'Wenzhou' model had spread rapidly in Anhui, Henan, Shandong, Hubei, Hunan and Fujian provinces.[57]

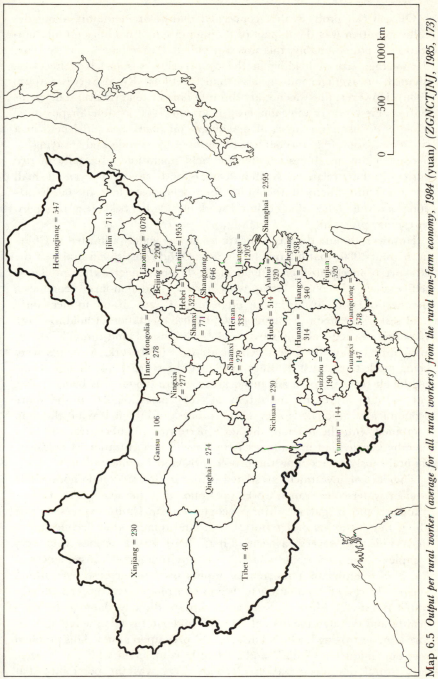

Map 6.5 *Output per rural worker (average for all rural workers) from the rural non-farm economy, 1984 (yuan) (ZGNCTJNJ, 1985, 173)*

Heilongjiang = 347

Jilin = 713

Liaoning = 1078

Beijing = 2200

Tianjin = 1955

Shandong = 646

Hebei = 523

Shanxi = 771

Henan = 332

Jiangsu = 1203

Shanghai = 2395

Anhui = 320

Zhejiang = 938

Hubei = 514

Jiangxi = 340

Fujian = 520

Hunan = 314

Guangdong = 378

Shaanxi = 279

Inner Mongolia = 278

Ningxia = 277

Gansu = 106

Qinghai = 274

Sichuan = 230

Guizhou = 190

Guangxi = 147

Yunnan = 144

Xinjiang = 230

Tibet = 40

0   500   1000 km

One special problem that concerned many commentators about de-collectivization was the impact of fragmentation of holdings on mechanization. Unquestionably, this was a problem. As we have seen, by 1984, the average size of holding in the countryside was just 0.56 hectares, divided, on average, into no less than 9.7 plots (Rural Survey Group, 1986). However, this was not an absolute barrier to agricultural mechanization. First, where the same crop is grown, it is possible for peasants' to agree to use large items of machinery on many peasants' land in a single operation (e.g. mechanical ploughing, harvesting and spraying).[58] Second, many machines suitable for field operation (especially in rice agriculture) are relatively small and can operate effectively even on small parcels. Third, fragmentation of holdings is no obstacle to the mechanization of a wide range of agricultural work outside the fields (e.g. transport, threshing, processing).

However, despite these qualifications, it was widely admitted in China in the mid-1980s that fragmentation indeed did constitute a brake on the advance of mechanization in field tasks. To some degree the problem is self-resolving. In poorer areas with undeveloped non-farm economies, the level of rural surplus labour often made it undesirable to mechanize field tasks. The main problems posed by fragmentation of holdings here were time wasted walking between plots and loss of land through boundaries rather than too little mechanization of field work. Attempts were being made to readjust holdings to reduce these problems, though it was a difficult task. In more advanced areas where labour was being drawn out of agriculture mechanization of field tasks tended to be more economically rational. However, the process of labour leaving the land combined with the freedom the state permitted in subcontracting land thereby vacated led in some areas to a rapid concentration of holdings, spontaneously overcoming the problem of land fragmentation.

The data on investment presented earlier in this section do not include land or water conservancy works (as opposed to the machinery used or drainage and irrigation). Many people outside China expressed fears about the possibility of deterioration in land quality after decollectivization. This had several aspects. First, there was a serious (but very complex) long-term concern about the environmental consequences of the high quantity of agrochemical inputs used to increase agricultural yields. The run-off from nitrogenous and phosphate fertilizers can damage water resources. Many agrochemical inputs directly damage people's health, and threaten the lives of other animals, in turn damaging agriculture (e.g. destroying birds and insects that prey upon pests). This problem was not unique to China[59] and had little connection with the issue of agricultural de-collectivization. Second, there was the possibility that individual farm households would have a shorter time horizon than collectives, and sacrifice long-term soil fertility to short-term profits. This was a serious issue prior to the fixing of land contracts (in 1984) at a minimum of 15 years. The extension of contracts to 50 years in 1987 and the granting of rights to inherit contracts resolved this problem.

Third, there was the possibility that de-collectivization might lead to broader environmental deterioration, notably de-forestation and soil erosion, which would have adverse effects on agriculture. After de-collectivization there were three principal types of forested area in China: state-owned, collectively owned, and individual forests. Both before and after the reforms, state-owned forests were much the most important,[60] The bulk of China's forests were not, therefore, affected directly by de-collectivization. State forests are usually located away from major centres of population, and, hence, transport costs for lumber often are relatively high. Pre-1980 the state-run forests were analogous to state factories, handing over all profits (if any) to higher authorities, and losses were subsidized without penalties. In the early 1980s, a profit sharing scheme was introduced — in Sichuan for example, 40 per cent was retained locally and 60 per cent handed to the provincial government (Nolan, 1983b). This greatly increased the incentive of the locality (*diqu* or *xian*) to look after forestry resources well, though still, as in the lumber industry anywhere, there remained conflicts between short- and long-term interests. At least if the forests are mainly state-owned there is a reasonable chance of regulations being enacted to ensure the preservation of long-term interests. Forestry managers who wantonly deplete resources are unlikely to be reappointed by the local government, which now has a greatly enhanced interest in maintaining forestry resources. This situation contrasts favourably with that in many timber-rich developing countries. Often, desperate to increase foreign exchange earnings, governments have provoked wasteful 'timber booms', by leasing the rights to large areas at low prices compounding the problem by offering only short-term leases, requiring concessionnaires to begin harvesting at once, and adopting royalty systems that induce loggers to harvest only the best trees while doing enormous damage to the remainder (World Commission, 1987, 152–3).

The (less important) collective forests also underwent considerable changes in the early 1980s. Under the Maoist system collective forests were administered by peasants paid a time rate, with no direct financial interest in whether the forests were run well or badly. Taken in combination with the strict limits paced on the growth of collective distributed income such a system provided maximum incentive for peasants to pillage illegally the collectively owned resource, a process assisted by the difficulty of policing woodlands. This set—up was little better than the classic 'common land' case in which there are no private property rights, no state intervention and where it has not been possible to devise collective procedures for protecting common resources (see Wade, 1987, for a discussion of possible solutions to the 'tragedy of the commons'). In the early 1980s most collective forests were contracted out to groups or individuals. The contract period was variable, though typically much longer than for ordinary farmland (before 1987), so that there was a strong incentive to consider long-term interests.

Individual woodlands were virtually non-existent pre-1978. In the early 1980s peasants were encouraged to take responsibility both for uncultivated hillsides (*ziliushan*—'private plot hills') on which they could grow trees and for individual trees planted around the village. Individual property rights (ownership of the trees, not the land; rights to freely buy and sell the trees and the products of the trees) were delineated clearly, and were made inheritable, thereby ensuring a long-term perspective.[61]

There were still big problems in China's forestry industry in the mid-1980s, but far from making matters worse, the contract system was better able than the pre-1978 system (a combination of crude state and crude collective administration) to combine long- and short-term forestry interests. If China's data are at all accurate, its afforestation work was more successful after the reforms of the 1980s than in the 1960s and 1970s. The reported average annual afforested area[62] in 1980—3 was 4.9 million hectares, compared to 3.9 million in 1970 and 3.4 million in 1965 (ZGTJNJ, 1985, 266). Moreover, it appears that the maintenance of existing timber resources was improved. In Sichuan, for example, after the introduction of the reforms in the early 1980s, it was reported that the survival rate of saplings rose from 30 per cent pre-1980 to 62 per cent in 1982, and that the rate of tree loss through fires fell sharply (Nolan, 1983b).

In addition to fears about land quality, a related area of concern has been the irrigation system. I have already noted that the commune system was extremely successful in mobilizing vast quantities of labour to undertake work on water conservation projects. Many Western writers have been anxious that de-collectivization would result in a serious decline in water conservation. Such concern often is based on the simplistic assumption that only collective farms are capable of organizing the provision of lumpy inputs or resolving conflicts between farmers over access to water. This viewpoint is at odds with the evidence of much of China's history and from many other parts of Asia (see, e.g., Stargardt, 1983; Franks, 1983; Hayami and Kikuchi, 1981; Bray, 1986).

Under the Maoist system, the calculation of costs and benefits for any given project was (if done at all) of a very rudimentary kind. Although enormous expansion of the irrigated areas was achieved, relatively little attention was paid to the problems of maintenance of water conservation facilities[63] or to the efficiency with which water was provided or drainage achieved. By the late Maoist period, China already had attained an extremely high irrigation ratio. The drained and irrigated area reportedly increased from 18 per cent of the arable area in 1952, to 32 per cent in 1965, and had reached 45 per cent by 1978 (ZGNYJJGY, 1982, 9; ZGTJZY, 1986, 44). As one writer in the mid-1980s put it: 'After years of massive investments in irrigation/ drainage works, China seemed to have basically overpowered the traditional 'grand agony' . . .' (Kueh, 1984b, 131). Indeed, the returns to further expansion of the irrigation ratio might well have become quite low by the 1970s compared to the alternative use of resources. In the early 1980s, the Chinese Government decided to shift the focus in irrigation work away from expansion towards 'consolidating existing installations and raising the efficiency of water conservation projects' (ZGJJNJ, 1986, V, 20), and a marked shift took place in the way state and collective resources available for water conservation were used.

It is, indeed, quite possible that the total volume of resources devoted to rural water conservation fell. There is little doubt that the state's allocations for farmland capital construction declined in the 1980s,[64] though this was not especially disturbing, since the increased rural prosperity post-1978 meant that the rural sector's capacity to finance its own investment projects had expanded greatly (see above). At the local level, peasants in most areas after the reforms were still required to contribute labour or money for collective water conservation (and road construction), though there had been some decline in the ability of local authorities to enforce such payments,[65] However, the capacity of those responsible for irrigation/drainage to raise revenue, and their incentive to do so, had risen considerably. For example, the rights to use water resources for purposes other than irrigation (e.g. for fishing) were now typically contracted out (to collectives, groups and individuals), thereby securing an important source of rental income for water authorities. Moreover, under the post-reform structure, the incomes of the managers of irrigation and drainage projects were related both to the income from water fees, and to the efficiency with which water was provided.[66] Hence, under the post-reform system, there was far greater incentive to collect water fees (Hinton, 1983), thereby increasing the resources available to local water management authorities (generally state or collective) (Nolan, 1983b Hinton, 1983).

Estimating the net effect of these changes upon the total resources available for water conservation is extremely difficult. It is probable that there had been some decline by the mid-1980s, but it is probable also that the quality of management had risen and that the widespread use of specialized contract labour (paid according to the quality of work) had raised the standard achieved by water conservation teams (Nolan, 1983b). Moreover, it should be reiterated that it was probably economically irrational to attempt to expand the irrigation system much or, indeed, to have devoted as large a volume of resources to water conservation as China did in the 1970s. Further, it probably made sense to concentrate these resources on improvement to the already very large (relative to China's arable area) irrigated area.

What, then, were the results for water conservation in the early 1980s? The irrigated area in total did, indeed, fail to expand after 1978, remaining fixed at around 45 million hectares (see chapter 5). However, there were plenty of signs of improvements in the quality of irrigation. The total horsepower of motors used for drainage and irrigation in agriculture rose almost 20 per cent from 1978 to 1985 (ZGTJZY, 1986, 43),[67] and in the Sixth Five Year Plan (1981–5), the improvements in water conservation indicators shown in table 6.18 were reported.

Table 6.18 *Achievements in water conservation in the Sixth Five Year Plan, 1981–1985*

Increases in	*Area (m hectares)*
Effectively drained and irrigated	3.6
Improved drainage and irrigation	9.5
Flooding eliminated	1.2
Soil erosion brought under control	3.7
Saline soil eliminated	0.6
Drained/irrigated with mechanical pumps	3.4
Irrigation from mechanical tubewells	1.8
Drinking water supply resolved: people (m)	33.3
animals (m)	21.0

Source: ZGJJNJ, 1986, v, 20

POPULATION GROWTH

After two decades of policy fluctuations, China's leadership in the 1970s firmly committed itself to reducing the national fertility rate, which in the late 1960s still stood at around 37–38 per 1000, the same level as in the early 1950s (ZGTJZY, 1986, 21). The main measures through which the state attempted to achieve this were: (1) large-scale production of contraceptives; (2) expansion of rural hospital facilities, enabling a great increase in rural abortions; (3) strongly 'encouraging' late marriages; (4) administrative pressure to limit family size in accordance with the national 'birth plan',[68] exercised through allocation of housing (vital in the cities), rural grain distribution, ration tickets, private plots, etc. The results were striking. By the late 1970s, the national birth rate was reported to have fallen to 17.8 per 1000 (ZGTJZY, 1986, 21).[69] The American expert on China's demography, J.S. Aird, commented: 'Since the early 1970s, the People's Republic of China has been pursuing what has proved to be the most successful family planning program the world has ever seen. Its effectiveness can be demonstrated beyond all doubt from the official data' (Aird, 1986, 185–6).

In the mid-1980s, the Chinese birth rate and natural rate of growth of population began to rise once more: the birth rate reportedly rose from 17.5 per 1000 in 1984 to 20.8 per 1000 in 1986, while the natural rate of population growth rose from 10.8 to 14.1 per 1000 in the same period (ZGTJZY, 1986, 21; State Statistical Bureau, 1987).

Many observers outside China argued that the rural reforms of the 1980s must have played a major role in this. They considered, first, that the reforms increased the incentive for peasants to have children since the gains from extra labour had become privatized, and the 'returns to investment in reproduction' had risen with the sharp rise in rural labour productivity in the 1980s. Second, they believed that de-collectivization had greatly reduced the means (mainly penalties) by which rural cadres could influence peasant behaviour. Third, many Western observers thought the rural party apparatus' capacity to influence peasant life had been undermined deeply by a fall in its prestige and morale in the 1980s. Finally, de-collectivization was alleged to have greatly weakened the capacity of rural collectives to raise resources for basic-level health work, including birth control and abortion.

In fact, the picture is much more complex than this. Despite the rise in the natural rate of growth of population, the figure for 1986 simply returned China to the rate reported for 1981/2. This figure (1.4 per cent per annum) is very low in comparison with other developing countries: the average rate of population growth for all low-income economies (excluding China and India) in 1973–84 was 2.6 per cent (World Bank, 1986b, 228).

Moreover, taking other influences as given, one would expect considerable fluctuations in China's vital statistics throughout the 1980s and into the 1990s as a consequence of 'echo' effects from China's demographic

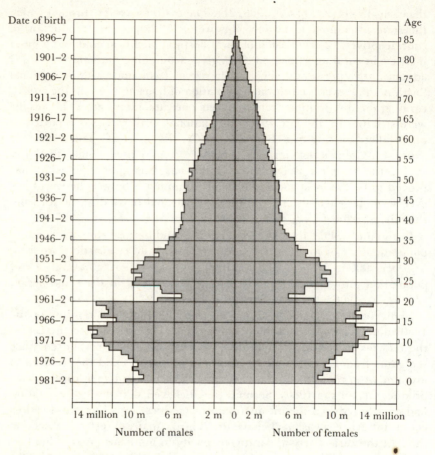

Figure 6.1 *Reported age—sex structure from the 10 per cent sample of 1982 census questionnaires (Banister, 1986, 164)*

upheavals in the late 1950s and 1960s. The 1982 census (see figure 6.1) revealed that the population cohort aged between 20 and 22 years of age (in 1981) was exceptionally small, owing to the collapse in fertility during the famine of 1959—61. *Ceteris paribus*, this would have tended to bring down the fertility rate as this relatively small cohort moved into the marriageable age groups in the early 1980s. Following close behind this relatively small cohort was a relatively very large cohort (figure 6.1) including people between the ages of 12 and 19 in 1981. Following the famine, the birth rate rose sharply, and stayed high during the mid and late 1960s until new policies were put into effect to bring it down. *Ceteris paribus*, the 'echo' effect of this would tend to raise the birth rate as this group moved into marriageable age from the mid-1980s through to the early 1990s. It is likely that a major part of the 'worrying' trends in China's vital statistics in the 1980s was due to these factors rather than to de-collectivization. However, critics argue that de-collectivization greatly reduced the capacity of China's leaders to control these pressures.

The leadership was deeply aware by the late 1970s of the problems likely to be encountered in controlling China's population growth after the mid-1980s on account of the 'echo' effect from the 1960s. As early as 1979 the government embarked upon a drastic programme — the 'one child policy' to control population growth:

> Upon careful study, the State Council deems it necessary to launch a crash programme over the coming twenty or thirty years calling on each couple, except those in national minority areas, to have a single child, so that the rate of population growth may be brought under control as soon as possible. Our aim is to strive to limit the population to a maximum of 1200 million by the end of the century. [Hua Guofeng, speaking in 1980 at the National People's Congress, quoted in Goodstadt, 1982, 381]

Official fears were expressed in the early 1980s too that de-collectivization would increase peasants' incentives to have more children.[70] It is not clear that this was, indeed, the case. First, it is unlikely that de-collectivization led to a general fall in the collective provision of benefits to elderly people in villages. In a large number of places pre-1978 such provision was rudimentary and often non-existent, as it still was in the mid-1980s. Consequently, over large parts of rural China the 'insurance' motive for reproduction was strong both before and after de-collectivization. In well-off areas the level of collective provision for old people was relatively good pre-1978 and improved significantly in the 1980s (thereby tending to reduce the incentive to reproduce). Secondly, it should not be forgotten that there was a strong incentive under the commune system for peasants to have many children in order to increase family income before the parents reached old age. Within communes' basic-level accounting units (usually 'production teams') there normally were quite wide differences in families' average per caput incomes, almost entirely dependent upon families' worker—dependant ratios (moderated to a small degree by skill and sex differences). Under this system there was a high incentive for an individual family to produce a lot of children so as to raise the family's share of (often static) collective distributed income. The tendency for families to think in quantitative ('more children') rather than qualitative ('fewer, but better educated children') terms was increased by the relatively low level of development of the more complex types of rural economic activities (farm sidelines and non-farm production) requiring higher levels of education. So, pre-1978, almost the only way to raise family income was to 'invest' in children.

These tendencies were reinforced by the low and slowly rising level of material and cultural consumption, which helped to perpetuate a traditional approach towards the family, in which children and family were given a prominent place in the peasants' set of values. The emergence of competing forms of self-fulfilment with rising living standards, as rapidly occurred in the 1980s, generally plays an important role in undermining the traditional approach towards the family.

The strong incentives to have large families under the commune system are reflected in the fact that even in the late 1960s, the birth rate still stood at the high level of the early 1950s. Enormous pressures were required to bring this down.

In fact, in certain respects the incentive to have children in the countryside was reduced post-1978. In rich areas the beginnings of a spontaneous transition towards small families was perceptible, attributable to rapidly expanding non-farm employment, improving collective provision of education (especially important in respect to women's attitudes to reproduction) and health facilities.

The key issue was how far the rural party apparatus wished and was able to control birth rates in those large areas of the Chinese countryside where the drive to have large families was as strong after as before de-collectivization.

The party's ability to coerce peasants into much lower reproduction rates than they would wish was, indeed, as strong as ever in the post-reform countryside. In the face of mounting concern about the huge numbers due to enter the marriageable ages from the mid-1980s to early 1990s, and reinforced by fears about the impact of rural reforms, the Chinese leadership panicked. From 1982 to 1984 a wide range of severe punitive measures was introduced to enforce the 'one child' policy rigorously.[71] The central authorities directed that all couples of child-bearing age with two or more children should be sterilized, that all women with one child or more should have an IUD inserted, and that all women pregnant without official authorization[72] should have abortions. A third child was to be 'absolutely prohibited' (Aird, 1986, 198).

After couples had received one-child certificates they were to be given 'health subsidies' in cash,[73] priority admission of the child to kindergartens and access to health facilities, priority in land allocation for housing and to be assigned lower sales quotas than other households ('Birth planning regulations', 1982). Severe fines were levied on those who exceeded the birth plan, and their real value was raised as the rural economy became more prosperous. Cadres could also manipulate the direct allocation of key inputs (e.g. petrol, chemical fertilizers, electricity) and licences for different types of business activity to penalize those not conforming to the birth plan. Ultimately, there was the possibility of straightforward physical coercion. As the campaign for the 'one-child family' reached a crescendo in 1983, there were widespread examples of extremely tough action by party cadres to achieve birth control targets. The most notorious case publicized outside China was that of Guangdong's Huiyang Prefecture, though it was far from unique. In this case, though, the leadership's activities in 1983 were reported in detail in the Hong Kong press:

In many communes in Dongguan County, where the campaign [in Huiyang Prefecture] was waged most fiercely, the pregnant women [who already had two or more children] were herded into 'study classes', where they were not allowed to talk to one another or to rejoin their families and were surrounded by 'work teams' who pressured them to have abortions regardless of the duration of pregnancy. Those who resisted were criticized in public meetings, harassed and humiliated. It was alleged that vehicles were sent to the villages to round up the pregnant women and take them to the hospital by force, creating a panic wherever they appeared. Individual respondents told of seeing women taken away in handcuffs, tied with ropes, or in cages used to transport hogs. In Huiding County it was said that arrest warrants were issued for some women on which the word 'pregnant' was written in the space indicating the crime committed. In urban areas, water and electricity were cut off for non-compliant households; in rural areas the electricity was cut off, the houses were sealed and fines were imposed. In one commune in Dongguan county, roof tiles were removed, the children of the family were turned out of doors and other families were warned not to feed them or they would be fined. In one instance, a pregnant school teacher fled to another community to save her second pregnancy, but her husband was arrested and confined in a 'water dungeon' until she returned and submitted to an abortion. The Dongguan Party secretary was quoted as saying that the purpose was to see to it that 'there is no road to heaven and no door in the earth' for the pregnant woman to escape through. [quoted in Aird, 1986, 208—9]

In face of the severity of this national party-led campaign to intervene in basic, intimate human rights, the ill-fated Indian campaign of 1976—7 pales into insignificance. The idea that the Chinese rural party apparatus had been rendered toothless by de-collectivization is seriously called into question by this campaign.

The wave of popular opposition that met this severe, effective campaign caused the Chinese government to pause and reconsider. The campaign to control the birth rate entered a new and rather more flexible phase in 1985—6. Greater variation in family size was permitted between regions. There was greater flexibility about allowing a second birth when the first child was a girl. This more relaxed, regionally differentiated approach played a considerable role in the upturn in the birth rate in 1985—6, allowing the underlying pressure arising from the exceptionally large cohort entering the marriageable age group to take effect.

INDIVIDUALISM AND MONEY-MAKING

Many Western admirers of the Maoist commune system and its collectivist ethos argued that 'making money' became the dominant goal of people's lives in China's villages in the 1980s. The collectivist thinking which, it is alleged, characterized the people's communes, had gone. In its place had been substituted a veritable obsession with making money. For example, writing about Hu Yaobang's speech of March 1983 entitled 'The Radiance of the Great Truth of Marxism Lights Our Way Forward', Orville Schell commented: '[W]hile I was in China I met no-one who was drawing "wisdom and strength" from Marxism, much less moving forward under the light of its "radiance" ... What I saw and felt instead was the "radiance" of people making money' (Schell, 1984). However, there are a number of points to make about this perspective. First, how many peasants in pre-1978 China were really guided by the 'radiance' of Mao Tsetung's thought? If peasants really were prepared to work selflessly for the collective would the results not have been better? Second, if Mao's ideals were far removed from the masses' outlook, what right did Mao and his followers have to impose their views on the masses? A case can be made for strong leadership with certain limitations on democratic rights in some cases, but there surely is no case for attempted mass thought control? Third, I have argued that there was, indeed, a wide gap between the peasant masses' outlook and that which Mao attempted to instil in them, and that the policies stemming from this (e.g. on workpoint differentials and income ceilings) were a major cause of poor collective performance and mass dissatisfaction. It should be noted, however, that, given Mao's desire to establish collective farms, his attempts to change peasant consciousness — to 'fight self and 'serve the people' — made sense, for only if peasants indeed were prepared to work hard for the collective could mutual trust be established and the 'free rider' problem overcome. Fourth, it has been argued that it is misleading to suggest that the only force at work in China after the reforms was individual money-making. There was still a powerful set of policies complementing individual pursuit of profit in the pursuit of other goals — those which attempted to provide collective goods, those which assisted the local poor and others living in regional concentrations of poverty. In these respects China was still doing well compared to most poor countries. Fifth, of course the pursuit of individual money-making had become vastly more important than pre-1978, but it has to be recognized that this drive, with suitable assistance from co-operative, collective and state action, proved a much more potent weapon for raising China's level of labour productivity and standard of living than Maoist collectivism. The narrow-minded short-term pursuit of 'socialist' goals, such as 'more equality' can damage the achievement of more important long-term goals, notably relieving poverty and raising mass living standards. Indeed, the achievement of these (latter) goals can be regarded as the prerequisites for a truly socialist society, since without them it is in effect impossible for the general public to run their own affairs — education and a certain amount of leisure are essential for this.

CONCLUSIONS

This chapter has examined eight areas in which it is argued by many Western observers that de-collectivization of agriculture was accompanied by serious problems in the Chinese countryside: (1) faltering agricultural growth rates, (2) undesirable shifts in the structure of farm production, (3) increased class inequality, (4) widening spatial inequality, (5) deterioration of the rural welfare system, (6) decline of rural capital accumulation, (7) population growth, (8) obsession with money-making. The major conclusions reached on each of these issues are as follows:

1 Faltering agricultural growth rates. Chinese agriculture enjoyed a period of extraordinary dynamism from the late 1970s to the mid-1980s. This formed the basis of a major improvement in the Chinese population's diet. I have argued that the institutional changes of the late 1970s and early 1980s were the main cause of this. Over the long term in a country of China's size and given reasonable assumptions about the income elasticity of demand, it would be unlikely that farm growth would

continue at the high per caput rate of this period. Indeed, in 1984–6
growth slowed down, though it was still quite fast compared to other
developing countries. Predicting the likely future growth rate of farm
output is extremely difficult. There are, indeed, uncertainties about
rural institutions, but the main question mark hangs over farm price
policy in its multiple aspects. Without further substantial increases in
the relative price of agricultural products it is hard to see how output is
going to increase rapidly in the future. This is a highly politicized issue,
because of the consequential effect on urban prices and it is impossible to
predict the outcome. Should the Chinese leadership take the path of
substantially raising farm purchase prices it is essential that the poorest
urban groups are, at least partially, protected from the effects.

2   Structure of the rural economy. Two issues were examined here. The
first was that of the balance between the farm and the non-farm economy.
Unquestionably, the fastest rural growth rates in the mid-1980s were in
the non-farm sector. However, there is not necessarily a contradiction
between growth in the rural farm and non-farm sectors. Indeed,there is
often a positive, symbiotic relationship between them; as labour moves
out of agriculture it opens up the possibility for raising agricultural
labour productivity more rapidly. The second issue examined in this
section was that of grain production. Undeniably, grain output grew
much less rapidly than other parts of the farm economy in the 1980s.
However, direct human consumption of grain was relatively high by
mid-1980s. Across the whole spectrum of the Chinese leadership there
was a deep commitment at least to sustain this level of per caput grain
output. In the mid-1980s this was being achieved by a combination of
administrative measures (the 'fixed contract purchase system') and price
policy. Insofar as it was possible to judge, it seemed likely that 'administrative' methods in this vital objective would remain important for many
areas. Given the fundamental importance of grain it was, surely, correct
that this should be so? Even the 'pro-price reform' Chinese Academy of
Social Sciences' Price Reform Group argued that this ought to be so: 'In
China, the conditions needed for completely regulating [grain] output
through the market have very far from matured (*hai yuan yuan mei you
chengshou*) . . . Thus, within agricultural commodity prices, the system of
market prices and state-unified prices with fixed contract prices as the
principal form cannot but co-exist for a relatively long period of time.'
(Chinese Academy, 1987, 20). Despite de-collectivization the state still
possessed a wide array of administrative powers to enforce the desired
level of grain output and marketings, should 'economic' (i.e. price)
measures fail to do so. Indeed, it is worth remembering that the Chinese

state was able to influence deeply the structure of farm output and marketings in the 1950s prior to the collectivization of agriculture through a combination of price policy and administrative measures (Perkins, 1966, ch. 3). The main question concerned the degree to which there would be growth of grain output in order to raise meat consumption. If the state allowed meat prices to reflect costs of production fully then it is unlikely that demand would be such as to stimulate a rapid growth of grain output for this purpose. On the other hand, if the state continued to use administrative means to depress the grain price and profitability then the supply response from peasants would be unlikely to produce a rapid growth of grain output to be used as animal feed.[74]

3 Village class relations. In the absence of detailed studies of the kind available for most developing countries, only superficial analysis of this issue was possible. It is extraordinary that in a country in which Marx and Lenin are taken so seriously, their methodology for the analysis of class relations is not applied in conducting village studies in China in the 1980s. Judgements must be tempered, also, by awareness of the great diversity of class relations that one would expect to find in a country of China's huge land area and population, though this chapter did try to draw some tentative general conclusions. The number of rural wage labourers certainly rose rapidly after 1978, mostly employed in non-farm work. However, wage labourers still constituted a small proportion of the rural workforce, mostly working for collective enterprises—though neither small size nor collective employment implies good working conditions. The removal of income ceilings, combined with the increased impact of market forces, unquestionably led to a much wider range of income and consumption differentials within any given village, especially in certain areas. Although the rural tax system is far from perfect, the Chinese state quickly introduced measures to attempt to control the incomes of the highest rural income earners via a progressive income tax on individual enterprises. The operation of the credit system, however, gives cause for concern in relation to its class impact.

Already, by the mid-1980s, there were signs that some permanent 'congealing' of class relations within villages was occurring, reducing the high degree of flexibility in socioeconomic structure characteristic of the Maoist period. However, there were some important factors tending to sustain mobility between stratificational positions. Compared to most poor countries, access to education and health facilities was, in most areas, relatively easy for all social strata, so that permanent stratified inequalities in human capital were likely to be relatively small. Access to land was guaranteed to all rural dwellers by the egalitarian redistribution of farmland in the early 1980s, and a competitive market for rented land should be able to meet changing future requirements (as worker − dependant ratios alter, for example). Access to necessary lumpy inputs (such as crop spraying, processing and irrigation) was still open to all villagers via the collective ownership of many of these facilities (irrigation, in particular). Easily divisible inputs (especially chemical fertilizer) were mainly allocated through state administrative channels rather than market forces. Whilst this meant that local political processes played an important role in their distribution, state control of the allocation of some inputs could enable it to influence the rural economy in socially desirable ways.[75] The rapid expansion of employment opportunities in rural non-farm enterprises in the 1980s almost certainly had an equalizing effect on intra-village income differentials. Most importantly, perhaps, for a wide range of rural economic activities (both agricultural and non-agricultural), start-up costs were low, there was ease of entry and few scale economies. These characteristics of 'petty capitalist commodity production' should ensure in the foreseeable future a reasonable degree of fluidity in the village class structure.

4   Spatial inequality. Areas with locational advantages were held back under Maoist policies. The reforms of the late 1970s and early 1980s enabled well-placed areas to achieve relatively large increases in labour productivity and income per person. Poorly located (often mountainous) districts, with inferior natural conditions, poor transport and, often, with weaker human capital resources, generally experienced much smaller absolute (and, often, relative) increases in labour productivity and incomes. Both at the end of the Maoist period and in the mid-1980s, poverty was highly concentrated spatially. In the mid-1980s, the range of spatial income and consumption differentials was very wide − in most respects, much wider than at the end of the Maoist period. However, many policies in this period, either intentionally or unintentionally, helped poorer areas to achieve absolute growth (even though their relative position frequently became worse): de-collectivization, increased freedom to determine the production structure, and improvement in the agricultural−industrial terms of trade benefited these areas in addition to well-located ones, while the rapid growth of the whole rural economy made possible an increase in state assistance to poor regions and provided opportunities through the market for poor areas to increase their prosperity (e.g. via remittances from migrants, and by producing specialist products to meet growing demands as incomes rose in other areas). Even though growth was uneven, it was deeply-rooted, and virtually all *xian* experienced at least some increase in average real incomes from the late 1970s to the mid-1980s.

Indicators of inequality for the whole rural population combine both local and spatial processes. Overall indicators of income inequality show a clear increase (table 6.19).

Table 6.19   *Share of rural income taken by different sections of the rural population, 1979 and 1984*

	Proportion of total rural income in:	
Segment of rural population	1978	1984
Top 25% of income earners	47.7	51.7
Middle 50% of income earners	43.0	40.1
Bottom 25% of income earners	9.3	8.2

National sample survey of over 37 000 rural households.
Source: Rural Survey Group, 1986, 7

The spatial range of production conditions and incomes in rural China is now enormous. The Maoist path of tightly holding back rich areas was deeply unsatisfactory, stifling the growth from which could come the resources to help resolve poverty. The state did much in the 1980s to assist poor areas. However, it must be stressed that, despite huge achievements, a large number of Chinese peasants still live in abysmal conditions. Looking at the enormous disparities in rural incomes between different areas, one cannot help feeling that still more should be done to transfer resources from rich to poor areas, and that it could be done intelligently through, for example, a well-constructed tax system without adverse effects on rich areas' 'production enthusiasm'.

5 Welfare and human capital. Problems with maintaining individual contributions to collective welfare funds certainly were encountered after de-collectivization. However, increases in funding occurred from other sources — increased revenue from collective enterprises, increased fees (paid by a now much better off peasantry), and increased state (especially *xian*) outlays. The increased funding was made possible by a more prosperous rural economy, albeit that a smaller proportion of total income might now have been allocated to these purposes. In education, peasants' demands shifted sharply, with a rapid decline in numbers attending secondary schools. However, attendance at primary school was still at a high level compared with other poor countries. Moreover, there was a massive increase in rural education obtained via informal channels such as television, radio and magazines. In the health system, there also was a big structural shift, with a decline in part-time health workers, and a big increase in the provision of professional health care.

Help for the locally poor in aggregate expanded considerably in the 1980s, based mainly on increased provision by collectives, which, in turn, rested on increased rural prosperity stimulated by the reforms. In welfare provision, as in personal income, the regional disparities in the mid-1980s still were extremely wide, but simply because much more information is now available about the low quality of welfare in poor areas, one should not be misled into thinking that conditions have deteriorated.

6 Accumulation and physical capital. Far from declining, as many commentators feared, total rural investment grew rapidly after 1978. Naturally, given the nature of the rural reforms, a large increase occurred in the share of private investment, and in poorer areas where the non-farm economy was weak, the collective's share in total investment was very small indeed by the mid-1980s (the 'Wenzhou' path). In addition, a substantial shift took place in the structure of fixed investment away from agriculture towards the rural non-farm economy, and, within agricultural investment, away from fixed investment towards current inputs. Fragmentation of holdings reappeared with many accompanying problems. The worst of these was the obstacle this provided to mechanization of field work, though this was to some degree found to be self-resolving, in that the areas where such mechanization was economically desirable were those in which the process of land consolidation was most advanced. The possibility of severe deterioration in land quality due to privatization was greatly reduced by the establishment of long tenures on land contracted from the collective and by the granting of inheritance rights to land contracts. In addition, changed methods of organising care of forestry resources probably resulted in a net decline in soil loss through deforestation. Total resources allocated to water conservation probably fell in the eighties. However, this was not necessarily a problem, since China had already achieved an extremely high irrigation ratio, and it was probably rational to allocate fewer resources to this activity than in the past, and to concentrate those resources on improving the quality of water control work.

7 Population growth. A renewed upward movement in birth rates occurred in the mid-1980s. To a considerable degree this was attributable to an exceptionally large population cohort entering the marriageable age rather than to an increased motivation for peasants to have children after de-collectivization. The severity of the 'One child family' campaign in the early 1980s, culminating in the often brutal excesses of 1983, does not support the belief that the party's capacity to influence peasants' birth plans had been greatly reduced. Moreover, it lends support to the

view that, despite considerable problems in the rural party apparatus in the early 1980s as policies changed violently from 'serve the people' to 'take the lead in getting rich', the party still wielded considerable power in the villages. The party's back-tracking in 1985–6 in the face of great popular discontent helpled allow the birth rate to rise again, but the rate was still low compared to other developing countries.

8   Obsession with money-making. It was argued that the main change had been in official ideology and in what constituted legitimate behaviour. It may have been illegal for peasants, under Mao, to produce, buy and sell at a profit for themselves and their families, but it is quite improbable in the light of what happened before and after Mao (and, indeed, under him) that the drive to do so was ever transformed. This chapter argues, moreover, that this productive, useful drive was central in propelling the advance of China's rural productive forces after 1978 just as it had been in often disadvantageous circumstances, pre-1955.[76] Furthermore, I have argued that this force was not wholly uncontrolled, but rather that the parameters within which it operated were powerfully influenced by state action in the interest of socially desirable goals at different levels.

7

Conclusion

Mo shi guo he, 'crossing the river by touching the stones under the water' (i.e. groping one's way across the river).

    A description of China's economic reforms in the 1980s

Contrasting visions of rural development This book has argued that in the socialist countries from the time of the Soviet debates in the 1920s through to the present day, there have been two fundamentally opposed visions of rural development. The 'Bukharinist' vision is sympathetic to individual farming, and to the positive role of market forces, while recognizing the crucial function both of co-operation and appropriate state action. The 'Stalinist' vision is hostile to individual entrepreneurship and to 'petty capitalistic' production, and confident in the state's ability to control directly the rural production process in the broader social interest. Even over the long periods in the socialist countries when Stalinist collective farms were the only permitted form of rural institution, the appeal of an alternative approach remained alive, if only as an unpublished, stigmatized sub-culture in political life. Indeed, the very virulence with which the 'capitalist' road in the countryside has been attacked in the socialist countries is eloquent testimony to the enduring presence of Bukharinist, 'NEP' ideas − whether in the form given them by such diverse figures as Deng Xiaoping, Liu Shaoqi, Chen Yun or Zhao Ziyang. This can be easily seen by the speed with which these ideas surfaced on the occasions when ideological controls were lifted. In China, the most vivid examples of this were the 'Hundred Flowers' in 1957, the relaxation in the early 1960s prior to the 'Socialist Education Movement', and, finally, in the late 1970s after the death of Mao. In the Soviet Union, the 'NEP model' re-emerged as an explicit rallying point for market socialist ideas in the post-Stalinist period (Lewin, 1975). Gorbachev is reported as having said to top party officials in 1986:

'When NEP was introduced, people's living standards rose fourfold. Why should you object to such an improvement today?' ('A 1921 lesson for Russia', 1987, 51).

Even in advanced economies with huge accumulations of capital petty commodity production can perform a useful role in certain sectors.[1] In poor developing countries, with limited development of transport and modern industry, petty commodity production carried on in small units of production (not just in the villages, but in cities too) is an immensely powerful force. It rests generally on intense exploitation of self, family, or of a small number of wage labourers. The principal motivation for the hard labour of the myriads of entrepreneurs involved is, simply, to improve the living conditions of their families, but it can prove a powerful engine for the development of the productive forces, unleashing the physical and intellectual activity of large numbers of people in response to widening market opportunities. To stimulate of this force requires a reasonable degree of security for the petty commodity producers, in terms of their property rights and the inheritance of those rights, and rights to retain a certain proportion (not necessarily all) of the income deriving from their efforts. The stifling of that force in the Soviet Union under Stalin and in China under Mao placed a severe constraint on overall growth and helped reduce the efficiency of resource use since petty commodity producers tend to squeeze out the last drop of output from capital goods. The liberation of that long-suppressed force in rural China after 1978 was a major factor in the explosion of productivity that occurred in that period.

Collective farms and China's rural economic performance   The issue of collective farms has been at the centre of this difference of vision. The question is deeply important, directly affecting the lives of hundreds of millions of peasants in the socialist countries, and having a powerful influence on the whole shape of those countries' politics and economics. China is not the first country to have de-collectivized agriculture, but it is much the most important and the only one to have done so after such a long history of collective agriculture. At the time this book was being written (Autumn 1986—Summer 1987) the Chinese rural reforms had been in place for over eight years since their tentative beginnings in late 1978 and for four years since their full flowering in 1982—3. It was, therefore, a timely point at which to examine the performance of the de-collectivized Chinese countryside and to see what general lessons could be learned from it for other socialist countries and for those outside them interested in rural economic policies.

The contrasts in China's rural economic performance pre- and post-reforms is extraordinary. Whether one looks at growth of output per caput, or at productivity of land, labour and capital, a massive change took place that provided the basis for a major leap forward in the standard of living in both town and countryside. By any criterion, this was an event of major historical importance. Unfortunately, it is impossible to reach unambiguous conclusions about this phenomenon. Other factors intervened in producing the results observed, notably a whole set of both demand- and supply-side interactions between the urban and rural economies. However, the logic of the analysis in this book suggests that an important part of the explanation for the observed results lies with the nature of collective farms. This view is strengthened by analysis of the post-war Soviet economy, in which many (though not all) of the urban industrial supply-side problems were eased, with only limited improvement in collective farm performance.

Labour supervision in collective farms In most circumstances, there are generally high costs in organizing agricultural labour in large centrally directed units. These costs affect not just the rural economy's output from given resources, but also its capacity to grow: the peasants' drive to improve their skills, to seek better ways of producing output, to branch into producing new types of output, is reduced; also, of course, if at each period of time, less is produced from given resources, then the potentially investible surplus for growth at each point is reduced. Only under quite exceptional conditions is it likely that collective cultivation will work well. Indeed, it is these small number of exceptions (e.g. Israeli *kibbutzim*), in which peasants' mutual trust is, indeed, established that shed so much light on what generally is absent in socialist countries' collectives. It is not a coincidence that under private agriculture one rarely encounters farms with a large number of hired workers. Nor is it a coincidence that it is rare for peasants voluntarily to pool their farmland.

Collective farms do not necessarily have to operate with a narrow range of earnings differentials. However, in practice, they have generally been characterized (both in China and elsewhere) by a fairly narrow band of earnings per labour day in respect to ordinary farm work. This is only partially due to an ideological preference for narrow differentials. It reflects also the fact that it is impossible in agriculture to devise a payment system which rewards workers in a large unit in proportion to work accomplished. It is much less troublesome to pay all workers more or less similar amounts for each day that they turn up for work. Unless collective workers trust each other and/or are highly motivated to work for the collective good irrespective of their remuneration compared to others, then a narrow band of differentials in remuneration for a day's collective labour is likely to produce an adverse effect on labour motivation. Unfortunately, the conditions necessary to avoid this problem are rarely encountered, and 'free riders' are commonplace in collective farms.

Moreover, agricultural production is critically dependent on the workers' flexible response to unpredictable natural conditions, so that, much more even than in industry, lack of diligence on the worker's part reduces output below its potential level with the available resources.

Inadequacies of the free market   In analysing the reasons for the relative prosperity of Britain in the eighteenth century, Adam Smith formulated his famous hypothesis concerning the importance of competitive entrepreneurs:

> Little else is required to carry a state to the highest level of opulence from the lowest barbarism, but peace, easy taxes, and a tolerable administration of justice. ... The natural effort of every individual to better his own condition, when suffered to exert itself with freedom and security, is so powerful a principle that it is alone, and without any assistance, not only capable of carrying on the society to wealth and prosperity, but of surmounting a hundred impertinent obstructions with which the folly of human laws encumbers its operation... [Smith, 1776, vol. 1, 540]

Smith, surely, was correct in his identification of competitive entrepreneurship as a dynamic force in economic development? However, subsequent experience suggests that simply removing obstructions to entrepreneurship is far from sufficient to lift an economy from poverty to prosperity.[2] Logic and the practical experience of rapidly growing economies such as Meiji Japan, Singapore, Taiwan and South Korea, suggest that market failure has to be overcome through activity above the level of the individual entrepreneur. Indeed, it is often forgotten that Smith himself devoted a large part of volume 2 of the *Wealth of Nations* to analysing the ways in which the state needed to supplement for market failure, 'erecting and maintaining those public institutions and those public works which, though they may be in the highest degree advantageous to a great society, are, however, of such a nature that the profit could never repay the expence to any individual or small number of individuals, and which it therefore cannot be expected that any individual or small number of individuals should erect or maintain' (Smith, 1776, vol. 2, 244).

Although collective cultivation of the soil and collective income distribution are formidable barriers to good farm performance, co-operation of one kind or another is frequently essential. The state (central or local) often has acted as the agency to ensure (more or less voluntarily) that activities vital to the farm economy, but which the market fails to provide, are carried out. The most striking instances of this are state-directed irrigation and drainage projects using conscripted peasant labour.

However, they include also a wide array of state-funded (or partially state-funded) schemes – research institutions (whose potential contribution to growth is enormous), rural transport networks, provision of information, organizing food stores, support for rural education and health, insurance schemes, marketing agencies, provision of credit, etc. These vital activities rarely take the form of a free transfer from the non-farm sector, but are more generally financed directly or indirectly by peasant contributions, and can be regarded as a form of state-led co-operation. It should be noted that such 'state'–directed activity has by no means always been organized by the central government. For example, in Imperial China, an important part of the organizational network for such schemes was the local 'gentry' who often had only quasi-official positions, not even being paid a salary by the state apparatus. In China in the 1980s, the most important level at which the state organized such activities was the *xian*, i.e. the 'local' state apparatus embracing up to around one million people (mostly peasants).

Throughout history peasants have also, to different degrees in different types of political, social and ecological environments, and under different degrees of population pressure, themselves devised co-operative arrangements of one kind or another. These do not necessarily enable villagers to benefit equally, nor are they necessarily democratically run, but they are, indeed, locally evolved, non-state institutions which do permit a higher level of rural productivity to be achieved. These range from the widespread practice in Asian rice agriculture of labour exchange at peak times in the agricultural season, to co-operative purchase of lumpy inputs both traditional (e.g. draft animals) and modern (e.g. tractors), to locally run institutions to control water supply, and, of course, include a myriad of organizations found in the agricultural sector of the advanced capitalist countries.

Arriving at the correct solutions to questions of lumpiness and economies of scale in the rural economy is complex, and there are few general rules that apply. The desirable outcome in each case is likely to be a different blend of individual provision, state-organized co-operation and co-operation organized independently by groups of peasants. However, only if these problems are solved and a suitable framework established can the dynamic force of rural petty commodity production be released to full effect.

Spatial issues in rural development   Analysis of massive economies such as China and the USSR makes one acutely aware of the importance of spatial issues in rural development. Collective farms *per se* do not have big implications for this question. However, the policies associated with collective farms, and facilitated by that institutional form, do affect it substantially. Collective farms can be used, as they were under Mao, as a vehicle to 'solve' spatial inequality through simply intervening to prevent collectives in well-located areas from raising the level of distributed income. However, such a solution is crude, and has the effect of seriously damaging production incentives in well-located areas' collectives, thereby tending to slow the growth of the whole rural economy, which in turn tends to limit the resources available to the state to try to resolve the problems of poorly located areas. Indeed, under the Maoist system, the state had so few resources available to help backward peasant communities that the main path for these areas to improve their position was '*ziligengsheng*' — literally, 'regeneration through one's own efforts' or, less literally, 'pull oneself up by one's own bootstraps'. Under most collective farm systems, peasants' geographical mobility has been tightly controlled, this being made possible by the collectives' control over access to a large proportion of peasants' food consumption and by, of course, preventing peasants having access to farmland in areas to which they might wish to migrate. Collective farms have provided an effective mechanism for tying poor peasants to their own poorly-endowed regions—at least some people in the backward regions of other poor countries have been able to migrate to better lives. The capacity of socialist countries to pursue within the collective farm institution well-worked-out policies towards rural spatial issues is heavily reliant on their having a coherent approach towards differential agricultural 'rental' income. However, analysis of this issue under both Stalin and Mao was notable for its absence, owing, in part, to the sheer difficulty of measuring differential rental income in a non-market system in which most farm prices are set by the state according to crude and often inconsistent criteria.

Collective farms and intra-village inequality A major attraction of collective farms in the eyes of many people is their elimination of exploitation through land rent, usury and wage labour, which frequently combine in a set of 'inter-locked' markets in non-socialist poor economies. Not only is this form of socioeconomic relationship abolished in collective farms but the prospect is held out, too, of personal income distribution being conducted on fair principles ('to each according to their work') and with due consideration for the needs of the least well-endowed section of the village (a portion of personal income distributed 'according to need'). In addition, a striking feature of collective farms is the high degree of mobility in average incomes among their members (though it must be stressed, good data on this are absent). Elimination of most local inequalities in asset ownership, relatively equal access among the local community to the means of human capital formation, and guaranteed access to relatively equally remunerated collective employment, all tend to provide for a high degree of mobility over time in villagers' income positions.

No slogan has generated more ire in the socialist countries than that which Bukharin enunciated as the basis of Soviet NEP in the 1920s:

> Our policy in relation to the countryside should develop in the direction of removing, and in part abolishing, many restrictions which put the brake on the growth of the well-to-do and kulak farm. To the peasants, to all the peasants, we must say: Enrich yourselves, develop your farms, and do not fear that constraint will be put on you... However paradoxical it may appear, we must develop the well-to-do farm in order to help the poor peasant and the middle peasant. [quoted in Carr, 1970, 2801]

Similar slogans formed the underlying philosophy of China's brief periods of 'NEP' in the early 1950s and early 1960s. Faced with the desperate need to raise rural production, the party leadership appealed to individual peasant incentives, with calls to 'expand the household and become rich' (*fa jia zhi fu*) and 'become rich through hard labour' (*gin dong zhi fu*). In 1950 the official Chinese party journal 'Study' (*Xuexi*) argued:

> If the peasants are afraid to become rich they will do enough to be able to have enough to eat and drink but no more. They will have no enthusiasm for increasing the application of fertilizers, raising their technical level, and for expanded reproduction. Their productive power will decline, the harvest will get smaller. In order to do away with this sort of erroneous thinking and to sweep away the peasants' worries about expanding production, we should resolutely protect land and other property rights and determinedly protect the land and other property rights of rich peasants. We should allow unrestricted loans, interest fixed by the peasants themselves, and insist on repayment of loans. We should permit the hiring of labour. We should advocate that 'working hard to become rich' is glorious and that 'becoming poor because one has not produced anything' is shameful. [Shang, 1950]

In the Chinese countryside of the early 1980s no set of slogans better symbolized the sea change in leadership philosophy than the switch from the Maoist 'serve the people' (*wei renmin fuwu*) to 'take the lead in getting rich' (*xian fu·qilai*).

Encouraging individual peasants to become well-off was accepted by most commentators in the socialist countries to be inseparable from intra-village class polarization. Typical of such views was Shang Gedong's in the midst of China's post-1949 land reform campaign:

> There are some peasants who, due to relatively strong production conditions, because they work hard and are good at management, expand their economy and gradually get rich. Among them is a small group who may carry out exploitation and become new rich peasants. On the other hand there are some peasants who, due to deficient production conditions, or lack of work effort, or because they are not good at management, or because they endure unavoidable misfortune, cannot expand their economy, and gradually become poorer. Among them is a section that cannot avoid being exploited and which turns into the new poor and hired peasants. In this way class differentiation develops. Under the situation in which the Chinese economy is still backward, this differentiation is beneficial to the development of production. Quite a number of peasants hope that they themselves will become well-off, and so they are enthusiastic in production, and expand the household in order to become rich. The rich peasant economy is quite a bit above the small peasant economy in terms of productive strength. Because rich peasants have better conditions in respect to agricultural implements, technology and fertilizers, their land productivity is higher. Thus, at the present time, class differentiation should not be feared. [Shang, 1950]

Two major points can be made about this issue. The first is that, as Shang reminds us, the 'cost' of the development of unequal class relations has to be set against the 'benefit' of a possible stimulus to rural production with potentially beneficial consequences for the whole economy, and for the reduction of absolute poverty. The second is that the degree to which intra-village inequality develops under such circumstances is likely to be less than many critics (both inside and outside the socialist countries) of the Bukharinist 'take the lead in getting rich' approach imagine, especially if appropriate action is taken by the state. There are a number of reasons why this is so. First, the possibility of cumulative development of intra-village inequality is greatly reduced if farm modernization takes place in the wake of a reasonably egalitarian land reform. Second, many important modern farm inputs are non-lumpy, and can be purchased by all farm strata, giving them all the chance to benefit from new technology, albeit to different degrees. Third, as long as the state does not attempt to stifle it, and especially if suitable policies are taken to encourage it, it is likely that as incomes rise in a poor country there will be a lengthy period during which output and employment in small-scale rural non-farm enterprises expands rapidly. This generally has an equalizing effect on intra-village income distribution. Fourth, the possibility for all village strata to benefit from rural growth is increased greatly if the state apparatus (frequently locally) and/or peasants themselves co-operatively, are able to provide an array of public goods, including health, education, transport, information, irrigation, credit, processing facilities, marketing, insurance, research, crop spraying and so on. The more that such provisions are made, the more powerful, too, is likely to be the operation of intertemporal movements in positions in the village class structure, at-tributable to changes in worker–dependant ratios over the course of the family cycle (i.e. 'Chayanovian' elements in rural differentiation). Finally, although taxing rural wealth and/or incomes is not easy, it is not beyond the wit of a well-motivated state to devise methods to tax extremely high rural incomes should these emerge. One obvious, and relatively straight-forward method is a rates levy on the size or value of domestic housing. However, since most rural economic activities, given reasonable state policies in the respects outlined above, are characterized by relatively easy entry, low economies of scale and very competitive product and factor markets, it is unlikely that exceptionally high incomes would remain so for any length of time. In the much-discussed Wenzhou case in China in the mid-1980s, for example, the extraordinarily high incomes of 'buyers and sellers' of buttons were unlikely to remain without attracting a host of new entrants, in turn driving down the income from this activity.

In sum, encouraging petty capitalist commodity production is, indeed, likely to encourage intra-village inequality in a modernizing poor economy. This was shown clearly in the analysis of post-1978 China. However, as this book has emphasized repeatedly, 'unequal growth' and 'polarization' are quite distinct phenomena. Even in the absence of appropriate state action the alarmist Leninist 'polarization' thesis seems to be based on a misconception about economies of scale in agriculture. If suitable state action is taken then there are real possibilities for making use of the market mechanism in the rural areas to stimulate growth in an unequal but not polarizing fashion, and in which there is considerable fluidity over time in peasant households' position in the village class structure.

Moreover, inequality of asset ownership and incomes is not the only meaningful kind of inequality. Although collective farms are able to perform 'well' in terms of these aspects of economic inequality, in respect to other kinds of inequality there is reason to be deeply concerned. A central impulse behind the formation of collective farms in the socialist countries was a desire on the part of the party leadership to remould peasant consciousness. One can question this as being plain unrealistic. It was far-fetched to imagine that the frequently impoverished, individualistic peasant populations of Russia, Eastern Europe, China, South-east Asia and Africa, could develop a collectivist mentality of the kind exhibited by a tiny number of highly committed (mostly intellectual) Jewish refugees. To persuade them to build on traditional forms of co-operation was feasible and sensible, but to attempt to create a fully collective rural society was, in hindsight, utterly unrealistic. Not only was such a project unrealistic, but it was highly questionable from the simplest moral standpoint. This was a gigantic exercise in social engineering – an extraordinarily arrogant, undemocratic attempt by a tiny minority to transform massively the thinking of the vast majority of these countries' population. Such an attempted revolutionary change involved enormous risks, especially in view of the essential economic role of the agricultural sector as the producer of food in a poor economy with only limited possibilities to trade non-food for food products internationally.

I have argued that not all collectivization was forcible. There is reasonable evidence to suggest that a large proportion of Chinese peasants were persuaded of the virtues of collective farms in the mid-1950s (there is even stronger evidence that very few Russian peasants in the late 1920s/early 1930s considered that collective farms were a desirable form of rural organization). However, even if peasants entered collective farms voluntarily, even if all cadres were extremely skilful and sensitive in their relations with collectives, which they were not, and even if the state had been committed to democratic operation of collective farms (so that collective farms might have been genuinely termed 'producer cooperatives'), which it was not, then the problems in principle with collective farms which this book identifies, especially those arising from the difficulties of devising an adequate payments system in the absence of mutual trust, would rapidly have led to peasant disillusion with the unsatisfactory aspects of the institution, necessitating considerable cadre pressure to keep peasants inside the institution and cadre control over peasants' collective labour. Through one channel or another, collective farms would have become characterized by tight control over the labour process exercised undemocratically by cadres, a small minority of the peasant population. The fact that Chinese local cadres under Mao followed the 'mass line' and often lived in physical conditions much closer to those of the mass of the peasants than was generally the case in Soviet and East European collective farms does not alter the similarity in the distribution of power within the collective farms.

Collective farms and capital accumulation To socialist countries' governments, the collective farm holds out an enticing prospect. The Stalinist and

Maoist 'growth models' had a common belief in the central role of capital accumulation in economic growth. The collective farm appeared to them to provide an instrument for ensuring high rates of rural saving and investment, and for transferring (initially at least) a portion of rural savings to finance urban industrialization.

Unfortunately, as has been seen, enforcing too high a rate of mobilization of 'surplus' labour for capital construction and reinvestment of increments to rural income can have a dampening effect on rural incentives. Moreover, given the low efficiency wih which collective farms have tended to use capital goods, a high rate of rural investment under collective farms can, in a sense, be regarded as a reflection of this failure to use resources effectively (indeed, a lot of capital is required in this system to sustain increases in output) rather than as an indication of success.

I have suggested too, that although collective farms do provide the state with the ability to control rural marketing tightly, 'siphoning off the rural surplus' (irrespective of whether or not this is a desirable thing to attempt) has proved (as both the Chinese and Soviet cases show) to be much more difficult than the supporters of collective farms imagined. Agriculture's need for industrial wage goods has been greater than anticipated owing to rapid rural population growth and slow change in the structure of employment (especially in China), as well as on account of the poor performance of rural handicraft production. Agriculture's need for industrial capital goods has also been much greater than anticipated, due to the low efficiency with which they have been used in collective farms and to the poor performance (disastrous in the Soviet First Five Year Plan) of animal motive power under collective farms. Thus, there have been powerful, unanticipated forces tending to produce a net import surplus for the farm sector.[3]

The evidence presented in chapter 6 of this book demonstrates that, given the appropriate conditions, individual peasant households have a high propensity to save and accumulate capital. The only circumstances under which collective farms are 'necessary' to 'force up the rate of accumulation in the villages' is where these conditions (e.g. security, reasonable prices, availability of industrial inputs and 'incentive' goods) are lacking. In these disadvantageous circumstances, such a strategy becomes a further factor in helping to reduce the effectiveness of collective labour and reducing the productivity of rural productive resources below their potential.

Poverty, inequality and economic growth   The relationship between poverty, inequality and economic growth is both extremely complex, and, yet, of central importance in poor countries.[4] This book has argued that collective farms tend to play the following role in this relationship. At the local level collective farms can serve as effective vehicles for ensuring that out of given resources a certain amount is set aside to meet the needs of poor people in the community, though it was argued that collective farms are not the only method through which this might be achieved. Other communities have achieved a great deal in these respects without collective farms. Local inequalities from rental income and in asset ownership tend to be greatly reduced in collective farms, and overall local income inequalities tend to be less than one would expect to find in the absence of collectivization, though the contrast with villages which had experienced an effective land reform but not collectivization (e.g. Taiwan in the 1950s and 1960s, the USSR in the 1920s, China in the early 1950s) is unlikely to be large. At the spatial level it has been seen that collective farms can serve as excellent vehicles for controlling regional income differences by simply preventing well-located collectives increasing distributed income. Unfortunately there are substantial costs to this strategy in relation to growth of output in such areas. There is little intrinsic to collective farms that helps them solve regional problems through resource re-allocation or local self-help better than alternative rural institutional set-ups. Indeed, because of the tendency of collective farms in various ways to slow down both the national and the rural economic growth below its potential, and, of course, their tendency to be associated with rigid controls on migration, collective farms are likely to be much worse at solving problems of regional concentrations of poverty than some other rural institutional forms. In sum, there is a serious danger that collective farms may tend to perform quite 'well' in solving local poverty and controlling both local and regional income inequality, but at the cost of slow growth and an inability to solve perhaps the most important problem of all in poor countries — large regional concentrations of poverty.

The rural non-farm economy   A serious problem for socialist countries has been the relative neglect of the rural non-farm economy. The potential contribution of this sector to development in a poor, labour-surplus country is large, as economists have pointed out since the debates of the 1920s in the USSR. For example, when production is located in the rural areas, there are often important savings on transport costs (compared to producing the same output in urban factories), which are, anyway, characteristically underdeveloped in a poor country. These industries often employ a large number of workers per unit of capital; consequently, their enlargement in appropriate sectors tends to change the structure of employment more rapidly than a strategy which concentrates mainly on large-scale, often capital-intensive, urban industry. Because they are located in the rural areas, expansion of these industries tends to economize on expenditures on urban infrastructure since the workers generally continue to live in their original residences. Because of the rapid absorption of labour, expansion of these activities tends to lead to more rapid growth of female employment outside the home, which will tend to produce a slow-down in the growth rate of population. These and many other arguments[5] support the idea of, in most poor countries, a mix of plant sizes, locations, and capital—labour ratios, and suggest that single-minded concentration upon urban, large-scale, capital-intensive plants involves serious costs. Socialist governments have tended to ignore their own countries' pre-revolutionary experience. In both the USSR and China before their respective revolutions, large parts of the rural handicraft sector were resilient in the face of competition from modern industry. This should have caused the post-revolutionary leadership to reflect on the reasons for this sector's continuing strength. These governments have also paid insufficient attention to examples of successful modernization elsewhere (notably Meiji Japan) in which this sector played an important role.

In principle, collective farms could include an active non-farm economy. In practice, this has mostly not been the case. Generally, collectivization of agriculture has been accompanied by collectivization of rural handi-crafts workers, with rural individual and co-operative non-farm activity strongly discouraged (apart from work on private plots), especially where it has involved employment of other workers. Unfortunately, many acti-vities in poor countries (e.g. pedlars, roadside food stalls, shoe repairs, barbers, entertainers, small carpentering jobs) are carried out most effectively by individuals or very small enterprises, so that suppressing them or collectivizing them has considerable costs. The rural non-farm sector has tended also to be severely handicapped by the priority given in the material supply system to the heavy industrial sector. Indeed, prior to China's post-Mao reforms, the most successful socialist country in respect to the rural non-farm sector was China, but even here there was a powerful bias towards a narrow range of collectively run small-scale 'heavy' industries producing inputs for agriculture. In the socialist countries, also, other kinds of supply-side difficulties have inhibited the development of the collective non-farm sector, such as the methods of remuneration for workers, lack of management independence, state control over prices and product types and lack of financial incentives for local authorities to encourage their expansion. On the demand side, the growth of these activities has been inhibited in the socialist countries by the national economic strategy which has produced generally slow growth of average real incomes and of international trade, and, hence, of demand for this sector's products — both directly, and via subcontracting from the large-scale urban light industrial sector.

Collective farms and the national economy   The impact of collective farms upon the national economic performance of socialist countries is, naturally, extremely complex. Some of the most important features of this are the following. Collective farms have tended to constrain the growth of rural labour productivity and living standards, thereby limiting the growth of the domestic market for industrial wage goods. Their inefficient use of capital goods has been a contributory factor to the socialist economies' heavy industry bias. The slow growth of output of agricultural inputs for light industry has tended to inhibit that sector's growth. Their constraints upon the use of rural resources (one of which labour, was often 'surplus') for small-scale non-farm production (other than capital goods for agriculture) has provided both a direct constraint on the supply of industrial wage goods and services and an indirect one, through limiting urban industry's access to low-cost rural assembly and input supply enterprises, as well as preventing surplus labour leaving agriculture and thereby providing an opportunity for agricultural labour productivity to rise. However, urban industrial performance has been constrained by supply-side problems stemming from the respective states' excessive concern with accumulation and from shortcomings of the industrial administrative planning system as well as by the internal methods of enterprise organization (especially in Maoist China). Together these have contributed to poor performance of industrial capital (and labour) productivity. As a result, the supply of industrial 'incentive' goods for both urban and rural workers tended to grow slowly. This has been unbalanced growth indeed, with the growth of heavy industry exceeding that of light industry and agriculture over a long period of time. This has permitted average living standards to grow only slowly and, in the case of China, mass poverty failed to decline.

Collective farms and rural development strategies   This book has argued that collective farms are a useful institutional form for raising the rate of rural saving and investment, for helping to solve local poverty, for ensuring limited intra-village income inequality and a high degree of mobility in income positions within the village, and for preventing beter-located areas from realising their locational advantages in the form of much higher incomes than other areas. However, it has questioned the desirablility of some of these goals, arguing that they, together with defects in principle in collective farms, as well as in some of the policies that have commonly been pursued through them have helped to produce a lower rate of growth of farm output than would have been possible with alternative institutions and to have necessitated the use of a relatively large volume of resources in order to achieve that growth. Collective farms have, in consequence, contributed to relatively poor performance in the non-farm sector (as well as being influenced by its shortcomings). The detrimental impact of collective farms upon the growth of rural productivity has meant that their capacity to deal with the most fundamental dimension of poverty — the regional one — has been very limited. Moreover, while collective farms have enabled certain kinds of inequality to be avoided, they have substituted new kinds of inequality, with tight controls over the peasants' economic, political and social freedoms exercised by a tiny minority of the population. For all its inequalities, the market provides breathing space for the growth of individual and group independence, and the assertion of rights against the state. The collective farm, with its fusion of economic and political power, provides the ideal vehicle for comprehensive control over its members.

The only kind of collective farm that should appear on socialists' agenda is a truly independent, voluntary, 'agricultural producers' co-operative'. This book argues that such an institutional form is likely to be a rare occurrence. Whereas co-operation offers huge advantages, at different levels, in many aspects of the farm economy, comprehensive co-operation in all aspects of production, even where voluntary, offers few advantages and requires exceptional conditions in order to be sustained voluntarily.

Statistical Appendix

Table A.1 Distribution of peasant population in xian with different levels of average per caput net income, 1985 (yuan)

Area	Total peasant population (m)	<100 yuan		100–300 yuan		300–400 yuan		400–500 yuan		500–600 yuan		600–700 yuan		>700 yuan	
		No. of peasants (m)	% of peasant pop.	No. of peasants (m)	% of peasant pop.	No. of peasants (m)	% of peasant pop.	No. of peasants (m)	% of peasant pop	No. of peasants (m)	% of peasant pop.	No. of peasants (m)	% of peasant pop.	No. of peasants (m)	% of peasant pop.
All China	818.1	21.5	2.6	424.9	51.9	190.7	23.2	119.5	14.6	40.06	4.9	13.41	1.6	8.01	1.0
Beijing	3.8	–	–	–	–	–	–	0.060	1.6	0.45	11.8	1.09	28.7	2.23	58.9
Tianjin	3.6	–	–	–	–	1.11	30.8	1.57	43.6	0.94	26.1	–	–	–	–
Hebei	47.4	1.63	3.4	13.63	28.8	16.79	35.4	12.84	27.1	2.02	4.3	0.28	0.6	0.19	0.4
Shanxi	20.8	–	–	5.71	27.5	8.23	39.6	5.49	26.4	0.78	3.8	0.32	1.5	0.28	1.3
Inner Mongolia	13.5	–	–	8.98	65.8	4.29	31.8	0.20	1.5	0.026	0.2	0.014	0.1	0.05	0.4
Liaoning	21.5	1.40	6.5	4.92	22.9	2.00	9.3	5.52	25.7	4.78	22.2	1.77	8.2	1.08	5.0
Jilin	14.1	–	–	–	–	0.28	2.0	7.39	52.4	5.26	37.3	1.14	8.1	–	–
Heilongjiang	17.1	–	–	1.69	9.9	7.18	42.0	6.26	36.6	1.72	10.1	0.25	1.5	–	–
Shanghai	4.2	–	–	–	–	–	–	0.59	14.0	0.95	22.6	1.61	38.3	1.09	26.0
Jiangsu	50.6	–	–	5.42	10.7	16.58	32.8	19.49	38.5	5.32	10.5	3.82	7.5	–	–
Zhejiang	33.4	–	–	6.95	20.8	15.09	45.2	4.51	13.5	6.77	20.03	0.14	0.4	–	–
Anhui	42.5	–	–	21.66	51.0	18.36	43.2	2.50	5.9	–	–	–	–	–	–
Fujian	21.6	–	–	13.75	63.7	7.19	33.3	0.67	3.1	–	–	–	–	–	–
Jiangxi	27.8	–	–	17.97	64.6	6.49	23.3	3.11	11.2	0.22	0.8	–	–	–	–
Shandong	66.6	–	–	10.08	15.1	21.06	31.6	27.29	41.0	6.76	10.2	1.16	1.7	0.28	0.4
Henan	67.1	2.57	3.8	54.71	81.5	8.11	12.1	1.19	1.8	0.54	0.8	0.06	0.1	0.004	neg.
Hubei	36.3	–	–	12.45	34.3	12.82	35.3	11.01	30.3	–	–	–	–	–	–
Hunan	47.5	–	–	32.00	67.4	13.85	29.2	1.45	3.1	0.21	0.4	–	–	–	–
Guangdong	46.8	–	–	21.46	45.9	13.85	29.6	4.86	10.4	2.07	4.4	1.72	3.7	2.79	6.0
Guangxi	33.2	1.75	5.3	30.36	91.4	1.07	3.2	0.006	neg.	–	–	–	–	–	–
Sichuan	87.1	1.37	1.6	73.67	84.6	9.27	10.6	1.83	2.1	0.95	1.1	–	–	–	–
Guizhou	25.8	–	–	24.92	96.8	0.78	3.0	0.11	0.4	–	–	–	–	–	–
Yunnan	29.4	4.67	15.9	22.66	77.1	2.12	7.2	–	–	–	–	–	–	–	–
Tibet	1.7	–	–	0.95	55.9	0.50	29.4	0.14	8.2	0.010	0.6	0.068	4.0	0.013	0.8
Shenxi	24.5	–	–	24.00	98.0	0.32	1.3	0.22	0.9	0.010	neg.	–	–	–	–
Gansu	17.0	7.42	43.6	8.48	49.9	0.49	2.9	0.43	2.5	0.16	2.2	–	neg.	0.004	neg.
Qinghai	2.9	–	–	2.49	85.9	0.25	8.6	0.056	1.9	0.052	1.8	0.006	0.2	–	–
Ningxia	3.1	0.64	20.6	1.02	32.9	1.07	34.5	0.38	12.3	–	–	–	–	–	–
Xinjiang	7.1	–	–	5.10	71.8	1.58	22.3	0.33	4.6	0.062	0.9	–	–	–	–

Source: ZGNYNJ, 1985, 240–3

Table A.2 *Zhejiang province: average per caput agricultural and industrial output in different xian, 1984 (yuan)*

	Gross value of agricultural and industrial output	Gross value of agricultural output	Gross value of industrial output	Gross value of output from xiang and cun (and below) level industries[a]
1 Hangzhou city:				
1.1 Yuhang xian	1536	573	963	565
1.2 Xiaoshan xian	1815	642	1174	653
1.3 Fuyang xian	975	507	469	309
1.4 Tonglu xian	1309	508	801	399
1.5 Jiande xian	1310	398	912	125
1.6 Chunan xian	620	328	292	66
1.7 Linan xian	1025	483	541	269
2 Ningbo city	–	–	–	–
3 Wenzhou city	–	–	–	–
4 Jiaxing diqu:	–	–	–	–
4.1 Hushou city	–	–	–	–
4.2 Jiaxing city	–	–	–	–
4.3 Wuxing xian	1527	699	828	398
4.4 Jiashan xian	–	–	–	–
4.5 Jiaxing xian	–	–	–	–
4.6 Pinghu xian	1530	679	851	368
4.7 Haiyan xian	1557	697	860	536
4.8 Haining xian	1843	779	1064	690
4.9 Tongxiang xian	1555	720	835	550
4.10 Deqing xian	1445	554	892	320
4.11 Anji xian	857	390	467	137
4.12 Changxing xian	934	430	504	202
5 Zhoushan diqu	–	–	–	–
5.1 Dinghai xian	779	323	455	241
5.2 Daishan xian	954	450	504	177
5.3 Shengsi xian	985	627	358	219
5.4 Putuo xian	1165	746	419	259
6 Ningbo diqu:				–
6.1 Yin xian	2166	897	1269	1251
6.2 Zhenhai xian	1714	663	1051	708
6.3 Xiangshan xian	1010	498	511	301
6.4 Ninghai xian	864	429	456	262
6.5 Fenghua xian	1201	517	684	408
6.6 Yuyao xian	1736	784	952	790
6.7 Cixi xian	1527	731	795	723
7 Shaoxing diqu:				
7.1 Shaoxing city	–	–	–	–
7.2 Shaoxing xian	2180	1062	1118	1313
7.3 Shangyu xian	1069	587	481	407
7.4 Sheng xian	792	390	401	180
7.5 Xinchang xian	814	308	507	177
7.6 Zhuji xian	727	402	325	180
8 Taizhou diqu:				
8.1 Linhai xian	563	296	276	109
8.2 Sanmen xian	514	303	211	90
8.3 Huangyan xian	820	335	486	227
8.4 Wenling xian	576	363	213	138
8.5 Yuhuan xian	800	541	259	353
8.6 Xianju xian	621	372	249	65

Table A.2 continued

		Gross value of agricultural and industrial output	Gross value of agricultural output	Gross value of industrial output	Gross value of output from xiang and cun (and below) level industries[a]
8.7	Tiantai xian	474	276	198	111
9.	Wenzhou diqu:				
9.1	Yongjia xian	414	232	181	154
9.2	Yueqing xian	640	387	253	289
9.3	Dongtou xian	768	556	212	391
9.4	Ruian xian	708	387	312	149
9.5	Pingyang xian	503	320	183	111
9.6	Taishun xian	272	219	53	20
9.7	Wencheng xian	239	164	75	26
10.	Lishui diqu:				
10.1	Lishui xian	823	331	492	54
10.2	Jinyun xian	426	263	162	70
10.3	Qingtian xian	346	216	130	83
10.4	Yunhe xian	488	258	230	33
10.5	Qingyuan xian	457	290	164	28
10.6	Longquan xian	612	395	217	53
10.7	Suichang xian	667	385	282	51
11	Jinhua diqu:				
11.1	Jinhua city	—	—	—	—
11.2	Quzhou city	—	—	—	—
11.3	Jinhua xian	1255	452	803	126
11.4	Lanxi xian	671	345	326	136
11.5	Pujiang xian	1279	516	356	255
11.6	Yiwu xian	757	427	330	233
11.7	Dongyang xian	749	386	381	168
11.8	Yongkang xian	849	424	425	77
11.9	Wuyi xian	—	—	—	—
11.10	Qu xian				
11.11	Jiangshan xian	715	362	353	72
11.12	Changshan xian	492	318	174	49
11.13	Kaihua-xian	699	387	312	74
	xian not included in the map on p. 171				
10.5	Cangnan xian	495	328	167	140
10.6	Songyang xian	516	372	144	32
10.7	Jingning zizhixian	313	236	77	18
	Panan xian	370	284	86	56
11	Longyou xian	693	378	315	98

[a] The output of xiang level industries is included in 'gross value of industrial output'; the output of cun (and below) level industries is included in 'gross value of agricultural output'.

High output per caput xian (over 1000 yuan) are marked by triangles; low output per caput xian (below 500 yuan) are marked by circles in the map on p. 171.

The numbers (1–11) on the left hand side of the table refer to the map on p. 171.

Source: ZJJJTJNJ, 1985

Table A.3 *Average per caput output and income in different parts of Anhui province, 1978–1984 (all data at current prices)*

Area		Gross value of agricultural and industrial output per caput				Average net income per peasant			
		1978 (yuan)	1984 (yuan)	Increase, 1978–84 yuan	%	1978 (yuan)	1984 (yuan)	Increase, 1980–4 yuan	%
1	Hefei city	—	—	—	—	112	416	304	271
1.1	Changfeng *xian*	248	453	205	83	62	330	268	432
2	Huainan city	—	—	—	—	—	—	—	—
2.1	Fengtai *xian*	242	459	217	90	46	291	254	532
3	Huaibei city	—	—	—	—	94(1981)	300	(206)	(219)
3.1	Suixi *xian*	161	491	330	205	45	352	307	682
4	Bengbu city	—	—	—	—	76	400	324	426
5	Maanshan city	—	—	—	—	121	451	330	272
6	Wuhu city	—	—	—	—	120	384	264	220
6.1	Wuhu *xian*	325	451	126	39	77	311	234	304
7	Anqing city	—	—	—	—	134	357	223	16
8	Tongling city	—	—	—	—	149	420	271	182
8.1	Tongling *xian*	267	390	123	46	241(1981)	340	(99)	(41)
9	Suxian *diqu*	[261]	[484]	[223]	[85]	[80]	[288]	[208]	[260]
9.1	Suzhou city	—	—	—	—	55	385	380	600
9.2	Suxi *xian*	211	523	312	148	52	320	268	515
9.3	Xiao *xian*	246	456	210	85	54	311	257	476
9.4	Dangshan *xian*	254	461	207	81	53	247	194	366
9.5	Lingbi *xian*	252	429	177	70	46	278	232	504
9.6	Si *xian*	199	429	230	116	46	244	198	430
9.7	Wuhe *xian*	267	582	315	118	60	366	306	510
9.8	Guzhen *xian*	225	532	307	136	55	377	322	585
9.9	Huaiyuan *xian*	254	567	313	123	65	387	322	495
10	Chuxian *diqu*	[273]	[711]	[438]	[160]	[107]	[396]	[289]	[270]
10.1	Chu *xian*	—	—	—	—	—	—	—	—
10.2	Laian *xian*	337	645	308	91	123	423	300	244
10.3	Tianchang *xian*	420	886	466	111	141	453	315	223
10.4	Quanjiao *xian*	412	827	415	101	91	450	359	395
10.5	Dingyuan *xian*	224	480	256	114	52	304	252	485
10.6	Fengyang *xian*	243	625	382	157	81	403	322	398
10.7	Jiashou *xian*	256	501	245	96	61	338	277	454
11	Chaohu *diqu*	[304]	[437]	[133]	[44]	[103]	[302]	[199]	[193]
11.1	Chao *xian*	—	—	—	—	—	—	—	—
11.2	Hanshan *xian*	335	509	174	52	113	330	217	192
11.3	He *xian*	369	518	149	40	122	344	222	182
11.4	Wuwei *xian*	269	371	102	38	97	295	198	204
11.5	Lujiang *xian*	248	333	85	34	122	273	151	124
11.6	Feidong *xian*	259	476	217	84	68	342	274	403
12	Xuancheng *diqu*	[277]	[413]	[136]	[49]	[88]	[306]	[218]	[247]
12.1	Xuancheng *xian*	295	400	105	36	81	337	256	316
12.2	Dangtu *xian*	477	640	163	34	183	413	230	126
12.3	Langxi *xian*	183	370	187	102	61	242	181	297
12.4	Guangde *xian*	245	397	152	62	54	304	250	463
12.5	Ningguo *xian*	299	408	109	36	134	276	142	106
12.6	Jing *xian*	385	501	116	30	93	277	184	198
12.7	Qingyang *xian*	236	404	168	171	91	314	223	245
12.8	Nanling *xian*	325	361	36	18	106	313	207	195
12.9	Fanchang *xian*	310	515	205	66	96[1]	319	223	232

13	Huizhou *diqu*	–	[574]	–	–	–	[388]	–	–
13.1	Tunxi city	–	–	–	–	114	384	270	237
13.2	Xiuning *xian*	363	653	290	80	102	355	253	248
13.3	Taiping *xian*	–	–	–	–	–	–	–	–
13.4	Jingde *xian*	322	461	139	43	85	294	209	246
13.5	Jixi *xian*	336	430	94	28	–	285	–	–
13.6	She *xian*	293	507	214	73	124	323	199	160
13.7	Yi *xian*	254	492	238	94	104	283	179	172
13.8	Qimen *xian*	300	633	333	111	106	310	204	192
13.9	Shitai *xian*	334	507	173	52	106	302	196	185
14	Anqing *diqu*	[263]	[407]	[144]	[55]	[74]	[175]	[101]	[136]
14.1	Tongcheng *xian*	266	515	249	94	143	315	172	120
14.2	Zongyang *xian*	155	241	86	55	73	199	126	173
14.3	Guichi *xian*	282	409	127	45	100	316	216	216
14.4	Dongzhi *xian*	344	492	148	33	106	305	199	188
14.5	Wangjiang *xian*	310	450	140	45	111	324	213	192
14.6	Susong *xian*	239	354	115	48	81	308	227	280
14.7	Taihu *xian*	222	322	100	45	106	231	125	118
14.8	Huaining *xian*	210	443	233	111	81	301	220	272
14.9	Qianshan *xian*	196	396	200	102	111	301	190	171
14.10	Yuexi *xian*	161	267	106	66	63	172	109	173
15	Liuan *diqu*	[263]	[375]	[112]	[43]	[65]	[221]	[156]	[240]
15.1	Liuan city	–	–	–	–	83	460	377	454
15.2	Liuan *xian*	218	352	134	61	64	256	192	300
15.3	Huoqiu *xian*	247	339	92	37	102	214	112	110
15.4	Shou *xian*	251	349	98	39	65	240	175	269
15.5	Feixi *xian*	255	469	214	84	73	352	279	382
15.6	Shucheng *xian*	265	366	101	38	81	259	178	220
15.7	Huoshan *xian*	300	351	51	17	77	149	72	94
15.8	Jinzhai *xian*	184	242	58	32	52	173	121	233
16	Fuyang *diqu*	[202]	[40]	[199]	[99]	[74]	[228]	[154]	[208]
16.1	Fuyang city	–	–	–	–	72	300	228	317
16.2	Fuyang *xian*	126	348	222	176	83	240	157	189
16.3	Bo *xian*	220	424	204	93	47	256	209	444
16.4	Guoyang *xian*	204	486	282	138	41	305	264	644
16.5	Mengcheng *xian*	195	542	347	178	42	308	266	633
16.6	Lixin *xian*	184	372	188	102	35	218	183	523
16.7	Yingshang *xian*	162	284	122	75	34	185	151	444
16.8	Funan *xian*	151	321	170	113	51	174	123	241
16.9	Linquan *xian*	164	269	105	64	59	174	114	195
16.10	Jieshou *xian*	168	493	325	193	48(1981)	345	(297)	(619)
16.11	Taihe *xian*	178	329	151	85	38	232	194	511
Not included in map on p. 169:									
	Huangshan city	–	–	–	–	126	334	208	165
	Chaohu city	–	–	–	–	123	336	213	173
	Chuzhou city	–	–	–	–	103	497	394	383

Figures in square brackets are averages for *diqu*: figures in parentheses are not comparable with the other figures.

The numbers (1–16) on the left of the table refer to the map on p. 169.

Source: Calculated from AHJJNJ, 1985

Table A.4 *Differences in consumption levels among peasants in different provinces, cities, and autonomous regions (average per caput)*

Area	Grain (unhusked) (jin)		of which fine grain (jin)		Vegetables (jin)		Edible oil (jin)		Meat (pork, mutton, beef) (jin)		Poultry (jin)	
	1980	1984	1980	1984	1980	1984	1980	1984	1980	1984	1980	1984
All China	514	533	326	418	254	281	2.8	4.9	15.5	21.2	1.31	1.87
Beijing	500	458	270	354	365	448	2.3	4.6	15.2	19.8	0.14	0.73
Tianjin	477	442	302	330	196	188	1.8	4.5	13.0	15.5	0.43	0.50
Hebei	452	434	136	228	226	247	2.1	4.7	9.1	13.0	0.16	0.20
Shanxi	484	467	97	229	170	206	2.0	4.4	6.2	8.0	0.13	0.11
Inner Mongolia	506	516	151	209	281	248	2.4	4.4	20.8	29.2	0.30	0.48
Liaoning	519	520	101	170	450	425	2.5	3.9	19.4	23.3	0.57	0.42
Jilin	599	647	130	137	205	606	2.6	4.7	17.8	24.9	0.89	0.98
Heilongjiang	508	535	117	235	290	345	5.4	8.4	14.8	15.4	0.70	1.04
Shanghai	594	560	477	523	201	235	6.6	9.0	25.3	38.4	1.93	3.04
Jiangsu	591	622	485	554	224	263	4.6	7.9	13.8	19.1	1.59	2.41
Zhejiang	625	625	544	608	234	273	2.9	4.3	15.3	25.1	1.99	2.43
Anhui	557	565	459	531	219	226	4.1	5.9	12.3	15.3	4.00	3.44
Fujian	584	605	531	569	275	301	1.0	1.0	12.6	16.9	2.89	3.52
Jiangxi	613	669	593	658	310	370	4.0	6.0	13.1	19.2	2.17	2.25
Shandong	459	463	161	328	232	300	3.4	8.4	10.1	12.8	0.87	1.14
Henan	443	479	246	396	150	174	2.0	3.8	8.2	10.0	0.47	0.81
Hubei	540	631	454	569	296	431	3.6	8.1	17.8	25.4	1.20	1.76
Hunan	669	656	609	619	370	336	4.5	5.5	22.3	33.3	2.39	3.74
Guangdong	584	540	534	522	231	237	3.6	5.0	13.1	25.0	4.29	7.19
Guangxi	514	546	469	506	251	281	1.9	2.8	12.9	23.0	3.66	4.69
Sichuan	517	543	368	465	295	334	2.1	2.4	26.6	34.7	1.03	1.78
Guizhou	449	464	298	373	286	292	1.4	2.2	19.9	27.4	0.76	0.95
Yunnan	443	470	263	376	253	305	0.7	1.1	16.2	30.3	1.36	2.61
Tibet	–	–	–	–	–	–	–	–	–	–	–	–
Shenxi	412	516	181	260	139	139	2.1	3.6	10.9	12.9	0.26	0.38
Gansu	477	475	240	380	87	121	2.9	4.1	17.7	11.9	0.24	0.19
Qinghai	–	470	–	366	–	106	–	8.8	–	25.1	–	0.28
Ningxia	452	483	361	408	152	207	3.9	7.0	7.4	14.0	0.43	0.37
Xinjiang	423	436	252	382	145	185	4.5	7.7	18.7	23.3	0.32	0.52

Table A.4 *continued*

Area	Fresh eggs (jin) 1980	1984	Fish and shrimps (jin) 1980	1984	Sugar (jin) 1980	1984	Alcoholic drink (jin) 1980	1984	Cotton cloth (chi) 1980	1984	Synthetic fibre cloth (chi) 1980	1984
All China	2.39	3.68	2.19	2.47	2.12	2.60	3.78	6.95	12.9	9.5	2.8	7.4
Beijing	3.90	13.68	1.52	2.41	1.95	3.60	4.96	10.71	15.6	9.1	3.9	10.3
Tianjin	3.12	6.38	4.69	7.06	2.47	2.62	3.13	5.06	15.0	9.1	3.4	9.3
Hebei	1.71	3.31	0.43	0.71	0.88	1.31	1.79	2.82	14.2	11.0	3.4	8.1
Shanxi	1.69	2.98	0.03	0.13	0.87	1.44	0.91	1.66	18.0	10.2	3.0	7.5
Inner Mongolia	2.50	3.04	0.24	0.43	1.01	1.41	3.33	4.59	15.3	9.6	2.4	6.1
Liaoning	3.89	6.81	3.38	3.75	1.09	1.21	3.73	6.52	14.1	9.4	4.4	9.3
Jilin	2.64	7.73	1.48	2.09	0.87	1.07	3.49	6.44	16.8	8.6	1.7	6.6
Heilongjiang	3.81	4.64	0.95	3.35	1.43	1.87	3.57	5.98	14.8	7.9	4.2	6.4
Shanghai	6.07	8.60	8.07	11.16	5.88	7.86	10.29	18.40	10.2	7.2	7.7	12.4
Jiangsu	2.78	6.77	3.88	6.00	2.12	3.66	4.31	9.47	12.9	7.5	3.9	11.0
Zhejiang	1.95	5.06	9.81	10.66	4.02	5.72	12.88	30.08	11.3	7.0	4.6	9.7
Anhui	3.24	3.54	2.61	3.01	2.26	2.48	3.12	4.67	14.3	7.2	2.7	8.3
Fujian	1.62	2.51	9.54	11.07	4.50	5.48	9.47	14.30	11.3	4.8	2.2	6.6
Jiangxi	2.05	2.99	3.01	3.82	1.99	2.45	2.74	7.96	11.1	6.3	2.5	7.7
Shandong	2.48	4.81	1.95	2.54	1.17	1.80	4.51	6.96	14.1	11.6	4.5	9.6
Henan	2.06	3.48	0.55	0.52	1.33	1.73	1.34	2.21	11.8	8.8	3.3	8.5
Hubei	2.19	4.07	3.45	5.43	1.89	2.65	3.61	8.09	11.0	7.0	3.4	9.4
Hunan	2.17	3.50	3.15	4.35	2.06	2.87	7.22	11.07	12.3	7.9	2.8	7.3
Guangdong	1.57	2.31	8.44	17.75	8.44	8.36	3.07	5.33	9.9	4.2	4.9	5.1
Guangxi	0.65	1.37	1.16	2.74	2.02	2.22	4.80	9.96	8.7	6.7	1.5	4.6
Sichuan	1.92	4.04	0.31	0.49	2.21	2.39	3.90	6.98	12.5	8.8	1.8	7.0
Guizhou	1.05	1.25	0.39	0.64	1.49	1.50	5.19	10.03	10.8	7.3	0.8	3.8
Yunnan	1.09	2.56	0.34	0.74	2.98	3.25	3.45	9.07	11.5	9.3	0.8	6.4
Tibet	–	–	–	–	–	–	–	–	–	–	–	–
Shenxi	0.87	1.63	0.05	0.03	0.77	1.16	2.22	3.58	15.4	10.0	2.4	6.5
Gansu	1.25	1.74	0.01	neg.	0.92	0.69	1.15	1.49	15.3	10.4	1.7	5.7
Qinghai	–	1.05	neg.	0.09	–	1.10	–	2.10	–	13.9	–	6.1
Ningxia	0.78	1.63	0.06	0.09	1.40	1.98	0.63	0.84	13.1	12.0	1.6	6.6
Xinjiang	1.59	2.11	0.07	0.17	2.12	1.33	0.91	1.60	19.4	11.0	3.5	7.1

Source: ZGNCTJNJ, 1985, 212–17

Table A.5 Differences in stocks of consumer durables between peasants in different provinces, cities and autonomous regions (average per 100 households)

	Bicycles 1980	Bicycles 1984	Sewing machines 1980	Sewing machines 1984	Radios 1980	Radios 1984	Wrist watches 1980	Wrist watches 1984	TV sets 1984	Tape recorders 1984	Washing machines 1984	Electric fans 1984
All China	37	74	23	43	34	61	38	109	7.2	2.8	2.0	5.9
Beijing	125	187	42	58	96	100	103	211	57.1	14.2	14.8	27.5
Tianjin	108	187	41	77	87	104	81	190	45.8	8.8	3.0	26.0
Hebei	76	119	33	62	59	90	31	99	5.3	1.1	0.9	1.6
Shanxi	62	100	36	69	25	69	39	124	8.6	2.3	0.6	0.6
Inner Mongolia	63	84	47	63	43	74	45	97	6.6	2.1	1.2	0.2
Liaoning	69	107	56	68	63	73	93	140	27.3	5.9	5.0	0.9
Jilin	37	74	41	60	69	83	75	118	14.6	3.9	6.8	1.0
Heilongjiang	47	67	45	53	68	73	58	103	13.5	3.6	6.0	27.9
Shanghai	81	122	41	68	44	73	126	203	24.2	4.7	neg.	34.2
Jiangsu	34	90	14	34	37	78	57	145	5.4	1.6	neg.	10.4
Zhejiang	14	70	14	46	13	31	61	178	3.5	2.0	neg.	20.3
Anhui	16	52	11	29	39	76	21	82	1.8	0.9	neg.	3.8
Fujian	16	42	20	51	19	37	71	164	5.2	2.9	neg.	13.1
Jiangxi	12	35	8	15	24	68	34	107	1.7	0.6	neg.	2.8
Shandong	70	129	28	51	53	96	33	104	4.6	1.2	0.3	1.8
Henan	36	84	30	53	40	80	16	74	1.9	0.7	0.1	1.1
Hubei	12	54	13	30	31	61	23	110	7.8	2.3	0.1	4.9
Hunan	4	32	10	21	11	32	26	99	1.1	0.9	neg.	2.3
Guangdong	104	125	53	58	77	66	112	158	8.0	10.4	17.9	43.4
Guangxi	54	97	19	51	13	32	25	108	2.8	1.5	neg.	9.6
Sichuan	9	19	4	12	12	36	17	91	3.7	1.2	0.1	1.3
Guizhou	4	11	6	15	4	16	1	68	1.8	1.1	0.1	1.4
Yunnan	7	37	7	26	14	42	17	115	4.3	6.7	0.5	0.3
Tibet	–	–	–	–	–	–	–	–	–	–	–	–
Shenxi	33	59	19	44	19	59	12	62	2.3	0.5	neg.	0.1
Gansu	41	58	19	35	16	47	24	71	2.3	1.6	neg.	neg.
Qinghai	–	51	–	47	–	38	–	89	1.5	4.6	0.4	neg.
Ningxia	90	116	25	58	17	67	51	122	15.0	6.3	1.5	0.2
Xinjiang	46	67	36	53	36	51	38	95	5.2	4.8	1.0	0.2

Source: ZGNCTJNJ, 1985, 218–21

Notes

Introduction

1 See, e.g., Nolan, 1976, Byres and Nolan, 1976.
2 The author is indebted to Dr G. C. Harcourt for this story.
3 At a conference of mainly Indian economists in New Delhi in October 1986 I encountered deep opposition to my sceptical view of the performance of China's collective farms.
4 It should be stressed that the relationship is not simple, as Carr-Hill's essay in Nolan and Paine (eds) (1986) points out.

Chapter 1 Bukharinism and Stalinism

1 The countries ruled by non-elected Communist parties are termed 'socialist' throughout this volume. The question of whether or not they are genuinely socialist is a more complex one than can be dealt with here.
2 For a perceptive analysis of the relationship of Maoism and Stalinism, see Friedman, 1982.
3 Aspects of the Stalinist model were quickly developed into formal schema, notably Fel'dman's (Domar, 1957) and Preobrazhensky's (Preobrazhensky, 1965). One of the reasons they were better able to do so than the Bukharinists is that the tightly controlled economic and political world of Stalinism assumes away (at great cost) the complexities of a world in which markets play a major role. Consider, for example, some of the key assumptions of the influential Fel'dman growth model: (1) constant prices, (2) capital is the only limiting factor, (3) absence of lags, (4) a closed economy (5) production independent of consumption (Domar, 1957, 153).
4 Among the most notable in the socialist countries are Bazarov (see, especially, the discussion in Erlich, 1967, ch. 7) in the Soviet Union in the 1920s, and Chen Yun in post-1949 China (see Lardy and Lieberthal, 1983). A

comprehensive account of Bukharinism and its influence in the Soviet Union is given in Lewin, 1975. The immense difficulty of developing market socialist growth models is well indicated by Dong's extraordinary schema published in China in the early 1960s, which relaxes just some of the constraints of a strict Stalinist world (Dong, 1963a, b, c). Dong's assumed setting is not that of full market socialism, yet it took him three long articles to merely summarise the main findings of his growth model (see the discussion in Lin, 1981, 32−4). It is noteworthy, and not at all surprising, that some of the most influential economic writings in the Bukharinist tradition are not presented as formal models. This applies to much of the most important Chinese economic writing post-1978 and to many of the leading market socialist works in the West (e.g. Brus, 1972; Nove, 1983).

5   This is not to deny either that there are important arguments between different groups within the ruling stratum or that mass views/actions do play a role in the political system.

6   It should be stressed that a definition such as this does not imply that certain socio-economic forms, such as 'workers' control' of the enterprise or firm, or 'abolition of the anarchy of the market' are a necessary part of socialism. It is conceivable that a democratic political system might decide, for various reasons, that it is better not to have workers running their firms or enterprises, and that the market is an extremely useful device which should play a central role in a socialist society.

7   See, especially, the excellent analysis of the role of the state in Taiwan in Amsden, 1979, and in the Asian NICs more generally in Little, 1979.

8   By 'informal' education is meant education acquired outside the classroom e.g. from discussion, radio, TV and newspapers.

9   A useful distinction can be made between 'moral' protests demanding greater democracy and 'economic' protest demanding, for example, state subsidies to compensate for price rises. In general, the former type of demand seems to inspire mass movements at a later stage in poor countries' development than the latter.

10   The only rapidly-growing economies in which the state has left the market largely to look after itself were Britain in the Industrial Revolution and Hong Kong in recent times. They are the exceptions that prove the rule of the necessity of 'planning in the context of a free economy'. They each enjoyed uniquely favourable conditions on both the supply side and the demand side, enabling rapid growth with a minimum of state intervention.

11   For a useful summary of the voluminous literature, see Ellman, 1979, ch. 3.

12   In the long term, it is true, he visualised eventual dominance of the large-scale state sector.

13   Even the famous 'de-industrialization' thesis for late-nineteenth-century India is far from proven (see, e.g., Bagchi, 1976, and Charlesworth's (1982) comments).

14   For a clear, comprehensive discussion of the rationale behind the development of rural small-scale industries, see Riskin, 1971.

15 Until the 'Lewis turning point' of drying up of the 'rural reserve army' of surplus, low wage labour has been reached, and until the transport system has been expanded.

16 The closest one comes to a contemporary economic justification is the Fel'dman model (Domar, 1957) which, as we have seen, rested on very restrictive, highly unrealistic assumptions. Subsequently, of course, much has been written to justify this approach (see, especially, Dobb, 1960, 1967, chs 3—4; Raj and Sen, 1961; Baran, 1957, ch. 8).

17 This, indeed was a dominant factor in the Soviet motivation. As Stalin expressed it in 1933:

> The fundamental task of the [first] five year plan was to convert the USSR from an agrarian and weak country, *dependent on the caprices of the capitalist countries*, into *an independent and powerful country, fully self-reliant and independent of the caprices of world capitalism*. [Stalin, 1933, 588, my emphasis — P. N.]

18 For contrasting views, see, for example, Bauer, 1981, ch. 14, and Sen. 1983.
19 Even Sen's 1983 data show this.
20 Still in 1987 around 56 per cent of non-agricultural consumer goods sold in the cities had state-fixed prices, and over 80 per cent of means of production were sold at state-fixed prices (personal communication from Tian Yuan, Executive Director, Research Centre for Economic, Technological and Social Development, State Council of China).

Chapter 2   Theoretical arguments concerning collective farms

1 It is quite conceivable that members of a co-operative might democratically decide to have rigidly hierarchical work organisation and wide income differentials: the key characteristic (in my view) of a co-operative is democracy in determining these key policy questions.

2 For further evidence on India under the Green Revolution, see, for example, Byres and Crow, 1983. ch. 4; for China see, for example, Nolan, 1983a.

3 See, for example, Bhalla and Chadha's (1982) careful study of over 1600 farm households in the Punjab. While the per caput gains from new technology were extremely uneven, related to differences in household land holdings, all farm sizes had adopted the new technology in the 180 villages surveyed.

4 For a vivid illustration of this proposition see Hayami and Kikuchi, 1981.

5 The key speeches of Mao (1955) and Stalin (1929a, b) hardly touch upon the reasons for the superiority of collective farms, but simply take it as given. One of the most interesting statements of the early post-revolutionary

period on the superiority of collectives farms is to be found in Bukharin and Preobrazhensky (1969, 352—7).

6   See especially, Bukharin and Preobrazhensky, 1969, 352—7; for the arguments put forward in China in the 1950s see Gray, 1970, 102—7.

7   One of the clearest discussions of this issue that the author has encountered is Mellor, 1966, ch. 20.

8   See, for example, Dasgupta, 1977.

9   See, for example, Bhalla and Chadha, 1982.

10   This, naturally, is quite a complicated calculation.

11   Even in China's densely populated countryside, the average area of the basic unit of rural work organization in the late 1970s was not small; each 'production team' (the 'basic unit of account') contained 54 workers and 16.6 hectares of arable area (24.2 hectares of sown area). The data are from 1979 and 1981. (ZGNYJJGY, 1982, 9; SYC, 1982, 133—4).

12   The distinction between voluntary peasant co-operation and local government-organized co-operation is a fine one.

Chapter 3   The Chinese rural economy under Mao

1   It is, naturally, extremely difficult to reach precise conclusions about extra mortality after the Great Leap Forward, without a great deal of detailed research. Unsurprisingly, the Chinese authorities are not keen to encourage research on this unpleasant subject. I have never discussed this subject with a single Chinese person who lived through this period, without it evoking deep, bitter memories concerning its impact among vulnerable groups in the population (especially old people).

2   See Michael Ellman's trenchant letter in *Marxism Today* (Ellman, 1986, 29).

3   For example, in the late 1970s the average number of people per production team varied from 27 in Guangdong province to 63 in Heilongjiang province (Nolan, 1983c, footnote 37).

4   See, e.g., Guangdong People's Bank, 1974; Hunan Province Revolutionary Committee, 1973; Liaoning Institute of Finance and Economics, 1973.

5   See, for example, the excellent account of life in a Maoist village in Chan et al., 1984.

6   On the ideological preference for time rates in the Cultural Revolution see the careful discussion in Parish and Whyte, 1978, 59—71.

7   Author's interview in 1983 with Xu Gaining, demographer at the Chinese Academy of Social Sciences, Chengdu municipality, Sichuan province.

8   Agricultural produce purchased by state commercial departments as a percentage of the gross value of agricultural production: 1952 = 18.6, 1957 = 29.2, 1965 = 46.5, 1970 = 43.8, 1975 = 32.2 (Ma and Sun, 1981, 72).

9   On the concept of rural 'surplus labour' in poor countries, see especially Nurkse, 1953, chapter II.

10   See, especially, the discussion in Ishikawa, 1982.

11   Gross value of agricultural output per agricultural worker (at 1970 prices, *yuan*): 1952 = 371, 1957 = 411, 1962 = 299, 1975 = 436 (Ministry of Agriculture, 1982, 28 and 85).

12   For example, in Anhui province in 1976, 1.7% of the communes' gross income (2.4% of net income after deducting material expenses) was allocated to the 'common welfare fund' (Nolan 1983c, table 3).

13   It is hard to say whether these charges generally covered costs.

14   This author knows of no study which is able to assess accurately the proportion of production teams using different systems (and their complex sub-variants) at different times.This statement is based especially on discussions the author had with Chinese officials at different levels in 1979 (Nolan, 1979).

15   For a detailed discussion of the situation in this respect in one village see Chan et al., 1984, 247−8.

16   Compared to India, for example, China did very well in these products: Swamy (1977, 379) has estimated that in 1955 China's output of the 'desirable consumer goods' group (comprising bicycles, radios and sewing machines) was 1.35 times that of India, by 1973, China had increased the output of this sector to 6.46 times the Indian level.

17   Closely analogous to Preobrazhensky's concept is the notion of 'double factoral terms of trade', used extensively in international trade analysis.

18   For example, national average per caput peasant consumption at constant (1952) prices was reported to have changed as follows: 1936 = 61.2 *yuan*, 1952 = 72, 1955 = 78.9, 1956 = 81 *yuan* (A discussion ... 1957). We still await a full-scale study comparing Chinese living standards in the 1930s and post-1949 (see Bramall, forthcoming).

19   The figure for 1949 is reported to be 20/1000 (SYC, 1982, 89).

20   In 1978, one third of peasants' net income reportedly came from non-collective sources (ZGTJZY, 1986, 110).

21   See also Nolan, 1981, 273−84, for a more detailed discussion of the data on intra-village inequality between land reform and collectivization.

22   The sex ratio also was important, as women were consistently paid less than men, which may help explain why the reported sex ratio in China remained so unbalanced throughout the post-1949 period (women as proportion of China's total population: 1949 = 48%, 1957 = 48.2%, 1978 = 48.5% (ZGTJZY, 1986, 21)).

23   For a more extensive discussion of the issues in this paragraph see Nolan, 1983a.

24   For one attempt to explore this issue see Nolan, 1983a.

25   National sample surveys for 1978 report that 66.3 per cent of peasant net income came from the collective (ZGTJNJ, 1985, 570).

26   Even grain re-sales to the villages usually had to be paid for (Maxwell and Nolan, 1980).

27   On differential rent in the USSR, see Ellman, 1973, 110−118; see also McAuley, 1977, chapters 5 and 7 on regional inequalities in rural income in the USSR.

28 To this degree there is a connection between collective farms and spatial differences, in that they provide an institution through which, if wished, such policies might be pursued. However, it is equally possible, in principle, to have used collectives to pursue quite different policies affecting regional inequality.

Chapter 4   The post-1978 reforms

1 See, especially, the careful accounts in Watson, 1983, and 1984/5

2 In the case of a model *xiang* in Sichuan province studied in detail by the author the electoral constituency consisted of just 15 villagers elected by the rest of the adult population. The total population of the *xiang* was over 13 000 (Nolan, 1983b).

3 For example, following de-collectivization in Xindu *xian* in Sichuan province the number of village accountants fell from 2 700 to 700 (Nolan, 1983b).

4 These demonstrations were much milder than those which were to rock South Korea later in the year.

5 See, for example, the four fat volumes covering just the years 1978–1983 (*Compilation of policies*, 1982; *Compilation of policies*, 1984).

6 These were still technically distinguishable by the fact that no state requisitions affected their product.

7 At the time of writing this decision still had not been published in full. No-one I spoke to in China in September 1987 (as the final revisions to this book were being made) doubted that the contract period would soon be announced as having been greatly extended.

8 Formerly the 'brigade' (*dui*).

9 See, e.g., Riskin, 1971, and Perkins, 1977.

10 Unless otherwise indicated, the information in the remainder of this section is taken from the author's field work in 1983 (Nolan, 1983b). Guanghan *xian*, where the author researched, was extremely advanced in the reforms undertaken and had already put into practice policies that were to be adopted later in other areas.

11 E.g. the manager of one village plastics factory reportedly earned a bonus of over 14 000 *yuan* in 1985 (Lu, 1986, 17).

12 Despite considerable growth in the 1980s of *xiangcun* enterprises' staff and workers' average wages (though at a much slower rate than their productivity), their average wages in 1985 still amounted to just 60 per cent of the level of those in state enterprises (ZGTJNJ, 1985, 100 and 105). Due to differences in the cost of living between town and countryside the difference in the real value of wages probably was somewhat less than this figure suggests.

13 The concept of 'surplus labour' is much easier to grasp intuitively than it is to measure. Most Chinese economists argue that at the present level of mechanization and cultivation in China there is 'substantial' rural 'surplus labour', amounting to as much as perhaps two-fifths of the rural workforce,

but there is considerable dispute about its dimensions. For a careful study in one area, see Song, 1983.

14   The 'state' in this case usually meant local authorities, notably the *xian*.

15   Kung and Chan in their (1987) account of rural export industries in Guangdong's Dongguan *xian* provide a similar view. The 'entrepreneurial spirit' of *xian* and *xiang* cadres was vital in establishing the framework within which small rural enterprises could expand successfully.

16   Net of material costs of production, wages and state taxes. Data are from a survey of 272 villages (*cun*) in 71 *xian*.

17   From a survey of 272 villages (*cun*) in 71 *xian*.

18   The main argument being that if peasants pay closer to the real cost of providing health care they will insist on a higher level of service.

19   'Basic construction investment' in state industry (current prices) (100 m *yuan*)

	1978	1982	1985	*% change* 1978−82	*% change* 1982−5
Heavy	244.0	214.0	383.0	−12	+79
Light	29.3	46.4	63.4	+58	+37

Source: ZGTJZY, 1986, 77

20   The proportion of state enterprises' profits retained by the enterprises rose from 13 per cent in 1978 to 35 per cent in 1982 (Field, 1984, 749).

21   The share of wages in the state sector taken by bonuses and subsidies rose from 9 per cent in 1978 to 29 per cent in 1984 (ZGTJNJ, 1985, 560).

22   Welfare outlays in state enterprises rose from an amount equivalent to 14 per cent of the wage bill in 1978 to 24 per cent in 1984 (ZGTJNJ, 1985, 560).

23   By early 1986, just 30 per cent of industrial consumer goods reportedly were sold at state-fixed prices, the rest either at floating or free market prices (Dong, 1986a), though the degree of float for floating prices was fixed by state authorities. Of industrial sales in 1986 (capital plus consumer goods) 40 per cent of the total value was reportedly at state-fixed prices (Gao, 1987).

24   From 1970 to 1985, collectively owned industry (urban plus rural) increased its output by 193 per cent compared to just 70 per cent in state-owned industry (both at 1980 prices). By 1985 collectively owned (including urban, *xiang*-run and *cun*-run) industry's share of national industrial output (at 1980 prices) stood at 35 2 per cent (ZGTJZY, 1986, 48).

25   Index of real wages of staff and workers in state enterprises: 1952=100, 1957=130, 1975=114, 1984=154 (ZGTJNJ, 1985, 556).

26   Average per caput peasant net income reportedly rose from 134 *yuan* in 1978 to 355 *yuan* in 1984 (current prices) (ZGTJNJ, 1985, 571). The total volume

of retail sales (current prices) in the cities rose by 139 per cent from 1978 to 1985 while in the villages the increase in the same period was 210 per cent (ZGTJZY, 1986, 88). Over the same period the price index for staff and workers reportedly rose by 34 per cent (ZGTJZY, 1986, 100).

27 As it was bound to in the absence of continued reform in state-run industry.

28 Already, by 1980, the number had fallen to 132 (at the peak, 230 types of farm produce were compulsorily purchased) (Duan, 1983).

29 From 1952 to 1978, the index of retail prices in state-run trade rose just 19 per cent. From 1978 to 1984 the index rose 16 per cent overall, while for grain the increase was 12 per cent and for subsidiary foodstuffs the increase was 36 per cent (ZGTJNJ, 1985, 332).

30 'Unified' (*tong gou*) and 'allocated' purchase (*pai gou*).

31 'Fixed contract purchases' (*hetong ding gou*).

32 'Market purchase' (*shichang shou gou*).

33 This was a major contributory factor to the substantial government budget deficits in the 1980s (ZGTJNJ, 1985, 523).

34 This figure is not, therefore comparable with the figure for *xiangzhen* enterprises, for which the gross profits figure excludes wages.

35 In 1982 their gross value of output amounted to 44 per cent of that of agriculture plus sidelines (Nolan, 1983b).

36 It was reported that the proportion of urban residents' food expenditure in free markets rose from 17 per cent in 1984 to 36 per cent in 1986 ('Free markets ...', 1987).

37 Prices would, presumably, settle at somewhere between the state and free market prices.

38 Oi (1986a, 234) gives data for parts of three provinces in 1984 indicating that for chemical fertilizer the ratio between the state quota price, the state 'negotiated' price and the free market price was in the order of 1:2:3.

39 See the perceptive discussion in Oi (1986a).

40 This, for example, was the view of Huang Changgong, head of Price Research Institute of Sichuan province (Nolan, 1983b).

41 On the Soviet farm sector see e.g., Gregory and Stuart, 1986, ch. 9; US Congress, 1979, vol. 2, Section 3; US Congress, 1982, vol. 2, Section 6.

Chapter 5   Performance of the rural sector since 1979

1 That is still the case in mid-1987 as this book is being completed.

2 i.e. a linked index using different sets of constant prices for different parts of the index.

3 Indeed, the growth rate from 1978 (a year of above-average natural disasters)

to 1985 (at 1980 prices) was reported to be 10.2 per cent (average annual compound growth rate) (ZGTJZY, 1986, 32).

4   For example, the number of peasant households included in the annual survey of income and expenditure increased from 6 095 in 1978 to over 66 642 in 1985 (ZGTJNJ, 1985, 570).

5   The World Bank, for example, conducted major missions in China, in 1980 (World Bank, 1981b) and 1984 (World Bank, 1986a), as well as other smaller projects.

6   Stone is one of the most knowledgeable Western experts on China's agricultural statistics.

7   For example, the average annual area affected by natural disasters was, reportedly, 43 million hectares for 1975−7 compared to 37 million hectares for 1983−5 (ZGTJNJ, 1985, 302; ZGTJZY, 1986, 46).

8   Though estimation of China's cultivated area is notoriously difficult, and there is much dispute both inside and outside China about the precise figure.

9   This is discussed in chapter 6.

10 The renewed upward movement in the rate of growth of population in the mid-1980s is discussed in chapter 6.

11 It must stressed that these data are rough indications only. Apart from the statistical problems discussed above, measuring changes in gross value of agricultural output in the late 1970s and early 1980s was complicated by the big changes in the composition of output, and the usefulness of any particular year's prices as the basis for constructing an index of output at constant prices is reduced by the large changes that occurred in relative prices.

12 This issue will be analysed in more detail in chapter 6.

13 Discussed in detail in chapter 6.

14 I have not been able to obtain an index of rural non-farm prices. The overall index of retail prices of consumption goods reportedly rose 28.1 per cent from 1978 to 1985, but much the fastest growth was in foodstuffs which reportedly rose 49.4 per cent. For clothing the index fell 3.3 per cent and for 'daily use goods' rose just 6.3 per cent (ZGTJZY, 1986, 100). Also it should be remembered that rural non-farm enterprises had obtained much more independence in price-setting than state enterprises, which they frequently undercut. It seems most unlikely that the price index for rural non-farm enterprises rose by as much as the overall retail price index; therefore, the vast bulk of the reported increase in output value probably was 'real'. This is suggested too by the fact that the real gross value of *cun*-run industry reportedly increased in the following fashion (billion *yuan*, 1980 prices): 1980 = 25.9, 1984 = 57.5, 1985 = 96.1 (ZGTJZY, 1986, 32).

15 See, especially, Griffin, 1979.

16 See especially the excellent discussion in Fields, 1980.

17 For a detailed account of local policies to help poor peasants in advanced *xian*, see Hinton, 1983, 22−3.

18 In mid−1987 the going rate in Beijing for a young female domestic help

(usually from a poor part of China, such as Anhui) was reportedly 50 *yuan* per month plus food and lodgings, or 100 *yuan* exclusive of food and lodgings.

19 This account is from the author's discussion with Yu Dechang of the Chinese Academy of Social Sciences, Agricultural Development Research Unit.

20 For example, in Sichuan, the state in 1983 was providing poor areas with 3000 *yuan* for the purchase of materials (e.g. explosives) for every kilometre of road constructed (Nolan, 1983, b).

21 In Sichuan in 1983 teachers who worked in poor areas (defined for this purpose to include 20.9 per cent of the province's total population) were allocated to one grade higher than they would have been in the normal plain areas (equivalent to a 10 per cent increase in income) (Nolan, 1983 b).

22 See Stone's careful formulation of this point (Stone, 1985, 117).

Chapter 6   Problems

1 The average annual real growth rates of agricultural output in developing countries in 1973–84 were (per cent):

Low income countries (excluding China and India)	2.4
India	2.3
Middle-income oil importers	2.9
Lower middle-income	2.4

(source: World Bank, 1986b, 182).

2 This does not imply that variations in the level of agricultural imports are unimportant for overall economic strategy.

3 In 1984, exports of 'food and live animals chiefly for food' amounted to just 2 per cent of the gross value of agricultural output (ZGTJNJ, 1985, 241 and 494–5).

4 Value of China's exports of silk and satin, cotton yarn, cotton cloth, woollen blankets and garments (excluding man-made fibres, million *yuan*): 1981 = 4190, 1985 = 8940 (ZGTJNJ, 1983, 414–16; ZGTJNJ, 1985, 503–5). These figures may be slight overestimates as some of the knitted garments may be for man-made fibres.

5 See ZGTJNJ, 1985, 566–7; the income elasticity of demand for consumer durables and housing is said to be 'higher than three' (China Rural Development Research Group, 1986, 16).

6 Indeed, in the early 1960s, farm output under the temporary de-collectivized agriculture, grew rapidly (index of agricultural output at 'comparable' prices: 1957 = 100, 1958 = 102, 1961 = 75, 1963 = 89, 1964 = 102, 1965 = 110 (ZGTJNJ, 1985, 238), simultaneously with a fall in the state purchasing price index from agriculture (1957 = 73, 1961 = 100, 1962 = 100, 1963 = 96, 1964 = 94, 1965 = 93 (ZGMYJJTJZL, 1984, 401)), and a deterioration

in the 'price scissors' between the industrial and agricultural price index (agricultural purchase price as percentage of rural industrial retail price index: 1957 = 100, 1961 = 123, 1962 = 117, 1963 = 115, 1964 = 116, 1965 = 120 (ZGMYWJTJZL, 1984, 425). I am indebted to the late Mr Wang Lin for making this point.

7   It is hazardous to try to calculate the 'supply responsiveness' of agriculture in respect to price changes in a period when so many other relevant variables have altered.

8   Indeed, it seems to me that the principal problem with price reform in general in any economy moving away from administrative planning is not general inflation, which does not necessarily have to follow, but changes in relative prices (a rise of food, housing, transport and energy and a fall in the price of consumer durables) which affect different income groups in different ways.

9   The reported monthly average expenditure per caput (*yuan*), on food in 1984 for urban dwellers of different levels of average income (*yuan*) was as follows (per cent of total expenditure in): ‹25 = 162 (61.4), 25–30 = 221 (61.1), 35–50 = 285 (59.4), 50–60 = 349 (57.9), 60–70 = 400 (56.6), ›70 = 486 (54.8) (ZGJJNJ, 1985, 566–7).

10 The average value ('original value') of fixed assets per village (*cun*) rose from 0.24 million *yuan* in 1978 to 0.57 million *yuan* (Rural Survey Group, 1986).

11 The value of collectively owned agricultural fixed assets (not surprisingly) *fell* by 10.7 per cent over this period (Rural Survey Group, 1986).

12 However, it is hard to assess the degree to which the structure, as opposed to the level, of rural non-farm output would be affected.

13 All these figures are for those sectors within 'agricultural production'.

14 7.2 million in 1984, amounting to about 1.8 per cent of total grain output (ZGTJNJ, 1985, 407, 501 and 506).

15 Throughout this section the term 'class' is used loosely to mean differentiation between social groups in a given community in terms of access to economic resources, income level, distribution of political power, etc. I consider it self-evident that most communities are hierarchically organized, and believe that it is more useful to analyse these differences in a rough and ready way than to spend a lot of time debating the finer points of defining 'class'.

16 E.g. Problems of Agricultural Economics (*Nongye jingji wenti*), Rural Work Bulletin (*Nongcun Gongzuo Tongxun*) or Chinese Rural Economics (*Zhongguo Nongye Jingji*).

17 Croll terms this the 'aggregate family' to distinguish it from the 'extended family' living under one roof.

18 Of course, the same argument would apply to such a law if applied to the individual rural non-farm sector.

19 By 1985, the 'individual' sector included 19 million peasants, accounting for 27 per cent of the total number of people working in *xiangzhen* enterprises (ZGJJNJ, 1986, v, 42).

20 By 1985, these accounted for 9 million peasants, or 14 per cent of the total number of people in *xiangzhen* (township) enterprises (ZGJJNJ, 1986, v, 42).

21 Hinton [1983, 11] gives a detailed example of such an enterprise.

22 *Xiang* and *cun*-run enterprises in 1985 employed 41 million peasants, or 59 per cent of the total number working in *xiangzhen* enterprises (ZGJJNJJ, 1986, v, 42).

23 The term 'human capital' is used here in a non-technical sense, to indicate people's physical and mental capacities for economic activity.

24 For a detailed discussion of this element in intra-village differentiation see Shanin, 1972.

25 Of course, the nature, and direction, of the causal relationship is not straightforward.

26 One may usefully distinguish between education as a 'capital good', enabling one to acquire useful knowledge, and education as a 'current input', providing one with immediately useful knowledge.

27 it should be noted that this took the form of a 'right to buy' not a 'guaranteed supply'.

28 Andrew Watson, personal communication.

29 Andrew Watson, personal communication.

30 The comparative point is this author's not Bernstein's.

31 The ownership right pre-1949 was with the landlord.

32 Though their spatial concentration is marked and will be discussed later.

33 Only rough orders of magnitude can be given because (1) some of the data are for per caput income and some are for per worker income, and (2) the lowest figure is for a whole *cun*, not giving the breakdown of income within it.

34 See, for example, the debate in Economic Research (*Jingji Yanjiu*), 1986, no. 8, pp. 58−67.

35 This is a very high tax threshold, many times the average wage level.

36 For example, in remote, mountainous Jinzhai *xian* in Anhui province the local minority people have traditionally suffered from throat goitres and stunted growth, impairing their work ability. These problems are caused by poor diet and water quality − a vicious circle. Special Peoples' Liberation Army work teams have each year for many years gone to the area to provide assistance. Research on some minority peoples, such as the Naxi in Yunnan, has revealed very low natural rates of population growth since 1949, mainly due to exceptionally high mortality attributable to poverty.

37 This is generally the case with the data on 'poor' areas in State Statistical Bureau, Village Sample Survey Group, 1985.

38 Assuming 30 per cent of output was marketed in both 1978 and 1984, the real value of the self-consumed portion of output (at 1978 prices) rose by about 25 per cent, and the real value of the marketed portion (in terms of industrial goods that could be bought) rose by 70−80 per cent giving a total increase in average per caput real income of 30−40 per cent.

39 Though the figure might be slightly higher if proper accout is taken of inflation. It is not made clear how this figure was calculated.

40 At current prices; in real terms, the picture would probably appear even bleaker.
41 Already, by 1983, in central Sichuan province, the fee for a consultation with a doctor in a *xiang* hospital had risen from 5 *fen* pre-1980 to 10—15 *fen* (Nolan, 1983b).
42 Based on information from Sichuan province for 1982 (Nolan, 1983 b).
43 E.g. in 'rich villages' in Huairou *xian* in the Beijing suburbs (Nolan, 1986b).
44 Unfortunately, a change in the criteria for 'small towns' complicates the picture.
45 To be certain of this comparable data from the late 1970s on age structure and school attendance are necessary.
46 It should be noted that the sharpest fall in school attendance had already occurred by 1983: Index of numbers attending primary school in China: 1978 = 100, 1983 = 92.8, 1985 = 91.4 (ZGJJNJ, 1986, III, 70).
47 It should be stressed that international comparisons such as these are fraught with difficulties.
48 Indeed, a relatively high porportion of broadcasting time in China is taken up with material of direct use in production.
49 Health facilities in China's urban areas (index: 1978 = 100):

	1978	1985
Hospital beds (no.)	100	134
Technically qualified health workers (no.)	100	155

Source: ZGNCTJNJ, 1985, 275, and ZGTJZY, 1986, 21

50 Yu Dechang, 1986, personal communication.
51 68 *yuan* in 1985 (ZGTJZY, 1986, 107).
52 See, e.g., Hinton, 1983; Walker, 1984; Bernstein, 1986; Watson, 1986.
53 This view has been put to the author in various forms at many seminars in the past few years.
54 These data are from a national sample survey for over 37 000 households. In real terms, the increase was slightly less. For example, the index of prices paid for industrial means of production sold to agriculture via state channels rose a little in the early 1980s: 1978 = 100, 1984 = 118 (ZGTJNJ, 1986, 532).
55 Of total village investment finance in 1984, 74.5 per cent was self-financed by the villages, 1 per cent was state financed, non-repayable investment, and 24.5 per cent was financed by loans (Rural Survey Group, 1986).
56 In 1984, the figure was 54 per cent (Rural Survey Group, 1986).
57 Private communication from Li Shi, Research Fellow at the Economics Research Institute of the Chinese Academy of Social Sciences, Beijing.
58 Such practices were widespread for rice cultivation in the Chengdu plain in 1983 after de-collectivization (Nolan, 1983b).

59 See, e.g., World Commission, 1987.

60 In Sichuan province, for example, 80 per cent of the forested area was state-owned (Nolan, 1983b).

61 Indeed, in 1982, *ziliushan* accounted for 20 per cent of all the trees planted in Sichuan (Nolan, 1983b).

62 I.e. the area planted with trees in that year; China's total area of forests in 1983 was 115 m hectares (ZGTJNJ, 1985, 3).

63 The main success indicator for local cadres was the simplest one: ability to report expansion of the irrigated area, usually achieved through mass winter-time campaigns. Once built, water conservation facilities require a high proportion of resources available to be devoted to their maintenance – indeed the proportion probably rises as the system expands beyond a certain point (e.g. reservoirs are likely to be built further from fields and, therefore, canals become longer).

64 Total state outlays on basic construction investment in agriculture fell 30 per cent from 1978 to 1984 (ZGJJNJ, 1985, 424).

65 See, e.g., World Bank, 1985, Annex 2, 4–5.

66 E.g. an annual meeting of peasants in an area served by a given project would give its collective view on the degree of timeliness in water provision, which would have an important influence on the bonus paid to the drainage/irrigation management (Nolan, 1983b).

67 Though it should be noted that the figure hardly altered from 1983 to 1985 (ZGTJZY, 1986, 43).

68 Since the late 1960s each unit received a quota for the permitted number of births, under the national 'birth plan'.

69 In fact, the national census of 1982 found that only 82 per cent of births in 1981 had been reported, so that the official population series shows a jump in the national birthrate to 20.9 per 1000 in 1981 (ZGTJZY, 1986, 21).

70 See, e.g., 'Rural Population', 1982.

71 See, e.g., 'Birth planning regulations', 1982.

72 In addition to the compulsory sales 'contract', peasants also have 'reproduction targets' written into the contract with the collective (see, e.g., the details of the contract translated in Nolan and Paine, 1986.).

73 Special state assistance was provided for poor areas to enable them to do so ('Birth planning regulations', 1982).

74 There are, of course, a variety of intermediary possibilities.

75 In Taiwan in the 1960s and 1970s the state maintained a monopoly over chemical fertilizer sales, which had important consequences for the state's ability to influence the rural economy: 'A monopoly over fertilizers made every peasant – without discrimination – beholden to the state. Such a monopoly also allowed the state to determine the crucial equation in economic development: the transfer of surplus from agriculture to industry' (Amsden, 1979, 357).

76 The brief Chinese 'NEP' period came to an abrupt halt in the Autumn of 1953 with the announcement of the 'general line on the transition to socialism. 'NEP' conditions were to return again briefly in the early 1960s.

Chapter 7   Conclusion

1   It can, indeed, be argued that technical progress, especially in microelectronics, since the 1960s has rendered it possible for small scale, petty commodity production, albeit of a new, higher value-added type, to survive in competition with large organizations in a wider range of activities than in an earlier phase of capitalism (see Best, 1988, forthcoming).

2   Moreover, it should not be forgotten that a critical, though much-debated, element in Britain's industrialization was a state which was immensely strong internationally. The conquest of large parts of the globe and dominance of the main seaways provided a powerful stimulus on both the supply side and the demand side. On the supply side it enabled Britain to be the main beneficiary of Europe's 'ghost acreage' (Jones, 1981) and gave it access to a vast supply of raw materials (especially cotton). On the demand side it resulted in a funnelling through Britain of a large portion of the huge external rise in demand for Europe's products (Landes, 1972).

3   It should be stressed that this is very complex empirical question, which has not yet been resolved for either the USSR or China.

4   For a careful, rigorous exploration of the issue, see, especially, Fields, 1980.

5   For a full discussion, see, for example, Riskin, 1971, and the more extended analsyis in chapter 4 and 5 of this book.

Bibliography

A discussion of some ways of looking at the living standard of workers and peasants, 1957, *New Hunan Daily* (*Xin Hunan Bao*), 23 April.

A 1921 lesson for Russia, 1987, *The Economist*, 24 January.

Aird J.S., 1982 Population studies and population policy in China, *Population and Development Review*, vol. 8.

Aird, J.S., 1986, Coercion in family planning: causes, methods and consequences. In US Congress, 1986.

Amsden, A., 1979, Taiwan's Economic History, *Modern China*, July.

Anhui Province's Economic Yearbook, 1985 (*Anhui jingji nianjian*) [AHJJNJ], 1985, Anhui Economic Yearbook Compilation Committee.

ARTI, 1978, *Agrarian reform and Rural Development in Sri Lanka*, Colombo, Agrarian Research and Training Institute.

Ash, R., 1976, *Land Tenure in Pre-revolutionary China: Kiangsu Province in the 1920s and 1930s*, London, Contemporary China Institute.

Ash, R., 1987, China's agriculture − the food sector, unpublished paper.

Bagchi, A.K., 1976, De-industrialisation in India in the Nineteenth Century; Some theoretical implications, *Journal of Development Studies*, vol. 12, no. 2, January.

Bahro, R., 1978, *The Alternative in Eastern Europe*, London, New Left Books.

Banister, J., 1986, Implications of China's 1982 Census results. In US Congress, Joint Economic Committee, 1986.

Baran, P., 1957, *The Political Economy of Growth*, New York, Monthly Review Press.

Bardhan, P., and Rudra, A., 1978, Interlinkage of land, labour and credit Relations: an analysis of village survey data in East India, *Economic and Political Weekly*, February.

Bauer, P.T., 1981, *Equality, the Third World, and Economic Delusion*, London, Methuen.

Baum, R., 1975, *Prelude to Revolution*, New York, Columbia University Press.

Bernstein, T.P., 1986, Local authorities and economic reform, unpublished paper.

Best, M., 1986, Industrial policy and strategic planning in the New Competition. In Nolan and Paine, 1986.

Best, M., 1988, *The New Competition and Industrial Policy*, Cambridge, Polity Press, forthcoming.

Bettelheim, C., and Burton, N., 1978, *China Since Mao*, New York, Monthly Review Press.

Bhaduri, A., 1983, *The Economic Structure of Backward Agriculture*, London, Academic Press.

Bhalla, G.S., and Chadha, G.K., 1982, Green Revolution and the small peasant, *Economic and Political Weekly*, 15 and 22 May.

Birth planning regulations of Shanxi province, 1982, reproduced in *Population and Development Review*, vol. 9, no. 3, September 1983.

Bradley, M.F., and Clark, M.G., 1972, Supervision and efficiency in socialised agriculture, *Soviet Studies*.

Bramall, C., n.d., *Income and the standard of living in China before and after 1949: a case study of Sichuan Province*, Cambridge University PhD. thesis, forthcoming.

Bray, F., 1983, Patterns of evolution in rice-growing societies, *Journal of Peasant Studies*, vol. 11, no. 1.

Bray, F., 1986, *The Rice Economics: Technology and Development in Asian Societies*, Oxford, Basil Blackwell.

Brus, W., 1972, *The Market in a Socialist Economy*, London, Routledge and Kegan Paul.

Brus, W., 1975, *Socialist Ownership and Political Systems*, London, Routledge and Kegan Paul.

Bukharin, N., and Preobrazhensky, E., 1969, *The ABC of Communism*, Harmondsworth, Penguin Books, originally published 1920.

Bukharin, N.I., 1982, *Selected Writings on the State and the Transition to Socialism*, Nottingham, Spokesman.

Byres, T.J., and Crow, B., 1983, *The Green Revolution in India*, Milton Keynes, Open University.

Byres, T.J., and Nolan, P., 1976, *Inequality: India and China Compared, 1950–1970*, Milton Keynes, Open University.

Carr, E.H., 1970, *Socialism in One Country, 1925–1926*, Harmondsworth, Penguin Books.

Central Committee of the CCP, 1958, Resolution on the establishment of People's Communes in the rural areas, 9 August. In Selden, 1979.

Central Committee of the CCP, 1984, Circular on rural work in 1984 (Document Number One), 1 January, 1984, published in *People's Daily* (*Renmin Ribao*), 12 June.

Central Committee of the CCP and the State Council, 1985, Ten policies for enlivening the rural economy, 1 January, published in *People's Daily* (*Renmin Ribao*), 25 March.

Central Committee of the CCP and the State Council, 1986, Arrangements for agricultural work in 1986, 23 February, published in *Bulletin of Rural Work* (*Nongcun Gongzuo Tongxun*), 1986, No. 3.

Chakravarty, S., 1987, Marxist economics and developing countries, *Cambridge Journal of Economics*, vol. 11, no. 1, March.

Chan, A., Madsen, R., and Unger, J., 1984, *Chen Village*, London, University of California Press.

Chao, K., 1970, *Agricultural Production in Communist China, 1949–1865*, Madison, University of Wisconsin Press.

Charlesworth, N., 1982, *British Rule and the Indian Economy, 1800–1914*, London, Macmillan.

Chen, C.S., and Ridley, C.P. (eds), 1969, *Rural People's Communes in Lien–Chiang*, Stanford, Hoover Institution Press.

Chen, H.S., 1973, *Landlord and Peasant in China*, New York, Hyperion Reprint (first published 1936).

Chen, J.S., 1987, Why China must stick to socialism, *Beijing Review*, no. 4, 26 January.

Ch'en, J., and Tarling, N., 1970 (eds), *Studies in the Social History of China and South–east Asia*, Cambridge, Cambridge University Press.

Chen, K.G., 1982, A tentative enquiry into the scissors gap in the rate of exchange between industrial and agricultural products, *Social Studies in China*, June.

Chen, X.K., 1981, Input–output analysis, and investigation of the economic structure. In Ma and Sun, 1981.

China Rural Development Research Group, 1986, Economic growth and rural development, *Economic Research (Jingji Yanjiu)*, no. 10, 10 March.

Chinese Academy of Social Sciences, Price Reform Group, 1987, Prices: questions and thoughts on pressing ahead with reform, *Economic Research (Jingji Yanjiu)*, no. 4.

Coale, A., 1981, Population trends, population policy, and population studies in China, *Population and Development Review*, vol. 7, no. 1, March.

Cohen, S.F., 1974, *Bukharin and the Bolshevik Revolution*, London, Wildwood House.

Cohen, S.F., 1982, The afterlife of Nikolai Bukharin. In Bukharin, 1982.

Compilation of policies on the rural economy (Nongcun jingji zhengce huibian), 1978–81 (2 vols.), 1982, Beijing, Nongcun duwu chubanshe.

Compilation of policies on the rural economy (Nongcun jingji zhengce huibian), 1981–1983 (2 vols.), 1984, Beijing, Nongcun duwu chubanshe.

Concise and important materials on the 1954 survey of peasant household income and expenditure, 1957, *Statistical Work (Tongji Gongzuo)*, no. 10.

Constitution of the Communist Party of China (adopted 28 August 1973), 1973. In *The Tenth National Congress, 1973*.

Crisp, O., 1976, *Studies in the Russian Economy before 1914*, London, Macmillan.

Croll, L., 1987, New peasant family forms in rural China, *Journal of Peasant Studies*, vol. 14, no. 4.

Dai, Y.N., 1986, Beefing up rural co-operative system, *Beijing Review*, no. 25, 23 June.

Dasgupta, B., 1977, *Agrarian Change and the New Technology in India*, Geneva, UN Research Institute for Social Development.

Davis-Friedman, D., 1978, Welfare practices in rural China, *World Development*, vol. 6 no. 5, May.

Dobb, M., 1960, *An Essay on Economic Growth and Planning*, London, Routledge and Kegan Paul.

Dobb, M., 1963, *Economic Growth and Underdeveloped Countries*, London, Lawrence and Wishart.

Dobb, M., 1967, *Capitalism, Development and Planning*, New York, International Publishers.

Domar, E., 1957, A Soviet model of growth. In Nove and Nuti (eds), 1972.

Dong, F.R., 1963a, Questions on studying the practical applications of Marx's reproduction formulae from the angle of unifying the production and use of social products, *Economic Research (Jingji Yanjiu)*, March.

Dong, F.R., 1963b, The allocation and use of products in the proportional relationships between the two major categories of production, *Economic Research (Jingji Yanjiu)*, August.

Dong, F.R., 1963c, Proportionality in socialist reproduction under various types of expanded reproduction, *Economic Research (Jingji Yanjiu)*, November.

Dong, F.R., 1982, Relationship between accumulation and consumption. In Xu, et al., 1982.

Dong, F.R., 1986a, China's price reform, *Cambridge Journal of Economics*, vol. 10, no. 3, September.

Dong, F.R., 1986b, Questions concerning the path of development of Wenzhou's rural commodity economy, *Economic Research Materials (Jingji Yanjiu Ziliao)*, no. 94, 20 August.

Du, R.S., 1983, The contract system which links remuneration with output, and the new development of co-operative economy in the rural areas, *People's Daily (Renmin Ribao)*, 7 March.

Duan, Y.B., 1983, Some situations in and opinions on farm production procurement, *Economics for Agricultural Production Technology (Nongye jishu jingji)*, no. 7, July, translated in *Joint Publications Research Service, China Report, Agriculture*, 26 January 1984.

Duby, G., 1968, *Rural Economy and Country Life in the Medieval West*, Columbia, SC, University of South Carolina Press.

Eckstein, A., et al. (eds), 1968, *Economic Trends in Communist China*, Edinburgh, Edinburgh University Press.

Ellman, M., 1973, *Planning Problems in the USSR*, Cambridge, Cambridge University Press.

Ellman, M., 1975, Did the agricultural surplus provide the resources for the increase in investment in the USSR during the First Five−Year Plan? *Economic Journal*, vol. 85.

Ellman, M., 1979, *Socialist Planning*, Cambridge, Cambridge University Press.

Ellman, M., 1981, Agricultural productivity under socialism, *World Development*, vol. 9, no. 9/10.

Ellman, M., 1986, Real famines, *Marxism Today*, vol., 30, no. 2 February.

Ellman, M., 1987, The non-state sector in the Soviet economy, unpublished.

Elvin, M., 1973, *The Pattern of the Chinese Past*, London, Methuen.

Enterprise Bankruptcy Act, 1987, *China Economic Weekly*, 5 January.

Erlich, A., 1967, *The Soviet Industrialisation Debate*, Cambridge, Mass., Harvard University Press.

Feuerwerker, A., 1968, *The Chinese Economy, 1870–1911*, Ann Arbor, Mich. Papers in Chinese Studies, no. 5.

Feuerwerker, A., 1977, *The Chinese Economy, 1912–1949*, Ann Arbor, Mich. Papers in Chinese Studies, no. 31.

Fewsmith, J., 1985, Rural reforms in China: stage two, *Problems of Communism*, vol. 34, no. 4 July–August.

Field, R.M., 1984, Changes in Chinese industry since 1978, *China Quarterly*, December.

Fields, G.S., 1980, *Poverty, Inequality and Development*, Cambridge, Cambridge University Press.

Fifth National People's Congress, Third Session, 1980, Individual income tax law of the Chinese People's Republic. In Yunnan Province 1984.

First Five Year Plan for Development of the National Economy of the People's Republic of China in 1953–1957, 1956, Peking, Foreign Languages Press.

Forbes, I. (ed.), 1986, *Market Socialism: Whose Choice?*, London, Fabian Society.

Franks, P., 1983, *Technology and Agricultural Development in pre-war Japan*, New Haven, Comm., Yale University Press.

Free markets in China's cities and towns, 1987, *Beijing Review*, no. 20, 18 May.

Friedman, E., 1982, Maoism, Titoism and Stalinism: some origins and consequences of the Maoist Theory of the Socialist Transition. In Selden and Lippit, 1982.

Friedman, E., and Selden, M. (eds), 1969, *America's Asia*, New York, Random House.

Galenson, W. (ed.), 1979, *Economic Growth and Structural Change in Taiwan*, London, Cornell University Press.

Gao, S.Q., 1987, Progress in economic reform, 1979–86, *Beijing Review*, no. 27, 6 July.

Goodstadt, L.F., 1982, China's one-child family: Policy and public response, Population and Development Review, Vol. 8, no. 1, March.

Gould, B., 1985, *Socialism and Freedon*, London, Macmillan.

Government of India (GOI), Planning Commission, 1957, *Report of the Indian delegation to China on agrarian co-operatives*, New Delhi.

Gray, J., 1970, The high tide of socialism in the Chinese countryside. In Ch'en and Tarling, 1970.

Gray, J., and White, G. (eds). 1982, *China's New Development Strategy*, London, Academic Press.

Gregory, P.R., and Stuart, R.C., 1986, *Soviet Economic Structure and Performance*, New York, Harper and Row.

Griffin, K., 1979, *The Political Economy of Agrarian Change* (second edn), London, Macmillan.

Guangdong People's Bank, 1974, *Rural people's communes production team accounting* (*Nongcun renmingongshe shengchandui kuaiji*), Guangzhou, Guangdong renmin chubanshe.

Gunasinghe, N., 1982, Land reform, class structure and the state in Sri Lanka: 1970−1977. In Jones 1982.

Gurley, J., 1969, Capitalist and Maoist economic development. In Friedman and Selden (eds) 1969.

Han, B.C., 1987a, Farmers active in commercial sector, *Beijing Review*. no. 19, 11 May.

Han, B.C., 1987b, Grain production and diversified economy, *Beijing Review*, no. 22, 1 June.

Han, B.C., 1987c, Industry becomes important in countryside, *Beijing Review*, no. 23, 8 June.

Handling economic disputes, 1985, *Beijing Review*, no. 11, 18 March.

Hayami, Y., and Kikuchi, M., 1981, *Asian Village Economy at the Crossroads*, Tokyo, University of Tokyo Press.

He, K., 1986, Agriculture: the Chinese Way, *Beijing Review*, no. 19, 12 May.

Hinton, W., 1983, A trip to Fengyang county, *Monthly Review*, vol. 6, November.

Horvat, B., 1982, *The Political Economy of Socialism*, Oxford, Martin Robinson.

Hu, W., and Yu. Z., 1986, Differentials in peasant income and the goal of becoming well-off together, *People's Daily* (*Renmin Ribao*), 11 April.

Hunan Province Revolutionary Committee, Department of Agriculture and Forestry, and Hunan Province Finance and Accounting Training Squads, 1973, *Rural People's Communes' Production Team Accounting (Nongcun renmingongshe shengchandui kuaiji)* Hunan, Hunan sheng renmin chubanshe.

Institute of Pacific Relations, 1939, *Agrarian China*, London, George Allen and Unwin.

Investigation and analysis of issues in the agricultural economy (*Nongye jingji wenti diaocha yu fenxi*), 1982, Beijing, Nongye chubanshe.

Ishikawa, S. 1967a, Resource flows between agriculture and industry, The Developing Economies, no. 1, March.

Ishikawa, S. 1967b, *Economic Development in Asian Perspective*, Tokyo, Kinokuniya Bookstore.

Ishikawa, S., 1982, China's food and agriculture: performance and prospects. In Reisch, 1982.

Jackson, W.A.D., 1971, *Agrarian Policies and Problems in Communist and Non-Communist Countries*, Seattle, University of Washington Press.

Jasny, N., 1949, *The Socialist Agriculture of the USSR*, Stanford, Stanford University Press.

Jones, E.L., 1981, *The Europlan Miracle*, Cambridge, Cambridge University Press.

Jones, S., et al. (eds), 1982 *Rural Poverty and Agrarian Reform*, Bombay, Allied Publishers.

Kitching, G., 1983, *Rethinking Socialism*, London, Methuen.

Kueh, Y.Y., 1984a, China's new agricultural policy program: major economic consequences, 1979−1983, *Journal of Comparative Economics*, vol. 8, no. 4, December.

Kueh, Y.Y., 1984b, A weather index for analysing grainyield instability in China, 1952−1981, *China Quarterly*, no. 97, March.

Kung, J., 1986, Beyond subsistence: the role of collectivisations in rural economic development in post-Mao China, unpublished paper.

Kung, J.S., and Chan, T.M.H, 1987, Export-led industrialisation: the case of Dongguang in the Pearl River Delta in China, unpublished mss.

Landes, D., 1972, *The Unbound Prometheus*, Cambridge, Cambridge University Press.

Lardy, N., and Lieberthal, K. (eds) 1983, *Chen Yun's Strategy for China's Development*, New York, M.E. Sharpe.

Law Research Institute, Heilongjiang Province (compiled by), 1984, *Compilation of Selected Economic Laws (Jingji falu xuanbian)*, Harbin.

Lei, X.L., 1986, Diversified economy attracts surplus labourers, *Beijing Review*, 24 November.

Lewin, M., 1975, *Political Undercurrents in Soviet Economic Debates*, London, Pluto Press.

Lewis, W.A., 1954, Economic development with unlimited supplies of labour, *The Manchester School*, May.

Lewis, W.A., 1978, *Growth and Fluctuations, 1870–1913*, London, Allen and Unwin.

Liang, W.S., 1982, Balanced development. In Xu et al., 1982.

Liaoning Institute of Finance and Economics, Department of Agricultural Economics, 1973, *How to do a good job of production teams' finance and accounting work (Zenme zuohao shengchandui caikuai gongzuo)*, Shenyang, Liaoning renmin chubanshe.

Lin, C., 1981, The reinstatement of economics in China today, *China Quarterly*, no. 85, March.

Lin, Z.L., 1982, New forms in China's rural socialist co-operative economy, *Wen Hui Bao*, (Shanghai) 29 October, translated in *Joint Publication Research Service*, no. 82958, *China Report, Agriculture*, 28 February, 1983.

Lin, Z.L., 1983, On the contract system of responsibility linked to production, *Social Sciences in China* (English), no. 1, March.

Lin, Z.L., 1986, On the question of the components of Wenzhou's commodity economy, *People's Daily (Renmin ribao)*, 11 November.

Little, I.M.D., 1979, An economic reconnaisance In Galenson, 1979.

Little, I.M.D., 1987, Small manufacturing enterprises in developing countries. *World Bank Economic Review*, vol. 1, no. 2, January.

Livingston, I. (ed.), 1981, *Development Economics and Policy*, London George Allen and Unwin.

Lloyd, J., 1986, New markets for socialist ideas, *Financial Times*, 17 November.

Lockwood, W., 1968, *The Economic Development of Japan*, (second edn), Princeton, NJ, Princeton University Press.

Lu, Y., 1984, Gap between rich and poor is bridged, *Beijing Review*, no. 46, 11 November.

Lu, Y., 1986, Communists work for collective prosperity, *Beijing Review*, no. 26, 30 June.

Luo, H.S., 1985, *Economic Changes in Rural China*, Beijing, New World Press.

Ma, H., and Sun, S.Q., 1981, *Research on Problems of China's Economic Structure (Zhongguo jingji jiegou wenti yanjiu)*, Beijing, Renmin chubanshe.

Macpherson, C.B., 1966, *The Real World of Democracy*, Oxford, Oxford University Press.

Macrae, J.T., 1979, A classification of Chinese development strategy since 1949, *The Developing Economies*, vol. 17.

Mao, T.T., 1955, On the co-operative transformation of agriculture, 31 July. In *Selected Works*, 1977.

Marx, K., 1967, *Capital, vol. 1*, New York, International Publishers.

Marx, Engels and Lenin on the dictatorship of the Proletariat: questions and answers (3), 1975, *Peking Review*, 17 October.

Maxwell, N. and Nolan, P., 1980, The procurement of grain, *China Quarterly*, June.

McCauly, A., 1977, *Economic Welfare in the Soviet Union*, Madison, University of Wisconsin Press.

Mellor, J.W., 1966, *The Economics of Agricultural Development*, London, Cornell University Press.

Mellor, J.W., 1976, *The New Economics of Growth*, London, Cornell University Press.

Ministry of Agriculture, 1980, *Basic circumstances of China's agriculture (Zhongguo nongye jiben qingkuang)*, Beijing, Nongye chubanshe.

Ministry of Agriculture, 1982, Policy Research Office, *Outline of China's Agricultural Economy (Zhongguo nongye jingji gaiyao)* (ZGNYJJGY, 1982), Beijing Nongye chubanshe.

Morawetz, D., 1983, The kibbutz as a model for developing countries. In Stewart, 1983.

Myers, R., 1970, *The Chinese Peasant Economy*, Cambridge, Mass., Harvard University Press.

Myers, R., 1984, Economic trasformation of the Republic of China on Taiwan, *China Quarterly*, no. 99, September 1984.

Nickum, J.E., 1978, Labour accumulation in rural China and its role since the Cultural Revolution, *Cambridge Journal of Economics*, vol. 2, no. 3, September.

Ningxia Hui Nationality Autonomous Region, Village Sample Survey Team, 1985, *Ningxia's villages in the midst of progress (Qianjin zhong de ningxia nongcun)*, Ningxia, Zhongguo tongji chubanshe.

Nolan, P., 1976, 'Collectivisation in China: some comparisons with the USSR' *Journal of Peasant Studies*, vol. 3, no. 2, January.

Nolan, P., 1979, Trip notes from Queen Elizabeth House, Oxford, China Study Group, in which the author participated (unpublished).

Nolan, P., 1981, *Rural income in the People's Republic of China, 1952 to 1957, with special reference to Guangdong province*, London University PhD thesis.

Nolan, P., 1983a, *Growth Processes and Distributional change in a South Chinese Province: The Case of Guangdong*, London, Contemporary China Institute.

Nolan, P., 1983b, Author's notes from a two-month field trip (July-August) to investigate rural reform in Sichuan Province (unpublished).

Nolan, P., 1983c, 'De-collectivisation of agriculture in China, 1979-82: a long-term perspective', *Economic and Political Weekly*, vol. 18, nos 33–34, 13 and 20 August.

Nolan, P., 1986, Author's notes from a three−week stay at the Economics Research Institute in Beijing to discuss, and collect materials on, the effects of the rural reforms (unpublished).

Nolan, P., and Paine, S., 1986, *Re-thinking Socialist Economics*, Cambridge, Polity Press.

Nolan, P. and White, G., 1980, Socialist development and rural inequality: the Chinese countryside in the 1980s, *Journal of Peasant Studies*, vol. 7, no. 1, October.

Nolan, P., and White, G., 1982, The distributive implications of China's new agricultural policies. In Gray and White, 1982.

Nove, A., 1977, *The Soviet Economic System*, London, George Allen and Unwin.

Nove, A., 1983, *The Economics of Feasible Socialism*, London, George Allen and Unwin.

Nove, A., and Nuti, M. (eds), 1972, *Socialist Economics*, Harmondsworth, Penquin Books.

Nurkse, R., 1953, *Problems of Capital Formation in Underdeveloped Countries*, Oxford, Basil Blackwell.

Oi, J.C., 1986a, Peasant households between plan and market − cadre control over agricultural inputs, *Modern China*, vol. 12, no. 2, April.

Oi, J.C., 1986b, Peasant grain marketing and state procurement: China's grain contracting system, *China Quarterly*, no. 106, June.

Omvedt, G., 1981, Capitalist agriculture and rural classes in India, *Economic and Political Weekly*, Review of Agriculture, December.

Paine, S., 1986, Notes on late twentieth century socialism. In Nolan and Paine, 1986.

Parish, W., and M.K. Whyte, 1978, *Village and Family in Contemporary China*, London, University of Chicago Press.

Pei, X.G., 1986, Another possible way to promote the construction of small towns, *Economic Research Materials* (*Jingji Yanjiu Ziliao*), no. 94, 20 August.

Perkins, D.H., 1966, *Market Control and Planning in Communist China*, Cambridge, Mass., Harvard University Press.

Perkins, D.H., 1969, *Agricultural Development in China, 1368−1968*, Edinburgh, Edinburgh University Press.

Perkins, D.H., (ed.), 1975, *China's Modern Economy in Historical Perspective*, Stanford, Stanford University Press.

Perkins, D.H., (ed.), 1977, *Rural Small-Scale Industry in the People's Republic of China*, London, University of California Press. ·

Perry, E.J., and Wong, C. (eds), 1985, *The Political Economy of Reform in Post−Mao China*, London, Harvard University Press.

Plant, R., 1984, *Equality, Markets and the State*, London, Fabian Society.

Preobrazhensky, E., 1965, *The New Economics*, Oxford, Oxford University Press.

Present situation and trends in the rural reform, 1986, *People's Daily* (*Renmin Ribao*), 30 April.

Price reform: six months later, 1986, *Beijing Review*, no. 49, 9 December.

Questions and answers on agricultural work in 1986, 1986, *Rural Work Bulletin* (*Nongcun gongzuo tongxun*), no. 208, 5 February.

Raj, K.N., and Sen, A.K., 1961, Alternative patterns of growth under conditions of stagnant export earnings, *Oxford Economic Papers*, February.

Ranis, G., 1978, Industrial development. In Galenson, 1978.

Reisch, E.M., 1982, (ed.), *Agricultura Sinica*, Berlin, Duncker and Humblot.

Research Group for China's rural development, 1985, A new stage in the Chinese economy and rural development, *Economic Research (Jingji Yangjiu)*, no. 7, July.

Research department of industry and enterprises of the Institute of Development, 1986, On the development of rural non-agricultural production, *Economic Research (Jingji Janjiu)*, no. 8, August.

Riskin, C., 1971, Small industry and the Chinese model of development, *China Quarterly*, no. 46, April–June.

Robinson, J., 1964, Chinese agricultural communes, *Co-existence*, May.

Rural Population, 1982, *Beijing Review*, 1 November.

Rural Survey Group, 1986, The situation and trends in rural reform, *Problems of Agricultural Economics (Nongye Jingji Wenti)*, 1986, no. 6.

Saith, A., 1986, *Contrasting experiences in rural industrialisation: Are the East Asian successes transferable?*, New Delhi, ILO–ARTEP.

Sang, J., 1983, *Everyday knowledge on rural economic contracts (Nongcun jingji hetong changshi)*, Taiyuan, Shanxi renmin chubanshe.

Schell, O., 1984, A reporter at large, *New Yorker*, 23 January.

Schram, S., 1974, (ed.), *Mao Tsetung Unrehearsed*, Harmondsworth, Penguin Books.

Schran, P., 1969, *The Development of Chinese Agriculture, 1950–1959*, London, University of Illinois Press.

Schurmann, F., 1968, *Ideology and Organisation in Communist China*, second edn. Berkeley, University of California Press.

Selden, M., 1979, (ed.) *The People's Republic of China: A Documentary History of Revolutionary Changes*, New York, Monthly Review Press.

Selden M., and Lippit, V. (eds.) 1982, *The Transition to Socialism in China*, New York, M.E. Sharpe.

Selden, M., 1982, Co-operation and conflict: co-operatives and collective formation in China's countryside. In Selden and Lippitt, 1982.

Selected Works of Mao Tsetung, 1977, Peking, Foreign Languages Press.

Sen, A.K., 1983, Development: which way now?, *Economic Journal*, vol. 93, December.

Shang, G.D., 1950, The question of the differentiation of the small peasant economy after land reform, *Study (Xuexi)*, vol. 2, no. 9.

Shanghai County Party Committee, 1975, We must still struggle to fight: an understanding of 'On the question of agricultural co-operation', *Study and Criticism (Xuexi Yu Pipan)*, no. 7.

Shanin, T., 1972, *The Awkward Class*, Oxford, Oxford University Press.

Sheng, Y.M., 1986, Resource flows and terms of trade between the farm and non-farm sectors in China, 1952–1983, Thesis submitted for M Phil in Economics, Faculty of Economics and Politics, Cambridge.

Shi, S., 1980, Where is the breakthrough point to rapid agricultural growth in China?, *Problems of Agricultural Economics (Nongye Jingji Wenti)*, no. 2.

Shiba, Y., 1977, 'Ningpo and its hinterland'. In Skinner, 1977b.

Shue, V., 1980, *Peasant China in Transition*, Berkeley, University of California Press.

Skinner, G.W., 1977a, Cities and the hierarchy of local systems. In Skinner, 1977b.

Skinner, G.W., (ed.), 1977b, *The City in Late Imperial China*, Stanford, Stanford University Press.

Smith, A., 1979, *An enquiry into the nature and causes of the wealth of nations*, vol. I (originally published 1776), Glasgow edn. R.H. Campbell and A.S. Skinner, eds.

Snow, E., 1970, *Red China Today*, Harmondsworth, Penguin Books.

Socialist Collective Ownership System (Shehuizhuyi jiti suoyouzhi), 1976, Guangxi, Guangxi renmin chubanshe.

Song, L.F., 1983, The employment of the surplus labour force in the countryside – A survey of Nantong country, Jiangsu province, *Social Sciences in China* (English), no. 1, March.

Song, P., 1986, 'Report on the 1986 plan for national economic and social development', *Beijing Review*, no. 20, 19 May.

Stalin, J., 1929a, A year of great change. In Stalin, 1976.

Stalin, J., 1929b, Concerning questions of agrarian policy in the USSR. In Stalin, 1976.

Stalin, J., 1933, 'The results of the First Five Year Plan, 7 January. In Stalin, 1976.

Stalin, J., 1976, *Problems of Leninism*, Peking, Foreign Languages Press.

Stargardt, J., 1983, *Satingpra I: The Environmental and Economic Archaeology of South Thailand*, Oxford, British Archaeological Reports.

State Council, 1984, 'Temporary regulation on expanding the autonomy of state-run industrial enterprises' (10 May). In ZGJJNJ, 1985.

State Statistical Bureau, 1980, 'Communique on fulfilment of China's 1979 national economic plan', *Beijing Review*, 30 April.

State Statistical Bureau, 1981, 'Communique on fulfilment of China's 1980 national economic plan', Beijing Review, 11 May.

State Statistical Bureau, 1982, Communique on fulfilment of China's 1981 national economic plan, *Beijing Review*, 17 May.

State Statistical Bureau, 1983, Communique of fulfilment of China's 1982 national economic plan, *Beijing Review*. 9 May.

State Statistical Bureau 1986, Communique on the statistics of 1985 economic and social development, *Beijing Review*, 24 March.

State Statistical Bureau, 1987, Communique on the statistics of 1986 economic and social development, *Beijing Review*, no. 9, 2 March.

State Statistical Bureau, Village Sample Survey Group, 1985, *A compilation of research investigation materials on peasant income and expenditure for each province, autonomous region and directly administered city (Ge sheng, zizhiu, zhixiashi nongmin shouru, xiaofei diaocha yanjiu ziliao huibian)*, Beijing, Zhongguo tongji chubanshe, 2 vols.

Stavis, B., 1978, *The politics of Agricultural Mechanisation in China*, London, Cornell University Press.

Stewart, F., 1981, Capital goods in developing countries. In Livingstone, 1981.

Stewart, F., 1983, (ed.), *Work, Income and Inequality*, London, Macmillan.

Stone, B., 1985, The basis for Chinese agricultural growth in the 1980s and 1990s, *China Quarterly*, no. 101, March.

Su, X., 1965, The struggle between the socialist and capitalist road in the countryside after land reform, *Economic Research (Jingji Yangjiu)* nos. 7–9 (3 parts).

Swamy, S., 1977, The economic distance between China and India, 1955–73, *China Quarterly*, no. 70, June.

SYC, 1982 (Statistical Yearbook of China 1981), Hong Kong, Economic Information and Agency.

SYC, 1983 (Statistical Yearbook of China 1983), Hong Kong, Economic Information and Agency.

Tan, Z.L., 1957, Preliminary survey of China's rural income and standard of living, *New China semi-Monthly (Xinhua Banyuekan)*, no. 11.

Tata Services, 1984, *Statistical Outline of India*, Bombay Tata Services Ltd.

Tawney, R.H., 1932, *Land and Labour in China*, London, George Allen and Unwin.

The Tenth National Congress of the Communist Party of China, (Documents), 1973, Peking, Foreign Languages Press.

Thorbecke, E., 1979, Agricultural development. In Galenson, 1979.

Tian, J.Y., 1986, On the present economic situation and restructuring our economy, *Beijing Review*, Nos. 6–7, 10 February.

Unger, J., 1978, Collective incentives in the Chinese countryside: lessons from Chen Village, *World Development*, vol. 6, no. 5 May.

US Congress, Joint Economic Committee, 1979, *Soviet economy in a time of change*, Washington, US Government Printing Office.

US Congress, Joint Economic Committee, 1982, *Soviet economy in the 1980s: problems and prospects*, Washington, US Government Printing Office.

US Congress, Joint Economic Committee, 1986, *China's Economy Looks Towards the Year 2000*, Washington, US Government Printing Office.

Venturi, F., 1960, *Roots of Revolution*, London, University of Chicago Press.

Volin. L., 1970, *A Century of Russian Agriculture*, Cambridge, Mass., Harvard University Press.

Wade, R., 1987, The management of common property resources: collective action as an alternative to privatisation and state regulation, *Cambridge Journal of Economics*, vol. 11, no. 2 June.

Walker, K.R. 1965, *Planning in Chinese Agriculture*, London, Frank Cass.

Walker, K.R., 1968, Organisation for agricultural production, in Eckstein et al (eds), 1968

Walker, K.R., 1984, Chinese agriculture during the period of the readjustment, 1978–83, *China Quarterly*, no. 100, December

Wan, L., 1984, Developing rural commodity production, *Beijing Review*, no. 9, 27 February.

Wang, D.C., 1985a, Will peasants be polarized by changes?, *Beijing Review*, no. 46, 18 November.

Wang, D.C., 1985b, no relaxation in grain production, *Beijing Review* no. 49, 9 December.

Watson, A., 1983, Agriculture looks for shoes that fit, *World Development*, vol. 11 no. 8, August.

Watson, A., 1984/5, 'New structures in the Organisation of Chinese agriculture: a variable model', *Pacific Affairs*, vol. 57, no. 4, Winter.

Watson, A., 1986, The family farm, land use and accumulation in agriculture, manuscript.

Webb, S. and B., 1937, *Soviet Communism: A New Civilisation*, (second edn). London, Longmans, Green and Co.

Wenzhou Rural Research Group, Chinese Academy of Social Sciences, Economics Research Institute, 1986, an investigation of Wenzhou's rural commodity economy, and an exploration of China's paths of rural modernisation, *Economic Research* (*Jingji Yanjiu*), 1986, no. 6.

White, G., 1985, The impact of economic reforms in the Chinese countryside: towards the politics of social capitalism?, manuscript.

Wittfogel, K.A. 1971, Communist and non-communist agrarian systems with special reference to the USSR and Communist China. In Jackson, 1971.

Wong, C., 1985, Material alocations and decentralisation: impact of the local sector on industrial reform. In Perry and Wong, 1985.

World Bank, 1981a, *World Development Report, 1981*, Washington, DC, World Bank.

World Bank, 1981b, *China: Socialist Economic Development*, Washington, DC, World Bank.

World Bank, 1985, *China: Agriculture to the Year 2000*, Washington, DC, World Bank.

World Bank, 1986a, *China: Long-term development issues and options*, Washington DC, World Bank.

World Bank, 1986b, *World Development Report 1986*, Oxford, Oxford University Press.

World Commission on Environment and Development, 1987, *Our Common Future*, Oxford, Oxford University Press.

Xin Yu Brigade, Jiang Jin People's Commune, Suzhou Municipality, 1978, *Xin Yu Brigade's Labour Management Norms for Recording Workpoints*, given to the author by Mr N. Maxwell, Oxford University.

Xu, D.X., et al., 1982, *China's Search for Economic Growth*, Beijing, New World Press.

Xue, M.Q. 1985, Rural industry advances amidst problems, *Beijing Review*, no. 50, 16 December.

Yan, Z.P., et al., 1955, *Statistical Materials on Modern Chinese Economic History* (*Zhongguo jindai jingjishi tongji ziliao xuanji*) Beijing, Kexue chubanshe.

Yang, C.K., 1965, *Chinese Communist Society: The Family and the Village*, Cambridge, Mass., MIT Press.

Yu, G.Y., 1980, Planting trees and growing grass, all round development of agriculture, forestry and animal husbandry: an agricultural survey of the drought-stricken, low output areas of Central Gansu and Xihaigu area of Southern Ningxia', no. 1, *Problems of Agricultural Economics* (*Nongye Jingji Wenti*).

Yunnan Province High Level People's Court, 1984, *Handbook of Economic Law Work*, (*Jingji sifa gongzuo shouce*) (vol. 2), Kunming, Yunnan minzu chubanshe.

Zaleski, E., 1980, *Stalinist Planning for Economics Growth, 1933—1952*, London, Macmillan.

ZGJJNJ, 1981 (*Chinese Economic Yearbook, 1981; Zhongguo jingji nianjian*) 1981, Beijing, Jingji guanli zazhishe.

ZGJJNJ, 1985 (*Chinese Economic Yearbook, 1985; Zhongguo jingji nianjian*) 1985, Beijing, Jingji guanli chubanshe.

ZGJJNJ, 1986 (*Chinese Economic Yearbook, 1986; Zhongguo jingji nianjian*) 1986, Beijing, Jingji guanli chubanshe.

ZGMYWJTJZL (*Statistical Materials on China's Commodity Trade Prices, 1952—1983; Zhongguo maoyi wujia tongji ziliao*), 1984, Beijing, Tongji chubanshe.

ZGNCTJNJ, 1985 (*Chinese Rural Statistical Yearbook, 1985; Zhongguo nongcun tongji nianjian*), Beijing, Zhonggou tongji chubanshe.

ZGNYJJGY, 1982 *see* Ministry of Agriculture, 1982.

ZGNYNJ, 1985 (*Chinese Agricultural Yearbook, 1985; Zhongguo nongye nianjian*) Beijing, Nongye chubanshe.

ZGTJNJ, 1984 (*Chinese Statistical Yearbook, 1984; Zhongguo tongji nianjian*), Beijing, Zhongguo tongji chubanshe.

ZGTJNJ, 1985 (*Chinese Statistical Yearbook, 1985; Zhongguo tongji nianjian*), Beijing, Zhongguo tongji chubanshe.

ZGTJZY, 1984 (*Chinese Statistical Summary, 1984; Zhongguo tongji zhaiyao*), Beijing, Zhongguo tongji chubanshe.

ZGTJZY, 1985 (*Chinese Statistical Summary, 1985; Zhongguo tongji zhaiyao*), Beijing, Zhongguo, tongji chubanshe.

ZGTJZY, 1986 (*Chinese Statistical Summary, 1986; Zhongguo tongji zhaiyao*), Beijing, Zhongguo tongji chubanshe.

ZJJJTJNJ, 1985 (*Zhejiang Yearbook of Economic Statistics; Zheijiang jinji tongji nianjian*), Zhejiang, Zhejiang sheng tongjiju.

Zhang, Y.R., 1965, The road to the elimination of the rich peasant economy in China, *Economic Research* (*Jingji Yangjiu*), no. 6.

Zhao, R.W., 1986, The question of the gaps in individual incomes in the course of the development of Wenzhou's rural commodity economy, *Economic Research Materials* (*Jingji Yangjiu Ziliao*), no. 94, 20 August.

Zhong, C.Z., 1961, On differential rent in China's rural communes, *Red Flag* (*Hong Qi*), no. 23, 1 December.

Zhong, D.B., 1974, *A discussion of distribution policy in the rural people's communes* (*Tantan nongcun renmin gongshe fenpei zhence*), Guangzhou, Guangdong renmin chubanshe.

Zhou, Q.R., 1986, The rediscovery of household management, *Social Sciences in China* (English), no. 2, June.

Index

Index by Chris McKay